"The appearance of a book .... ins worlds as thorough, clearheaded, and insightful as Calt's should be considered a gift of fate. To say *I'd Rather Be the Devil* is the best book on the subject of 'country blues' for the layperson would be an understatement on the order of 'Air is good for your body.'"
—**Don Howland,** *Voice Literary Supplement*

"[Calt] seems, like James, more than a bit brilliant. His analyses of blues history and James's music are penetrating and idiosyncratic, and the harsh skepticism with which he views blues-collector culture and the music it lionizes is something like a pleasure after decades of adulatory 'air pudding.' . . . A remarkable book."
—**Robert Christgau,** Minneapolis *City Pages*

"In light of the romanticism that permeates most works on blues, Calt's vituperation is refreshing. He writes with anger and iconoclastic zeal and he generally knows what he's talking about. The result is a fascinating and disturbing book, containing a lot of truth, a lot of interesting historical research, and a lot of food for thought. . . . Unlike the hagiography that often passes for blues scholarship, Calt's book shows James as a real person. . . . In a world where Robert Johnson is on a stamp and the House of Blues is making the juke joint into a flavor of the month, [Calt] offers a valuable counterweight."
—**Elijah Wald,** *Living Blues*

"[Calt] writes with a knowledge and intelligence that make even his most extreme statements interesting. . . . His greatest virtue is his insistence on painting James as a real, albeit infuriating, person. . . . Calt's perspective is badly needed." —*Boston Globe*

"Less a biography of one blues legend than a biography of Mississippi blues, this account chronicles Skip James's life in part to make a more important, more affecting point. . . . Calt depicts James, born on a plantation in 1902 and abandoned early by his bootlegger father, as a man whose life before and after a single 1931 recording session *was* the blues. . . . Calt's interviews with James just before his death in 1969 imbue this book with a true survivor's voice." —*Publishers Weekly*

"Entertaining and on the mark . . . Calt's narrative is always interesting and often spellbinding. . . . Fascinating reading." —*Acoustic Guitar*

I'd Rather Be the Devil

Skip James and the Blues

STEPHEN CALT

DA CAPO PRESS
New York

Library of Congress Cataloging in Publication Data

Calt, Stephen.
   I'd rather be the devil: Skip James and the blues / by Stephen Calt.
     p.   cm.
   Includes index.
   ISBN 0-306-80579-0
   1. James, Skip, 1902–1969. 2. Blues musicians–United States–Biogra-
phy. I. Title.
ML420.J234C35 1994
781.643'092–dc20
[B]   94-28398
                                                                       CIP
                                                                        MN

Published by Da Capo Press, Inc.
A Subsidiary of Plenum Publishing Corporation
233 Spring Street, New York, N.Y. 10013

Manufactured in the United States of America

For Joe Costelloe, and Pete Whelan

When our enemies deceive us,
when our friends betray us,
we are not to be consoled;
yet we are quite willing to
deceive and betray ourselves.

La Rochefoucauld

AUTHOR'S NOTE

With the exception of a few isolated comments, the Skip James quotations in this book were drawn from tape recordings made by the author at irregular intervals between 1964 and 1969, in New York City, Palisades, New York, and Philadelphia. The ellipses within quotations represent the elimination of redundancies and superfluities, rather than pauses in speech. James' quoted letters are rendered in their original spellings.

Most of the material I obtained from James was gathered in the course of social visits. Recording reminiscences was an incidental aspect of the visits themselves, at least to James. He did not share my interest in documenting his life; for the most part he appeared to be indulging a peculiar whim of mine. He had no interest in anything that might be written about his life, and no awareness that anything he said about himself could conceivably tarnish his reputation. The only subject that appeared to make him skittish were the road camps that had employed him as a youthful laborer; he felt that young people would be better off not knowing that such "dirtier than dirty" places existed. "I don't think it would be worthwhile to have that published, in a way," he said, after recording his reminiscences about it. "That wouldn't be etiquette."

James also had a general aversion to discussing his musical development or past experiences as a blues musician, and almost never volunteered anything on the subject. He was more responsive to questions about his musical career when his remarks were not being recorded, and I thus made a practice of annotating his passing musical tidbits by hand.

The recordings were discourses rather than interviews: because James was resistant to anything resembling probing, the author found it politic to interrupt as infrequently as possible. It was expedient to assume such a passive role because James was an extremely fluent speaker, who enjoyed making monologues more than participating in two-way conversation. For the most part, James simply rambled on a topic he wanted to talk about, or that the author suggested, until he ran out of comments, or until (after half an hour) one side of a tape reel had been expended. In some instances, his recorded remarks were rehashes of or elaborations upon matters he had previously brought up on that particular day.

At best the author can hope to have succeeded in conveying something of the flavor of Skip James' life, and illuminating his personality from my own perspective. I cannot pretend to have written a work of legitimate biography. It is only legitimate within the framework of blues history, which is for the most part legend and fancy. James' story is quasi-history, its pre-1960s content determined by what he cared to reveal about himself. His disclosures are selective and often self-serving. His recollections cannot be corroborated or their accuracy verified; the dates that are assigned to his various activities may in some instances be approximate.

The particular history I have assembled of James is one that would not have been possible had he perceived me as a blues enthusiast or a writer. The face James gradually disclosed to me was not the one he wore for the benefit of "fans" and interviewers, particularly as he began to fancy himself a father figure to me. The ensuing portrait may make James appear uniquely jaded, but that is less a reflection on James than on the superficiality of most blues research. Most of the writers who have chronicled professional blues singers had perfunctory (if any) contact with them. Most of the blues singers who became familiar to latter-day writers and audiences, such as Sam Chatmon, John Hurt, Mance Lipscomb, and Jack Owens, were never professional musicians. As a rule, these amateurs were far more wholesome and earnest than career blues singers; their predominance on the blues circuit of the 1960s fostered illusory (and still prevalent) ideas as to what typical blues singers were like. To form an impression of the career blues singer from the example of a farmer whose hobby was playing blues is like attempting to depict professional gamblers on the basis of encounters with recreational card players. In order to recount certain episodes, it was necessary for me to refer to myself in the narrative. On principle I have a great aversion to such self-reference, and it was only at the insistence of the editor that I cast these references in the first person. I have attempted to spare myself no less than James, or other assorted characters on the blues scene of the 1960s, some of whom have never outgrown their perceptions and enthusiasms of the period.

Incidents pertaining to James' 1960s concert career were noted as they occurred. Quotations from Sam Chatmon, David Edwards, Gary Davis, Son House, Tom Shaw, and Booker White were drawn from various tape-recorded interviews the author made between 1966 and 1973. Quotations from Henry Stuckey were taken from a joint interview conducted by the author and Gayle Wardlow in Satartia, Mississippi in July, 1965. The quotations from Ishmon Bracey, H.C. Speir, Booker Miller, and Johnnie Temple were transcribed from tape recordings made by Gayle Wardlow in Jackson, Mississippi between 1967 and 1971. Quotations from Jack Owens were drawn from a 1993 tape-recorded interview conducted in Bentonia, Mississippi by Edd Hurt, to whom I owe a special debt of gratitude. Various people have been kind enough to answer the inquiries I have put to them: Bill Barth, David A. Jasen, Skip Henderson, Donald Kent, Bernard Klatzko, the late Little Brother Montgomery (by mail), Gene Rosenthal, Maynard Solomon, John Steiner, and Pete Whelan, each of whom deserves my heartfelt thanks. As always, I have benefitted from musical, moral, and metaphysical musings with Woody Mann, who provided the transcriptions for this book. Finally, I owe my professional and personal thanks to my intrepid editor, Yuval Taylor, whose initially exasperating suggestions to a truculent author resulted (to my surprise) in a greatly improved product.

Draft portions of this book have appeared in 78 Quarterly (626 Canfield Lane, Key West, Florida 33041). The songs of Skip James that are referred to are generally available in compact disc form, and may be obtained in most record stores.

CONTENTS

PART ONE

1. *The Blues Singer*

In the winter of 1931, a blues singer boarded a segregated Illinois Central passenger train in Jackson, Mississippi. He was a small, dark, figure with a laborer's brawny build and a face that was memorable chiefly for its blue eyes. He carried no luggage, except for a sixty-five dollar guitar that had recently been given to him by a local record store owner. In his pockets were thirteen dollars, expense money the same man had given him.

He had no idea how much he would be paid for the records he was scheduled to make, or how many songs he would be allowed to record. Almost nothing concerning the session had been explained to him by his sponsor, who had given him his train ticket.

The man had been north of Memphis only once, two years before, and he was surprised to see a well-dressed, light-complexioned black woman board the train at Springfield, Illinois with a white man, evidently her lover. He had never seen a mixed couple. In his native Mississippi, a black man could not glance at a white woman without risking the wrath of Southern whites; if a white man consorted with a black woman, he did so surreptitiously.

Noticing his guitar, the man asked him if he could play *Am I Blue?*, a popular tune Ethel Waters had introduced a year and a half earlier in a movie musical.

"I think so," Skippy James replied. After singing a verse, he completed the song with kazoo accompaniment. Enraptured by his performance, the couple engaged him in conversation. When James explained that he was headed north to record for the Paramount label, the woman asked what songs he intended to record. She wrote down his address, and promised to buy his records.

A few moments after they concluded their conversation, the woman tapped him on the shoulder and handed him fifty cents. Silently, he snickered. Her lover was a wealthy Jew, he thought; he could have afforded a dollar tip.

At six o'clock the next morning the train pulled into Milwaukee, Wisconsin. In the station, James was startled to find himself hailed by a white stranger dressed in a business suit. As the man introduced himself as Art Laibly, the recording manager of Paramount, James wondered how Laibly had been able to recognize him. Together they rode an electric train to Grafton, a small town twenty miles north of Milwaukee. Laibly escorted him to a local hotel, where he was to rest before the session began that afternoon. Before leaving James, Laibly asked him how many records he could make. "As many as you want," James replied.

Soon James fell asleep. At eleven a bellhop woke him and took him to a cafe, where Laibly bought his lunch. As James ate, the 37-year old recording director explained the financial details of the recording session, offering him a choice between a deferred sales royalty and a flat fee for making records over the next two years. Believing that his records would sell abundantly, James decided to accept the deferred payment arrangement.

At one o'clock, he was taken to a nearby recording studio located on the second floor of a deserted factory. The room was empty except for an engineer and a tall, attractive black woman who evidently worked as Laibly's assistant.

A glance at the company's equipment satisfied him that it was "number one stuff."

Laibly asked him if he preferred to begin recording on guitar or piano. James replied laconically that it made no difference to him. Laibly suggested that he begin his session on a company guitar, which could accomodate twelve strings. As James tuned the instrument he marveled that it could hold a tone "just like a piano." In his mind, it was worth $350, far more than the five or ten-dollar instruments he was accustomed to owning.

After explaining recording procedures, Laibly gave him two mint tablets and a glass of whiskey, expedients the singer used to "scrape out" his throat. At Laibly's request, he began playing the first song of his session, *Devil Got My Woman.* After he finished a couple of verses he was beckoned to the control booth by an engineer who asked if he had ever heard his voice on record. The song fragment, which had been recorded to test volume levels, was played back to him for his reaction.

Then the session began. At the onset of a flashing green light James would begin playing a song of his own choosing. He was to continue until he saw a red light, which meant that he was to complete the song after finishing the verse he was singing. When a song was finished, Laibly would ask him for its title. In some instances, he would be asked to repeat a song.

One of James' songs, a dirge-like, minor key lament, appeared to impress Laibly:

> Hard times here an' everywhere you go
> Times is harder than ever been before.
>
> An' the people are driftin' from door to door
> Can't find no heaven, I don't care where they go.

Laibly expressed surprise that James had observed the effects of the Depression.

By the late afternoon James had recorded over a dozen tunes, most of them blues. On the following morning, he returned to the studio and recorded a succession of piano songs. For these tunes, Laibly placed a board beneath his feet to enhance the sound of his foot-stomping. When Laibly asked if he could compose or rearrange a song about a gun, James thought for a few minutes and reeled off an impromptu tune:

> If I send for my baby, and she don't come
> All the doctors in Wisconsin, sure won't help her none.
>
> And if she gets unruly, and gets so she won't "do"
> I'll take my 22-20, I'll cut her half in two.

As he repeated the second verse, he pummeled the board beneath him with his shoe, as if to demonstrate the violence he intended to wreak upon the imaginary girlfriend.

After he had completed four piano songs, Laibly informed him that he had recorded more tunes than any previous Paramount artist. He spoke of holding another session later that year.

James left Grafton that afternoon with eight dollars in expense money given by Laibly, and a promise of receiving payment by mail when his records were issued.

He anticipated attaining immense fame from his records. In the meantime, however, he would resume the footloose life style one of his songs had commemorated:

> You wake up, set out on a long ol' lonesome road
> "I got to leave from here, catch the first freight train
> that blow."

(Hard-Luck Child)

"I never was in anything too long or deep: that's why I reckon they called me 'Skip,' " he once remarked.

His immediate plans were no more exalted than an appearance at a weekend house party in Jackson. As the weekend was a few days away, he decided to get off when his train stopped in Memphis. He made his way to a barrelhouse on North Nichols Street, in the city's black red-light district. As always, he counted on ready money by introducing himself to the owner as a musician and playing an audition tune.

In the middle of his performance a brawl erupted. At the sound of gunfire, he stopped playing, and walked out.

2. *The Researcher*

Jazz collectors who first encountered the records of Skip James in the mid-1940s regarded him as a primitive jazz pianist. It was not until the mid-1950s that they became recognized as blues classics by a small circle of record collectors who began to specialize in such music, which had been retailed in the South for black consumers and had received no contemporary publicity.

His records, issued in minute quantities by a company that was on the verge of going out of business, were rarities. Six or seven of them had turned up in the thirty years that followed his session. Beyond the fact that all of James' records had been produced at one extended session, specialists knew nothing of the circumstances that surrounded them. Because the defunct company that had recorded him had discarded its recording ledgers during the Depression, it was not known how many songs Skip James had actually recorded, or how many of his records the company had actually issued. Only a few copies of each surviving Skip James record existed; two of them existed in the form of a single scratchy copy. Their rarity and obscurity added to their appeal: a collector who owned a Skip James record could bask in a feeling of exclusivity.

His records were all the more treasured by early collectors because his sound was completely esoteric. Like the blues of other Southern guitarists of the era, they had no seeming connection with either popular music or the band blues of celebrated singers like Bessie Smith. Most collectors regarded popular music with contempt: to them, it was bland and formula-ridden. The blues of a musician like Skip James, on the other hand, spoke of solitary passion. Its meanings could only be surmised by modern-day listeners. There were no studies of such music; it had arisen, existed, and died unrecognized.

Except as a name on a record label, Skip James had no identity. Collectors were puzzled by his proficiency on two instruments: other recorded blues artists either played one instrument, or dabbled amateurishly on a second one. His voice, too, was a curiosity: sometimes he sang in an understated tenor, and sometimes in a lush falsetto. His guitar-playing had an almost eerie sound. As they listened to his records, collectors often wondered what kind of person he had been. One collector supposed that he had been deranged, so unworldly was his music.

Such fantasies were all the more rampant among early blues collectors because none of them had set sight on an actual representative of the early blues era. As human beings, blues singers were ciphers. The culture that produced them was similarly opaque. The records were like artifacts of a lost, uncharted civilization.

In the absence of tangible knowledge about their favorite musicians, collectors coined a catch-all label for self-accompanied blues guitarists like Skip James. The music was called "country blues," and the musicians, "country bluesmen." In the minds of collectors, these phrases became musical superlatives. They signified that the musician forged his own songs, without the assistance of songwriters, and devised his own accompaniments. The essence of country blues, collectors thought, was a staunch musical individualism.

Having invented a genre, collectors sought to introduce it to the public by reissuing their most prized 78 rarities in album form. Between 1959 (when the term "country blues" took hold among collectors) and 1962, anthologies called "The Country Blues," "Really! The Country Blues," and "The Mississippi Blues" introduced records by James and other obscure Southern blues artists.

One of those who embraced the small but rabid cult of "country blues" was a recent high school graduate from Meridian, Mississippi, Gayle Wardlow. Wardlow had originally been a country and western enthusiast. Partly because old blues records were readily found in his home state, he became interested in collecting them. By the time Wardlow immersed himself in blues, however, the music was defunct. His only memory of a living blues guitarist stemmed from his childhood, when he had seen one perform at a depot in Louisiana. Sometimes he wondered if this figure had been one of the men who made the records he collected.

Periodically, Wardlow "canvassed" for blues 78s in tumble-down shacks occupied by elderly blacks. The blacks who still owned records from the 1920s no longer owned phonographs and no longer listened to blues. Most of the records he unearthed were in unplayable condition. Occasionally Wardlow would ask older blacks if they remembered certain musicians. For the most part, the blacks he spoke to were uncommunicative. Often he could not tell whether they were evasive, or simply uninterested in blues. His perfunctory encounters with them were always strained and tense. In Mississippi, segregation was still the order of the day, and a white person was not thought to have any proper business visiting a black household. Whenever he pulled his car abreast a row of houses in a black neighborhood, Wardlow was afraid that some local redneck would notice him and take him for a civil rights worker out to register blacks.

Like a detective searching for suspects, Wardlow kept a list of likely Mississippi bluesmen: Kid Bailey, William Harris, Skip James . . . All of them were biographical blanks. The most curious blank was Skip James, whom collectors esteemed as one of the two or three greatest blues artists of all time. For months Wardlow made inquiries concerning him in assorted Mississippi towns. For all of his efforts, he had nothing to add to the stark notation that appeared on the back of a reissue album:

> Skip James . . . No details. Said to have been from
> Louisiana. Was proficient on both guitar and piano.
> Present whereabouts unknown.

The notion that James had been from Louisiana had arisen from one of his own songs:

> I'm goin' I'm goin'
> Comin' here no more
> If I go to Louisiana mama Lord they'll,

They'll hang me sure.
(*If You Haven't Any Hay, Get On Down The Road*)

Yet Wardlow believed that James and most of the country blues greats of the 1920s hailed from his native state. This conviction had been fostered by northern record collectors, who took it as an article of faith that because blues arose from the oppressed condition of blacks, the repressive state of Mississippi necessarily produced the most intense blues singers. Their reasoning was supported by the fact that some blues greats were actually from Mississippi: Bukka White, Charlie Patton, and Robert Johnson.

Although Charlie Patton and Robert Johnson had been dead for three decades, it appeared that some Mississippi blues singers who had recorded in the 1920s might still be alive, and able to resurrect their old music. In March of 1963, Wardlow was startled to learn that a northern blues enthusiast had just rediscovered a 1920s guitarist named Mississippi John Hurt in a tiny Delta town. The discovery had been not entailed any clever detective work or even persistence. In 1928 Hurt had recorded a tune called *Avalon Blues* that began:

Avalon's my home town, always on my mind

The enthusiast had merely looked up Avalon on a Mississippi map, and driven there from Washington, D.C. It turned out that Hurt had spent all of his seventy years in Avalon, working at assorted manual jobs. He had never been a professional musician and did not consider himself a blues singer. Because his brother was a local bootlegger, he first took the white visitor for a revenue man.

Hurt had since moved to Washington and resumed his career in coffeehouses. Despite his advanced age, he was able to play all of his old songs exactly as he had recorded them thirty-five years before. He was an easy-going, self-effacing figure who found a ready niche in what was called the "folk revival." He had even appeared on the Johnny Carson Show.

It grated Wardlow that a northerner had accomplished Hurt's rediscovery, and that blues specialists were primarily Yankees and Europeans. In the fall of 1963, he located his own Mississippi blues singer, Ishmon Bracey, after the mention of Bracey's name to an elderly black in Jackson had prompted the response: "Bracey buried my brother." Bracey had become a minister.

Except for John Hurt, who didn't consider himself a blues singer, Bracey was the first Mississippi blues singer from the 1920s to be turned up in his original environment. But nothing about the crass creature whom Wardlow called "Preacher" evoked the kind of purity that Mississippi blues were taken to represent. He had nothing interesting or significant to say about music, his own or anyone else's. He was preoccupied with his place in the blues pecking order, as enshrined in episodic jousting affairs between himself and whatever entertainers he happened to cross in his travels. His proudest achievement was his ability to make a crowd applaud for himself, rather than a rival blues singer. Instead of priding himself on his own recordings, he prided himself on his ability to copy hits like *Tight Like That* and *Sitting On Top Of The World*, which sometimes gave him an edge in such jousting affairs.

Bracey's values were those of a pop musician, written on a small scale. He was a shameless name-dropper who did not know that when he spoke of accompanying Louis Armstrong, the name of the fabled jazz great excited his discoverer less than that of an obscure blues singer.

It did not occur to Wardlow that some of Bracey's reminiscences were fabricated, as when he claimed to have been a companion of Blind Lemon Jefferson. He had sometimes gone to Greenwood to meet Jefferson, he said; then the two would tour the Delta. It would have been extremely difficult for Bracey to make any arrangements to meet Jefferson in such a fashion, and even more difficult for him to acompany the artist's slapdash phrases. Although Jefferson had no need of any accompanists, the professional blues singers of the period had an incorrigible need to impress people. So it was that two other blues musicians, Josh White and Leadbelly, had concocted similarly unlikely stories of their association with Jefferson, who had been the best-selling bluesman of the 1920s.

The desire to impress, in fact, was almost the hallmark of the professional blues singer. It made his reminiscences problematic. When a blues singer came in contact with record collectors, and learned that it was the nonentities of the field rather than someone like Blind Lemon Jefferson who most excited them, his name-dropping would assume a new cast of characters.

Record collectors had already learned to distrust the breezy recollections of Big Joe Williams, a Mississippi bluesman who had been living in Chicago since the mid-1950s. Big Joe spent most of his nights in the basement of a local record store, the Jazz Record Mart. He conned gullible collectors into believing that he had recorded obscure Paramount sides under the name King Solomon Hill. When Williams (in 1957) spoke of the fabled bluesman Sleepy John Estes living in Brownsville, Tennessee, the owner of the Jazz Record Mart, Bob Koester, was skeptical. "He had told unbelievable stories about himself, the bluesmen he knew, and other bluesmen he claimed to know," Koester later recalled.

Big Joe believed that Skip James was dead, having been murdered in Mississippi. But he was already so discredited (he had claimed that John Hurt was dead) that no one bothered to ask him about James, even after an enfeebled Estes was turned up in Brownsville in November of 1962.

What was most exciting to Wardlow about talking to Bracey was that he appeared to have seen many obscure musicians, although in passing. Frequently, the mention of a name or a snatch of his recording would prompt Bracey to supply a home town for the singer.

Mention of Skip James brought only Bracey's skeletal recollection of a musician he had once seen in Jackson decades before. He played in a strange style and his fingers were a blur on the guitar, Bracey said. Apparently Bracey had taken no real interest in the man or his music; otherwise he begrudged mention of a one-time competitor.

In January of 1964, Wardlow learned that a Chicago blues singer named Johnnie Temple had returned to his native Jackson to visit relatives. Temple had been a successful band singer in the 1930s, recording nearly a hundred blues for the Decca label. His career had lasted some fifteen years, only sputtering out in 1949. Collectors regarded his works as boring and gave them a wide berth; they seemed to represent the antithesis of the music of a Skip James or John Hurt.

To Wardlow, the 55-year-old Temple was a figure of interest only for his recollections of Mississippi blues singers who had preceded him. After making perfunctory conversation with him, Wardlow asked Temple if he had ever heard of Skip James.

"Yeah, I knew Skippy," Temple said. "I learned guitar from him." James, he said, came from Bentonia, Mississippi.

Wardlow had never heard of Bentonia, a small plantation town in the hills halfway between Jackson and Yazoo City. On his first free weekend after talking to Temple, he drove there from Meridian in the hopes of finding Skip James. The town consisted primarily of a general store and a gas station. It looked indistinguishable from other pokey Mississippi towns that had existed to fuel the moribund cotton economy. In 1930 it had numbered only 170 persons.

One of them had been Skip James. Within minutes of arriving at Bentonia, Wardlow had picked up various scraps of information concerning James: that he was a small man whose real name was "Nemia," that he had learned guitar from an older localite named Henry Stuckey, that his song *Cypress Grove* had been named for a Bentonia lake in which James had swam and fished as a boy, that he had once had a nervous breakdown because a wife (the subject of *Devil Got My Woman*, it was said) had left him for a rival, that he had gone to Texas after his recording session, and had returned to Bentonia in the late 1940s.

But no one had seen James for ten years. A cousin named Lincoln Polk told Wardlow that he had staked a cotton crop for James in the early 1950s by borrowing five hundred dollars from a Yazoo City bank. Together they had raised a crop. One morning during the fall harvest season he awoke to find that James and a wife had disappeared. In the center of town was his own abandoned truck. Before his departure, James had cashed in the cotton crop it carried. When Polk reported the loss to his white boss, the man said of James: "You should kill that S.O.B." Ostensibly to recover his money, the cousin had since visited Tunica in search of James, without result.

Polk was convinced that James had fled to Tunica, a town in the northern part of the Delta. Wardlow wondered if he might have gone to West Memphis, Arkansas, where Johnnie Temple had last seen him in 1960 or 1961. On that occasion, Temple said, James had invited him to a tavern for some drinks, and had spoken of operating a night club.

On a street in Tunica, Wardlow met a gambler named "Hard-Face" who appeared to have known Skip James. "Hard-Face" described an elderly man of James' general appearance who played blues on piano and guitar. The man, whom "Hard-Face" knew only as "Curly," had operated a night-spot called the *Tin Top* or *Tin Roof Cafe* in West Memphis. In 1961 he had been arrested on a bootlegging warrant and had jumped bail.

Finding James, it now appeared, would be a difficult task. He was a man who did not want to be found.

3. *The Quarry*

Later, he would make up a morbid, sorrowful song about the experience. It began:

> Layin' sick on my bed
> I used to have a few friends but they wish that I was
>   dead.
>
> The doctor came in lookin' very sad
> He diagnosed my case and he said it was awfully bad.
>
> He walked away, mumblin' very low
> Say: "He may get better but he'll never get well no
>   more."

His desolation was not simply a song conceit: he had only one visitor, a common-law wife who found him incomprehensible. "He gets up at night and sits and thinks," she would say of him. "He won't tell anybody what's on his mind."

As he lay in the hospital ward, he brooded. Decades ago, when he was a child, his condition had been prophesied. At the age of four his mother had taken him to a fortune teller: the fortune teller had told him that he would travel widely in life and become a famous person, but would be ruined by a scandal. Her melodramatic words had made a lasting impression on him. Once he had traveled widely and had achieved some fame with music. Now the last part of the prophecy had come true.

The doctors hadn't explained what was wrong with him, and he would not have trusted their explanations. He had no confidence in their ability to heal him. The task of healing him

was up to Jesus. If Jesus wanted him to recover, he would recover. If Jesus wanted him to die, he would die.

But he was not resigned to death. He wanted to get off the
hospital bed and destroy the person who was responsible for
his condition—a wrenching growth on his penis.

The malefactor, he knew, was a girlfriend who had worked
hoodoo on him. She had done it to ruin his sex life after he
had refused to leave his wife for her. In the process she had
inflicted shame and disgrace upon him: he had looked forward
to equaling his father, who had boasted of leading a vigorous
sex life up to the age of 86.

She would not go unpunished for subjecting him to what he
called "this jinx of death." If he ever got out of the hospital,
he would shoot the woman dead. Even if he saw her on a public
street in broad daylight he would open fire, and keep firing
until he ran out of ammunition. Afterwards, the Tunica police
could do with him what they wished.

4. *Looking Back*

"There's no tellin' where I mighta wound up if I hadn't come off this music business," he once said, remarking on his religious conversion. "In Hollywood, I reckon." Yet by the time he had decided to forsake blues, James' recording career was already stalemated. Instead of the large initial payoff he anticipated from Paramount, he received a check for twenty dollars after the company released his first record, *Hard Time Killin' Floor Blues*. By the end of the year his wealth amounted to sixty dollars in royalty money.

The Depression only masked what would have been an inevitable failure on James' part. Though he traveled extensively in Mississippi in the 1920s, he had left no real mark beyond his home town. Johnnie Temple recalled that when he would sing *Devil Got My Woman* on the streets of Jackson, he sounded so sorrowful that spectators would pay him money to make him stop singing. Strife and sorrow had no entertainment value among audiences of his day.

Many blues singers paid lip service to the notion that blues was unhappy music, the antithesis of the spirituals that were supposed to uplift the spirits of listeners. Their songs were replete with rhetorical references to "having the blues," which became almost obligatory when blues became the popular music of blacks in the decade between 1910 and 1920. Yet most blues singers were simply entertainers. In Mississippi, the verbal content of most blues songs was superseded by a heavy dance beat that provided a livelihood for their performers, who entertained at rural "house frolics" (private parties organized by bootleggers as a means of selling their product) and "jukehouses" (commercially operated night-spots located in towns and cities). Even James respected this principle: his sorrowful *Hard Times* was played incongruously to a surging 1-2 beat. But the beat of his music was often secondary to its emotional content. His songs were expressions of his own bleak temperament. He was an aloof person who begrudged banter and mistrusted merriment. If blues had not existed in James' youth, he might have invented them.

For as long as he could remember, Skip James was a loner. "I myself was some kind of peculiar kid, I guess," he would say. "I wanted to be by myself: if the conversation wasn't so that I could . . . get a little logic from it, it didn't interest me. I always wanted to do somethin' for myself, and just decided I wouldn't stop till I made some kind of mark in life." In music he generally shunned duet partners. "I never did want to play in no group or band or nothin'," he said. "I just wanna be me, Skip." For the most part he was too egotistical to work with other musicians: "If I get out in the deeps in the water," he explained, "I don't expect to have two paddles . . . I'd get out there and mess around with you, I be pullin' this side and you be pullin' that side . . . I ain't about to tote you: tote yourself. That fair? If I don't drift, I'll sink. An' if I should drift and make it ashore . . . I made the landin' for Skip."

To James, other musicians were opponents. Using the metaphor Booker T. Washington applied to his race, he likened blues musicians to a barrel of crabs. "Those crabs'll be crawlin' to try to reach the height of that barrel. An' the lead one will be nearly at the top. And those behind him are apt to grab him and put him back, 'cause he don't take them with him." Whenever he played, he had no intention of taking other musicians with him: he wanted to scale the top of the barrel by himself. The thought that another musician might duplicate his music was almost unendurable to him. The sight of a musician in his audience was a summons to James to alter his own playing. "If I figure he have caught the least idea about a song, when he come back the next night it'll be so different that he can't understand it. Keep him graspin' at it all the time."

Listening to James rant about the barrel of crabs that represented the music world to him, one was tempted to think that music appealed to him because it reflected the alienation of a man in perpetual combat with the world. His music was the defiant product of an emotional hermit: "I wanted it different all the way—I always have had that intensity, to go contrary to the rest."

PART TWO

5. *Woodbine*

Many factors combined to imbue Skip James with a sense of haughty isolation from his peers. He was an only child in a plantation culture where large families predominated, and a member of a favored family in a downtrodden environment where "Southern white folks didn't wanna see the colored fellow with nothin' but a shovel or hoe handle or plough handle in his hands, and a mule to pull it." His mother Phyllis worked as a cook and babysitter for the wealthy owner of the *Woodbine* plantation, located a mile and a half from Bentonia and fifteen miles south of Yazoo City, where he was born in a "colored" hospital on June 21, 1902. He was christened Nehemiah Curtis James, his given name honoring the governor of Judea who rebuilt the walls of Jerusalem.

His native Yazoo County was a region of cotton plantations set in bluff hills just south of the Mississippi Delta. In an 1869 treatise on the Southern plantation system, an observer had written of its residents: "... the black population of this County in point of intelligence is very far ahead of any similar population heretofore manumitted ... "[*] Perhaps because its original surroundings were so desolate, *Woodbine* was treated as a town on nineteenth-century maps. (A synonym for the Virginia creeper, "Woodbine" had been a favorite allusion in nineteenth century romantic poetry.) The towns in the vicinity that would become James' primary musical outlets—Satartia, Pocahantas, and Flora—were even smaller than Bentonia, and the only ap-

---

[*]F.W. Luring and C.F. Atkinson, *Cotton Culture And The South* (A. Williams & Co., Boston).

preciable settlement in the vicinity, Yazoo City, was no city at all. In 1930 it numbered only 5580 residents.

Though the adult James spoke contemptuously of these "plantation towns," he also was wont to sentimentalize the character of their rustic residents, whom he felt were uncorrupted by self-interest. "There was such a close tie or relation in a community then," he said of his childhood years. ". . . Brotherly love was existin' so . . . When we raised cattle and would have an overplus of milk and butter, we'd divide and distribute among the people that didn't have any. I've walked miles a lots of times to take neighbors things like tomatoes, milk, and butter. But now if somebody got a surplus you got to pay for it, or else you don't get it.

"We'd have haystacks of peanuts, till we'd feed it to the cattle if nobody could use it. Now if you ain't got ten cents you can't get a bag of peanuts. If you want a piece of meat now, you can't get it: not unless you got the money. Regardless to the friendship.

"Christianity was really prevailin' then in a sincere and honest way. The people didn't get apart so much as now . . . "

Instead, they were divided along racial lines. The elderly woman who owned *Woodbine* exercised absolute control over its black tenants. "She would stand there sometimes at certain windows and then watch the labor in that big house, and if you would stop one minute she would tell her son: 'So-and-so stopped and he did such-and-such a thing. He didn't work so well.' That was in slavery time-ism . . .

"When freedom come (I don't know what they call it; whatever it is, I can't understand it) she would come to me more considerate and more 'compris,' more in sympathy . . . She believe in that slavery in this way: she want to see the Negroes work hard, but one thing about it: sometime her son would not want to give some of them as much justice as they deserved, but she would tell him sometimes: 'Son, I think that's wrong.' "

While all blacks stood legally on the same low Jim Crow level, sharp social distinctions abounded on every plantation. James' own family was marked by two polar extremes, exalted respectability and furtive criminality—warring identities that he was to reenact in his own life. Thanks to his mother's position in the

Whitehead household ("she wasn't no maid," James boasted), he considered himself a caste above the sharecroppers he disparaged as "plantation Negroes." His father Edward, on the other hand, was a local lowlife, whom James knew chiefly by legend and idealized as "very skillful." A guitarist and a bootlegger, he had left Bentonia as a wanted man around 1907. According to the story that James received from relatives, his father had been backed in the latter enterprise by a wealthy plantation owner from nearby Mechanicsburg, Dick Williams. The political control Williams had exercised over local police had been to no avail when state revenue agents decided to raid his plantation still, and when Williams got wind of their plans, he advised the elder James to flee.

"Son" James, as he was originally called, would believe that his musical gifts had been inherited from his father, whose music he never heard. Yet he had grown up feeling, as he put it, "like a forsaken child." He had only fragmentary images of his father, not all of them pleasant. "I remember that my daddy bought me a tall chair," he said, "a red chair with a back to it. 'Bout a four-foot chair, and 'cause I'se a little fella, he held me up in it. I remember eatin' at that chair many time." James thought this gift was presented to him at age two. "Now I don't remember this myself, but my mother told me that one day we were sittin' there, and my daddy said somethin' to me. Then I threw a fork at him. Now what did I do that for? Somethin' must have happened to me, I reckon. And my daddy got so angry . . . he wanted to whup me. Then him and my mother had it out. She said, 'You know you should not hit that baby,' and she wouldn't let him. And they had a little battle, but I don't know how it came out because I was too small."

His most enduring childhood image of his father was his recollection of seeing him somberly kissing his mother good-bye and pocketing two boxes of wooden matches as he prepared to take to the woods to escape the police.

It was partly owing to his lifelong sense of abandonment that his blues became desolate documents. He considered *Hard-Luck Child* "his song," a summation of his situation in life:

Been to the Nation, from there to the Territo'
And I'm a hard-luck child, catch the devil every-
    where I go.

Besides imbibing his mother's sense of social superiority, he
also imbibed the mantle of bitterness she took on after Mrs.
Whitehead, the owner of *Woodbine*, left the plantation to her
son R. K. "Kirk" Whitehead, for whom Skip's mother had often
baby-sat. Phyllis James claimed to have heard the son make a
deathbed promise to his mother that he would give Phyllis a
lifetime, rent-free home on the plantation, along with a cash
stipend. The promise never materialized, and Phyllis took on,
in her own mind, a sense of betrayed martyrdom. Perhaps in
unconscious imitation of a figure he idealized ("she mostly was
worked to death," he said bitterly of her), James would similarly
acquire a disgruntled sense of having been perennially short-
changed in life.

While his mother toiled in the Whitehead kitchen, Skippy was
raised by his maternal grandparents, who had been brought to
Yazoo County from Virginia on the slave market. They were
an industrious couple who would "raise everything themselves
but sugar and flour," and their efforts buffeted them from the
havoc wrecked by the boll weevil, which desolated Bentonia
around 1907. "Grandmother and them used to raise their own
rice and tobacco," he recalled. "They'd kill hogs and have meat
from one end of the year to the other and sometimes for two
years. We'd have cans of lard that we never did get to open.
We'd raise chickens. Then we'd kill beefs and pickle 'em. See,
we'd kill a yearling and carve it up; then put it in barrels with
vinegar and spices; what they call a pickel-pork . . . Sometimes
that food would last through the whole season."

The credo of his grandfather, which had been "If they beat
me today they'll have to beat me tomorrow," might have become
Skippy's own. He had an intractable disposition which his
mother attributed to his astrological sign (Leo). "I tell you, I
have always been very agreeable," he once said, "but I go as
far as I can and then I won't go no further. I'm just like a
mule: you can spur him and you can beat him, and he ain't
gonna do nothin' but stand there and kick up and wag . . . I'll

lead but I won't drive: you can lead me but you can't drive
me. I stay in one place and kick up and raise hell."

As a boy he tended cows for his grandparents but did no
plantation work, for which the overseer of the plantation
once recommended that he be flogged. According to James,
who learned of this event from his mother, the Whiteheads
sharply rejected this suggestion. James claimed that his boyhood "agreeableness" and intelligence eventually made a fine
impression on "Kirk" Whitehead. "He liked me cause I was
always very active and smart, you know; if I seen anything
to be did on the plantation I'd go there and do it: go out
and clean up the yard, feed the stock or somethin' like that,
an' he just taken a liking to me." Once the plantation owner,
who had no children, indicated to Phyllis James that he
would give Nehemiah a first-class education if she would let
him take charge of his upbringing. "I wished many times my
mother hadda given me to that man," James said. "I'd a-been
his godson."

Although James later boasted of being a "walking encyclopedia,"
his avid natural intelligence was blunted by a catch-can education.
"My mother, what little education I got, she did it; she give me
that privilege," he would say regretfully. "When I got eligible for
school, my mother started me. Sometimes I would take more
interest in myself than my teacher would." By the most recent
census of 1900, 49.1% of Mississippi's blacks were officially clas-
sified as illiterate; it was estimated that fewer than 40% of the
state's black youths between the ages of five and eighteen then
regularly attended school. "Those people at the time I was comin'
up was mostly illiterates," he recalled. ". . . Very few times could
you find one of the parents with an education . . . Usually none
of the parents did . . . If you had a high school degree, it was
'worthwhile' [worth money]." In later years, James would represent himself as a high school graduate, a claim that brought a
snicker from his blues-playing mentor, Henry Stuckey.

To compensate for his lack of formal knowledge, he acquired
a pretentious vocabulary, and brandished it at every opportunity.
A word like "speed" was too humble for him; in its place he
would say "velocity," even if the plantation blacks who heard
him speak listened uncomprehendingly.

At the same time, his mother's superstitiousness readily rubbed off on him, and he acquired an enduring belief in magic. "I learnt to sit under the feets of people who are styled as gazers," he recalled. "I've studied horoscopes right smart in my life."

Despite his alienation from his peers, he lent an attentive and often credulous ear to any fantastic notion uttered in his presence. "This guy was talkin' to someone that I was a friend to, and he say that he flew so high and so far till he couldn't come down," he once reported. "And he ran into a city up there. And that city had golden gates, that open at your call. The streets was pearl, and it was people there transferred: walkin' just like we're walkin' down here. And those gates opened at their own accord: you didn't have to touch 'em. . . . You know the Bible say there are first, second, and third heavens in the mid-airs.

". . . I thought over that, and I don't know how to accept that so well."

The segregated schools he attended did nothing to cure his superstitiousness. His most memorable formal educational experience consisted of a visit by a magician who performed sleight-of-hand tricks.

He also learned, from a black teacher, the meaning of the word "nigger." As James heard it, "nigger" was a quality of character, not of color.

"Mean disposition and dirty ideas—that's a nigger for you," he said.

This notion of negritude as a figurative property seems to have possessed James. In order to salvage self-esteem, he grew almost to regard himself as a figurative white man trapped in a black skin. "I think I have a white man's integrity," he once remarked. His blues would reflect his image of himself as an honorable victim of other people's evil machinations. Their implicit message was that he was white; his adversaries were black.

Even in childhood, James was wont to look down on his peers. "Kids in my day were just after rippin' and playin' and fightin' one another—they wasn't trained. They didn't wanna learn anything; they were bad kids." James had more exalted interests. While attending the St. Paul elementary school on *Woodbine* he was consumed by curiosity for strange words; whenever he found a scrap of paper he would attempt to read it. He often carried such scraps to older people in an effort to learn the strange words he saw written on them. In later years, James would speak in his own strange dialect, its curiously cultivated abstract nouns removed from the concrete speech of his contemporaries (which employed almost no abstract nouns), its grammar on the level of unlettered plantation speech. He often invoked archaic uses that reflected the bygone speech of the elders he had consulted in childhood:

At his departure [death], he was eighty-six.

And they was so many of them till the elements [sky] was just dark . . .

I'm so precautious [cautious] along the line of musical errors.

You can take a peach or pear . . . that is hangin' on the tree . . . After a while, it gonna ripen, after which it has reached its perfection [full growth].

. . . my step-daddy . . . he told 'im: '. . . you better not top [ascend to the top of] that hill.'

. . . when he bust that bottle open there was a pure [absolutely] dead jaybird in there.

. . . it tossed its tail around . . . like a fish in the water, make a flounce [twisting motion] or somethin' like that.

. . . if I'll contain [take up] with you . . . and see that you don't take heed to what I say, well then . . .

. . . This gentleman . . . threw out some very bad insinuations deferrin' [referring] to Mississippi.

Music interested him no less than language. "When I was just a little kid, I used to make a racket around the house by beating a bucket," he recalled. ". . . That was just about the first time I'd gotten an idea to make a tune." To the chagrin of his grandmother, he followed anyone he saw playing music "like they were the pied piper." His earliest musical memory consisted

of surreptitiously peering at a square dance held on *Woodbine*
when he was seven or nine years old, around the time his father
defected from his household: "I couldn't stay out no way, I had
to slip off; grandmother woulda whipped me to death, man,
she'd a-know I slipped off to a frolic..." At the frolic a middle-aged localite named Rich Griffin fiddled to *Drunken Spree*,
accompanied by the "rapped" (strummed) guitar of a youth from
Satartia, Henry Stuckey:

> I pawned my watch, pawned my chain
> Pawned my gold diamond ring
> If that don't settle my drunken spree
> I'll never get drunk again.
>
> I love my darlin', yes I do
> Love her till the sea go dry
> An' if I thought she didn't love me
> I'd take morphine and die.

This song made a lasting impression on him; soon he was
singing a rudimentary version of it. "I was quite a little yearling
boy, about seven, eight, or maybe nine or ten years when I
started to sing," he recalled. "Then I began to try to drag the
guitar around, frailin', playin' some chords of different things
I had heard." The first instrument he played was a $2.50 model
purchased by his mother. "After I got strong enough to make
a good chord, then I would harmonize it with my voice." His
early experiments took place at home: "My mother made me
put the guitar down to eat my meals, I was just that much interested," he recalled.

As a beginner James relied on his own ear. He never took
lessons from local musicians. "...If you're just musically inclined, you can just go on, hear somethin', and that sound
will stay within, until you get someplace where you can try
it," he generalized. "You got a send-off, right in the other
fellow's version which you hear; may not be one verse of a
song; you get that, you can hold it until you get home...
you can practice on it."

His aspirations as a guitarist were fueled by the example of
Charlie and Jesse Sims, two brothers from nearby Valley who were

considered Yazoo County's top guitarists, and Stuckey, who was five years older than himself. Stuckey lived on the Satartia plantation of Whitehead's cousin "Ky" Kirk. He had begun playing guitar in 1905 at the age of seven, learning chords from an older local musician named Rich Dickson. He developed a raucous style of heavy strumming. As a soloist, "he'd holler and stomp till you'd think there was two or three people," James said of him.

Stuckey frequently visited Bentonia to accompany Griffin and a 70-year-old fiddler known as "Old Man Green McCloud." McCloud played such works as *Sliding Delta* and *Alabama Bound*, two standards of the day, and *Turkey In The Straw*. In emulation of McCloud, James sometimes experimented with violin, but never learned to play it proficiently.

Before he was fifteen, James began practicing on an organ owned by his aunt Martha Polk. His original organ effort was a popular ditty known as *Coonjine Lady*. It was played chordally with an *oom*pah beat and featured a simple two-line refrain:

Coonjine lady, coonjine
Coonjine lady, coonjine

Mama don't 'low me to coonjine
Papa don't 'low me to try.

The dance that "coonjine" presumably represented was long obsolete when James learned the piece.

Another early James effort was *Slidin' Delta*, a Slow Drag ditty that alluded to an Illinois Central train he had never seen:

The Slidin' Delta runs right by my door (2).

I'm goin' where the Southern cross the Dog (2).

James learned to play a strummed version of this song, which had been a staple among black guitarists since the early 1890s. The song, he was to say in the 1960s, was "at least a hundred years old."

Before James became accomplished musically he developed a musical perspective. He considered *Drunken Spree*, an eccentrically phrased eight-bar ditty known among musicians of both races, a banal piece of music. "It wasn't deep enough suited," he said of the song, which was played with a lumbering 1-2 square dance beat. The version he acquired from Henry Stuckey and recorded some twenty years later was probably typical of plantation music in the early 1900s. Its melody, which did not span an octave, was drawn from the pentatonic scale that was the bedrock of contemporary hillbilly music, with the addition of a minor seventh. It featured an ungainly, colorless accompaniment in the A position, with no integration of guitar and vocal lines. Instead, a conventional IV^7-V^7 chord progression was used to harmonize its melody.

As soon as he was able to, James would discard strumming for plucked melody notes, often played on single strings. "I don't believe in no rappin' an' frailin'," he said, using Mississippi synonyms for guitar strumming. "Never did. When I started tryin' to learn, I always did wanna pick my music clear, where I could understand it."

James also yearned for a forlorn sound that would impress listeners: "I decided . . . I'd try to play somethin' just as 'lonesome' as I could. To try to take an effect." To the adult James, blues would become "lonesome songs," the product of aching loneliness:

> . . . you hear me singin' my true lonesome song
> These hard times can last us so very long.
> (*Hard Times Killin' Floor Blues*)

> Hey hey pretty mama, I ain't gonna be here long
> That's why you hear me, sing my lonesome song.
> (*Little Cow And Calf Is Gonna Die Blues*)

But the verbal content of his songs was second to their ability to assault the senses. He conceived of blues as having the mesmeric effect of spirituals. Instead of uplifting listeners, it would stun them. "Why did I like blues?" he once asked. "Well, I'll tell you . . . The blues will take more effect than any other kind of music." Unlike other blues singers, he was able to project forlornness even when performing spirited, uptempo music. One of the ways by which he was able to suggest "lonesomeness" was to sing in a falsetto voice that imitated his pre-pubescent vocal register, and, perhaps, the violin strains of musicians like Green McCloud. "I started singing when I first started a note," he recalled. "First note I made on the guitar I wanted to harmony with it or sing or say somethin' to it. That's the best way you can get your music harmonized. You don't sing, you might make a dischord anytime."

Although blues experts of later generations surmised that blues arose on rural plantations, James' early musical diet consisted of a meager assortment of bland eight-bar ditties. None of his pre-teenage mentors performed blues, and James never heard of blues in his youth. "Later on, when I got grown, I heard my mama and them talk about 'singing the blues.' I wondered what the blues was then," he would recall.

6. *The Birth Of The Blues*

Sometime shortly after 1820, a paternalistic white planter or missionary taught a group of Southern slaves a simple one-chord eighteenth-century Methodist hymn written by the celebrated composer Charles Wesley (1707-1788). The tune, *Roll Jordan,* had recently been published as part of a Kentucky camp meeting hymnal that was circulated in Kentucky and Virginia in the wake of the Great Revival that had erupted at a Kentucky camp meeting in 1801. The planter or missionary who passed it on to slaves no doubt intended to Christianize heathen Africans, and in so doing, make them more docile and tractable. Yet this transaction would achieve an improbable result: it would lay the basis for a rowdy form of music that would be developed within seventy years and would become America's only native compositional form. Ironically, this musical form, eventually known as the "blues," would gain notoriety among blacks as the "devil's music," the antithesis of godly music, and would be celebrated by whites as a simon-pure expression of black music.

How does one know that blues were a by-product of the Great Revival, issuing from the same cultivated pen (Charles Wesley's) that authored the words of *Hark! The Herald Angels Sing*? After all, blues music sprouted in complete obscurity. It was not until 1912 that any published song bore the name "blues," and not until the 1960s that researchers paid more than cursory attention to its conceivable origins.

The answer lies in the eccentric architecture that gives the blues phrase its distinctive character. The building block of the blues is a four-bar phrase divided into two unbalanced parts:

From *Hurst's History of Methodism*

CHARLES WESLEY

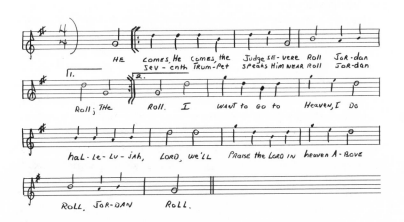

a ten-beat vocal phrase, followed by a six-beat instrumental phrase. It is this unvarying phrase, repeated three times, that makes for a twelve-bar blues, and is the unique insignia of the form, removing it from the realm of spirituals or any other song form.

The four-bar phrases of *Roll Jordan* likewise consist of a ten-beat line, followed by a six-beat refrain ("Roll, Jordan"). Substitute an instrumental phrase for the refrain, and one has an unmistakable blues phrase.

The six-beat instrumental snippet that completes most blues lines has a refrain-like character. Like a vocal refrain, it is normally repeated throughout the song, with no variation. As with a vocal refrain, it is musically complete, but incapable of standing apart from from the section it accompanies.

Two early blues recordings used a six-beat vocal refrain rather than an instrumental fill. Blind Lemon Jefferson's *Bad Luck Blues* (1927) began:

> I wanna go home but I ain't got sufficient clothes
> Doggone my bad luck soul

The phrase "Doggone my bad luck soul" is equivalent to the six-beat refrain of *Roll Jordan*. The initial vocal line of Tommy Johnson's crude one-chord *Cool Drink Of Water* (1928) is divided into two sections:

> I asked for water, an' she brought me gasoline
> Lord, Lordie, Lord!

The chorus "Lord, Lordie, Lord!" (sung in a falsetto) is also equivalent to the refrain "Roll Jordan."

In all probability, the earliest blues song resembled the format of *Bad Luck Blues* and *Cool Drink Of Water*, sung either a cappella or set to rudimentary accompaniment on the banjo or fiddle, the favorite black instruments of the nineteenth century. The unknown creator of the first blues probably based its phrasing on *Roll Jordan*, set to secular lyrics and a new melody. Its strictness indicates that blues arose as performance music, rather than as a formless expression of individual feeling. The likelihood is that the proto-blues singer who converted *Roll Jordan* into a secular song himself had no idea that a genre would eventually come of his effort. By the same token, his audience was probably unfamiliar with its musical predecessor, which was far less famous than Wesley's *Jesus, Lover Of My Soul* (1739).

A frequent armchair assumption that blues began as a spontaneous outburst of emotion was the result of reading Wordsworth's famous preface to *Lyrical Ballads* (1802), which held that poetry arose from the "spontaneous overflow of powerful feelings . . . " This notion was even applied to dance blues; as a 1929 newspaper ad for Charlie Patton's recording of the tune *Down The Dirt Road Blues* put it:

> He's had a lot of trouble at home and he's decided to hit the dirty, dusty road for parts unknown. He wants to forget everything and to go somewhere else, so he sings this novel blues as his lazy mule joggles him along the old dirt road.

The emphasis on the emotional tenor rather than the tangible components of blues obscured its links to a previous model, which had been long forgotten admist Wesley's output of 6500 hymns (many written spontaneously, for special occasions) by the time blues arose.

In itself, the derivation of blues from an old spiritual is unremarkable. For example, several songs of the early rock and roll era were filched from forgotten, decades-old songs. Laverne Baker's *Tweedle Dee* (1954), which disk jockey Alan Freed touted as the first rock and roll hit, copied the phrasing pattern and tune contour of the nineteenth century ballad *Careless Love*. Moreover, the line between black gospel and secular music has always been nebulous, causing the Mississippi blues singer Sam Chatmon to surmise: "The blues come from church songs." The concert singer Roland Hayes wrote of turn-of-the-century music in his native Georgia: "So nearly contiguous were the sacred and profane worlds in the Flatwoods that their music was nearly identical." A fiddler he knew maintained that "the profane music of city Negroes was simply the familiar religious music put to swing. The sacred words were dropped, and new texts, frequently meaningless, put the burden of sensation upon the notes." Secularized hymns of the era included *She'll Be Comin'*

'Round The Mountain (originally published in 1899) and *Hesitation Blues.*

What is remarkable is the likelihood that a single song should spawn a full-fledged musical genre. How and why this happened is a matter of guesswork. In all likelihood the pattern of *Roll Jordan* took root in nineteenth-century black music because it was among the earliest spirituals learned by slaves. The musical culture of both races was in a rude state in 1820, when *Roll Jordan* (written between 1740 and 1750) was published for camp meeting consumption. Owing to a paucity of native material, musical borrowings abounded everywhere: eight years earlier, when Francis Scott Key had written what would become the national anthem, he set its words to a German drinking song.

In any event, a transformed version of *Roll Jordan* became familiar to nineteenth century slaves as *Roll Jordan, Roll.* Although this famous song bore little resemblance to its predecessor, the phrasing pattern of the original *Roll Jordan* was adopted by a slave spiritual published in 1887, *Is Massa Goin' To Sell Us Tomorrow?.* Other spirituals approximated its phrasing pattern by pairing a nine-beat vocal with a seven-beat refrain: *Inchin' Along* (published in 1872), *He's The Lily Of The Valley* (published in 1872), *Let My People Go!* (published in 1872), and *Bye an' Bye* (published in 1902). This pattern, which was found in a white hymn (*Antioch*) published in 1854, would sometimes supplant the "ten/six" phrase in twentieth-century blues song.

Because the secular songs of nineteenth-century blacks were scarcely documented, one is left to guess when the pattern of *Roll Jordan* gave rise to blues. The blues phrase could have arisen in black song any time between 1820 and 1890, when one sees the first inklings of blues song. It might have existed for decades in the form of one or two songs. At some point another musician substituted an instrumental fill for a six-beat refrain, and created a recognizable blues. This unknown innovator laid the basis for the emergence of blues as a real genre, rather than a motley assortment of transient tunes. Indeed, it is the part-vocal, part-instrumental character of blues that constitutes its real claim to distinction: no other song form has a built-in instrumental phrase, and it is this aspect of blues that has exerted the greatest influence on rock music.

Even after it was transformed into a song that alternated vocal and instrumental phrases, blues probably existed indefinitely in the form of one or two uncelebrated songs. It was only when numerous musicians began to copy their format that it solidified into a genre, enabling its exponents to become blues singers by trade. In all probability, the transformation from song to songs to genre took decades to effect, and was suddenly accelerated by the turn of the century vogue for the guitar.

Individual songs bearing the blues phrasing pattern were familiar a century ago. *Careless Love*, a maudlin eight-bar ballad that W. C. Handy heard in 1892 and that became a staple of black entertainers, used a "ten-six" blues pattern for its first, second, and concluding phrases. Another hoboing song of the same vintage, *East St. Louis* (the same song James knew as *Slidin' Delta*), consisted of two four-bar phrases, the second of which was a familiar blues phrase.

A quartet W. C. Handy joined around 1890 in Florence, Alabama, adapted a twelve-bar guitar blues, *Got No Mo' Home Dan A Dog*, set in an ABA melody pattern. Between 1892 and 1895, Handy and local musicians performed the same song in Evansville, Indiana:

> Gwine take morphine and die, Lord (2).
> Gwine take morphine and die.
>
> Ain't not no friend nowhere, Lord (2).
> Ain't got no friend nowhere.
>
> Got no more home than a dog, Lord. (2)
> Got no more home than a dog.

Evidently its originator was a vagrant who used his lyrics to attract sympathy and handouts from listeners. Already a familiar conceit of blues lyrics had been established; in decades to come the songs would typically express turmoil and turbulence.

There were doubtless many other blues of the period, or from earlier decades, but no musicologist paid any attention to them. It was not until the first decade of the twentieth century that blues took on its familiar name or had any claim as the preferred music of blacks. By the time blues were first recorded in 1920, the music was recognizably old-fashioned. Mamie Smith, the first black singer to record blues, told a *Chicago Defender* reporter in 1921: "It is a peculiar and individual type of music which goes back for generations."

As blues developed, it acquired distinctive characteristics besides its peculiar phrasing pattern. For unknown reasons, it customarily settled into an AAB melodic and lyric pattern, which resulted in a twelve-bar stanza. Each phrase formed a complete, speech-like statement.

It is conceivable that the characteristic blues format was also suggested by *Roll Jordan*, which used an AABB pattern that differed from the typical blues only in its repetition of the second phrase. Moreover, the separate declamations of *Roll Jordan* formed complete statements, in the fashion of blues song:

> I want to go to heaven, I do.
>
> We'll praise the Lord in heaven above.

Another unusual characteristic of blues was its phrase endings: each blues vocal phrase invariably ended on the keynote, and its follow-up instrumentation on the tonic chord. This feature may also have been a legacy of *Roll Jordan*, which ended its first two ten-beat phrases on the keynote. In any event, it gave blues a crude, unmelodic cast, creating an air of finality with every blues phrase. Whatever its origin, the keynote phrase-ending indicates that blues were developed by musicians who had not assimilated much in the way of Western melodizing, which tends to suspend the keynote until the last phrase of a stanza, and to rely on other phrase-ending notes in the interim.

Virtually every blues song, regardless of its structure, has this keynote/tonic phrase-ending characteristic. If a blues vocal phrase does not end on the keynote, it ends on a note (such as minor third or dominant) that has been substituted for it. The same is true of a blues instrumental phrase. It is this feature that stamps numerous black songs (such as Skip James' *Devil Got My Woman*) as blues even though they contain eccentric phrasing patterns. In some instances musicians created blues songs simply by singing an arbitrary keynote-ending phrase, and following it with a similarly arbitrary instrumental one.

The tyranny of the blues keynote-ending is probably the reason that blues failed to mushroom into a more conventional sixteen-bar song, with four phrases instead of three. Although a few sixteen-bar blues were recorded in the 1920s, the lack of melodic development that was mandated by keynote endings made lengthy blues stanzas unecessary.

Among black performers, blues gradually gained ascendancy over two rival song types, both of which survived into the early twentieth century, only to wane as blues waxed. The first such form, which was sometimes called the "breakdown," was a simple medium or uptempo four-bar dance ditty phrased in single measures, given a 1-2-3-4 accenting pattern. It made use of a continuous banjo or guitar accompaniment involving two major chords (the dominant and the tonic) and featured a chord change on the accented first beat of each measure. Some breakdowns were instrumentals; others were set to vocal airs. Although black breakdowns remained a distinctive genre, the form was derived from white music; its essential ingredients can be found in Stephen Foster's guitar arrangement of *Old Dog Tray*, which was published in 1855 and was based on two four-bar phrases, involving the dominant seventh and tonic chord.

The breakdown was popular fare at pre-World War One plantation dances and may have dated to the 1850s, when the term "breakdown" entered American speech as a synonym for a black dance gathering. It probably died out because its musical possibilities were readily exhausted in the form of a few songs. By the time black music was recorded on a wide scale in the 1920s, vestiges of this once-fashionable form were still heard in half a dozen recordings: *Tear It Down* (a popular repertoire piece among black guitarists), *Drop That Sack* (a twelve-bar ditty recorded by Papa Charlie Jackson), *Shake It And Break It* (another twelve-bar song recorded by Charlie Patton), Bo Carter's eight-bar *Twist It, Babe*, Gus Cannon's *My Money Never Runs Out*, and Caldwell Bracey's *Stered Gal*. Other breakdowns were played by contemporary Southern guitarists, such as Mississippi John Hurt (*The First Shot Got Him*), Leadbelly (*You Can't Lose Me Cholly*), and Gary Davis (*Candy Man*). No musicians of the period specialized in breakdowns, however, and the only black entertainer of the era who showed a real flair for the idiom was William Moore, a guitar-playing barber from Virginia whose 1928 recording *Barbershop Rag* was (despite its title) a rollicking, intricately-picked breakdown.

The second song type, which some performers termed the "rag" (and which never acquired the firm nomenclature of blues), was an eight or sixteen-bar vocal ditty typically used for square dancing. This genre of songs had nothing in common with the familiar ragtime piano music, or Tin Pan Alley songs based on this music. "Rag" songs consisted of two-measure phrases (with the final beat or two beats of each phrase instrumentalized) that were more melodic than blues songs, thanks to their non-keynote cadences. Although the white public had no inkling of the existence of the "rag" idiom, isolated "rag" songs entered mainstream pop music. The chorus of *The New Bully*, which May Irwin popularized in 1895, was based on a version of *Pallet On The Floor* called *Looking For The Bully Of The Town*.

Numerous "rag" songs became standards among black entertainers: *Make Me A Pallet On The Floor, Stack O'Lee, Nobody's Business If I Do*. While the arrangements of such songs were often individualized, most performers who sang "rag" songs appear to have relied on their intrinsic melodies to carry the performance, rather than impose their personalities on the form in the fashion of many blues singers.

The format of "rags" was less distinctive than that of blues, having been conventional in hillbilly music and in spirituals, either of which could have given rise to the "rag" song. Although "rags" and blues had distinct and dissimilar structures, the dominance of blues as popular music among blacks led performers (or record companies) to sometimes mislabel "rags" as blues.

Although the blues would scarcely contain a single inherent structural feature, its performing conventions became so rigid and pervasive that they were often later taken as intrinsic attributes of the form, and would mistakenly find their way into musical definitions. The blues vocal phrase and the single-note riffs that were offshoots of it employed an Afro-American tonality that mixed major and minor tones in such a way as to make the music neither major nor minor. The bedrock minor tones were the minor third and seventh, freely mixed with major thirds; they had arrived by way of Africa, where they were common. When blues song first appeared in Tin Pan Alley via W.C. Handy, this departure from the diatonic pop scale was so striking that musicologists began referring to "blue notes" (minor thirds and sevenths), or a "blues scale," such as was employed by Gershwin's *Rhapsody In Blue* (1924). But the same tonal ingredients were found in spirituals, or any other black song. Nor were minor thirds and sevenths inherent in blues-singing. The title verse of Henry Spaulding's classic *Cairo Blues* (1929), for example, would be rendered with the conventional pentatonic scale employed by white country musicians, and Stephen Foster: because the character of blues actually derives from its phrasing pattern and juxtaposition of vocal and instrumental parts, such a departure is scarcely noticable.

The most familiar blues convention was the twelve-bar format of its typical stanzas, brought about by repeating its first phrase, and concluding with a rhymed line. It was often supposed that the twelve-bar presentation was the blues' intrinsic form, or that it represented a refinement of some earlier pattern. Since the essential building block of the twelve-bar pattern is the 10/6 (or 9/7) series of vocal/instrumental beats, which amounts to a four-bar phrase, it is likely that the earliest recognizable blues consisted of eight or twelve-bars, depending on whether two or three phrases were employed to create a stanza. Far from being a refinement of an irregular pattern, this pattern itself was awkward and irregular, involving fractional measures that were foreign to the basic mode of Western music-making. Even blues singers themselves did not naturally take to this pattern: virtually every blues guitarist who would attempt to render the standard blues instrumental phrase would split his instrumental work into two snippets, the first a conventional single measure riff, concluding on the tonic, followed by two harmonically superfluous beats of full chord strumming.

The twelve-bar stanza appears to have taken hold because its predictability allowed for easy ensemble playing. A more firmly fixed convention was the first-person premise of the blues couplet:

> I'd rather be the devil, to be that woman's man . . .
>
> I would rather be buried, in some cypress grove . . .
>
> I love my cherry ball, better than I love myself . . .

The subject of virtually every blues song was the singer himself. This hermetic outlook may have come from the Book of Psalms, where the first person predominates, or from a spiritual based on a psalm. Of the thousands of blues recorded between 1920-1941, there are probably fewer than half a dozen that are not sung from the first person.

It is likely that the average blues song heard at the turn of the century was simply a recitation of disconnected experience, without any theme or point of view. The self-conscious emphasis on autobiographical experience that marked blues was fostered by the black spiritual, which reflected the Wesleyan notion of religion as an "experience" of the convert, and sought to depict specific religious experiences. Most likely, they were sung from the first person because such was the premise of other contemporary black songs, such as spirituals and the boatman's song heard by Fannie Kemble in Georgia around 1838:

> Fare you well, and good-bye, oh, oh!
> I'm goin' away to leave you, oh, oh!

Some blues lyrics recorded nearly a century later were similar to such simple recitations:

> And I'm goin' away, I'm goin' away to stay
> That'll be all right pretty mama, gonna need my help
>   some day.
>
>   (Skip James: *Cypress Grove Blues*)

Wandering was the leading subject of male blues song, whose performer was typically an itinerant.

It was probably because many nomadic blues singers used their songs as panhandling gimmicks and thus blared (if not magnified) their reversals on the road that the songs came to be known collectively as blues. The persona of the homeless person in need of assistance was basic to the black street singer. When blues were used to entertain rather than attract sympathy from strangers, they had no express lyric content. Besides concocting his own couplets, a singer was likely to crib them from any convenient source. In some instances blues verses were drawn from European models transported to America. A London street rhyme, "Up in the North, a long way off/The donkey's got the whooping-cough" emerged in blues as:

> Now the cat's got the measles, the dog's got the
> whoopin' cough
> Doggone a man let a woman be his boss.
> > (Papa Charlie Jackson: *Cat's Got The Measles*, 1924)

Sleepy John Estes' *Brownsville Blues* (1929) paraphrased a pompous Irish ballad collected in 1913:

> Ah then, Mary you're my heart's delight, my pride
> and only care
> It was your cruel father, would not let me stray there.
> > (*Mary From Dungloe*)

Estes sang:

> An' the gal I'm lovin' she got this great long curly hair
> An' her mama an' her papa well they sure don't allow
> me there.

A nineteenth century Irish ballad, *Boston City*, was paraphrased by Estes' Brownsville, Tennessee mentor Hambone Willie Newbern in *Shelby County Workhouse Blues* (1929):

> The jury found me guilty
> And the clerk he wrote it down
> The judge he passed my sentence
> And I was sent to Charlestown.

Newbern sang:

> Judge found me guilty and the clerk he wrote it down
> "Says I'll give you ten days buddy, out in lil' ol'
> Shelby town."

Other blues stanzas were paraphrases of spirituals. Whereas the Fisk Jubilee Singers rhapsodized in the 1870s:

> My good Lord's been here
> And he's blessed my soul and gone

The blues singer complained:

> Oh listen fair brownie, somethin' goin' on wrong
> It's the woman I love she done been here and gone.
> (Blind Lemon Jefferson: *Shuckin' Sugar*, 1926)

Such borrowings were easily effected because blues lyrics were typically discursive, offering a string of self-contained couplets instead of a single theme or story.

Although the term "blues" did nothing to clarify the content of what was really a rag-tag lyric form, it helped attract attention to the idiom. Without such a label it is doubtful that blues would have stood apart from other types of black song in the minds of its performers, who could not have understood their songs in formal musical terms. While the dismal realities depicted by many blues would ultimately blight their appeal to future generations of blacks, the usual tenor of blues probably made them attractive to their original audiences, who had lacked an alternative to the obligatory optimism of spirituals, which bore no resemblance to the ordinary realities of black life. With its emphasis on annoying or despiriting tribulations and obstacles, blues became a necessary cultural counterpart to the Fundamentalist insistence that religious faith would induce perennial happiness on the part of the believer, whatever his earthly circumstances.

When early blues singers thought of blues, they did so in terms of church music. As Skip James said: "... A spiritual will revive you ... In the emphasis of the words, and in the style of music, the harmony that it carries will revive you ... This spiritual stuff, it'll make you rejoice and get up joyful and clap your hands and be sociable. There's a different feelin' in the blues ... It makes you feel like you're sad and misused and mistreated and so forth ..." Indeed, the Fundamentalist notion that happiness was only legitimate through church-endorsed activity no doubt caused many blues singers to make their songs conspicuously unhappy, if only in terms of bald declaration.

The real stronghold of the blues was the Deep South, where Fundamentalism was most fervent, and the real heyday of the blues was the early twentieth century, when the church dominated black culture.

7. The Buck Rabbit

When "Son" James was twelve his mother moved to the Delta town of Sidon to be with her husband, who was hiding there from the law. The reunion quickly eroded in the wake of an argument over a "whipping" the father meted out to "Son." "He gave me a few lashes with the belt, and then mother and him had a tie-up about that. I didn't see him after that." Between the ages of thirteen and fourteen, he was baptized at a revival meeting in Sidon, which then numbered 390 residents. While he became an intellectual believer in the Bible, his conversion had no effect on his life style. Describing his youth decades later, James said: "I was wild as a buck-rabbit."

A common-law wife said of him: "Skip was a bad child. He never listened to his parents." His early misadventures, whatever they consisted of, were an important and even indispensable prelude to his career as a professional blues singer. Although blues historians of the future would assume that taking up blues music was a normal activity on the part of any black youth of the period, the universal belief in James' plantation society that blues-singing led inexorably to an eternity in Hell belies this notion. Many sharecroppers who tinkered with blues remained fixed at an amateur level, largely because they were unwilling to assume the risks of occupational blues-singing, or become what James would term a "reprobate." Unless a singer was handicapped and unable to earn a conventional livelihood, only a pre-existing inner distortion on his part could make him indifferent to the fate that was thought to await blues singers, and the reputation he acquired as a devotee of "the devil's music." This was particularly true because blues singers could not rationalize their activity, which had been singled out by Southern black Fundamentalists as a uniquely evil calling, probably because long-lasting Saturday night revelry prevented patrons of blues singers from attending Sunday morning services.

Such finger-pointing, in fact, may have been a chief cause of the song conceit of "having the blues." It could well have caused blues singers to adopt a defensive sophistry by representing themselves as mere portrayers of feelings, feelings which could not in themselves be scored by Fundamentalist preachers. As James would say, referring to the vexations voiced in the Book of Psalms: ". . . in the Bible it states that a man can be blue, have the blues." Such was his flimsy defense of blues-singing in the face of his own Fundamentalism. But the representations of dismal feeling found in most blues songs, including James', involved the discontents and tribulations of someone who was bound up in the peculiar life style of the blues singer.

When he was first interviewed by the author, James claimed that blues singing had served as a form of inner expression, acting as a salve for unspecified sorrows. But this was a veil he had thrown over himself to avoid detailing the actual attraction blues-singing originally held for him. Eventually, he was to reveal that he had been drawn to blues singing on a professional level because he wanted to become a pimp. Becoming a blues singer was, in his immediate environment, almost an initiation rite for budding pimps.

For James to arrive at this pass required a previous disposition towards deviance. Although he was to say of himself, "I used to be a mean bastard," he gave no indication of any factors or experiences that hardened him, or set him in conflict with respectable society. However, he made passing mention of a youthful interlude that probably foreshadowed his blues career: at the age of thirteen or fourteen, he ran away from home and spent a year on the road, traveling as far as Florida and Georgia. James never discussed what he did during this period, but he could not have supported himself with honest toil.

It may have been during this mysterious period in his life that James acquired the attachment to weapons he was to display as a teenager in Bentonia. Though his mother taught him

Biblical precept "blessed are the meek," he made it a practice to carry a switch-blade knife for "protection," and prided himself on his willingness to use it. He also carried a gun, and made no secret of his readiness to use it. As a consequence of his cold-bloodedness, James discovered that his rivals rarely spoke against him to his face, or were willing to confront him physically; of one such local antagonist, he said: " . . . I always had me a little 'protection,' and he knew I'd pop him with it."

The silent fear that James was able to engender among neighbors was to facilitate one of his growing obsessions — that others were discreetly and mutely plotting his downfall. Over the years he would develop a morbid superstition that his musical talent would lead to a violent death. "When I recorded for Paramount, I didn't care nothin' about nobody else playin' at that time," he later said. ". . . Well quite naturally, that would cause enemies. 'Oh, Skip James, oh Skip James, they tell me Skip James has got to be famous . . . Boy, his fame has got mighty fast, too far. We gotta dip that guy.' See, *he* done had that fame, and then he think I'm gonna win it."

While it was expedient for James to place his hypothetical enemies in such an innocuous context, it was probably his delinquent life style that actually created enemies, insofar as they existed. "I didn't care nothin' about nothin' then," he said of his youth. "I wouldn't take nothin' in them times. I was young, and I was a fool, too. A fool about my 'protection,' and about defendin' for myself."

Unlike most Southern blacks of the age, he was willing to confront and antagonize whites. Around 1917, not long after his mother had returned to Bentonia, he heard "some of them old peckerwoods" standing in front of a Yazoo City drug store use the word "nigger."

"I could hear 'em, so I said: 'A nigger? . . . What is a nigger?'

" . . . 'A damn nigger is just a damn nigger. I don't give a damn how much eduction he get, he still is a damn nigger.'

"I say: 'Yeah? Nigger, nigger, nigger . . . ' I just stood there and said: 'Nigger.' I said: 'Well, I'll tell you somethin': I have an idea about that since you said it first . . . *You* can be just as bad a nigger as any black man in the world . . . I don't care what your color is and how red you are . . . If your heart is black and you have mean ideas and disposition, that's a nigger for you, right there.'

"They went to scratchin' their heads. Boy, they went to lookin' at one another. They wanna make a break at me *so bad* . . ." Had a "break" materialized, James maintained, he would have drawn his knife in self-defense.

For the most part, however, he was silently contemptuous of Jim Crow, and begrudgingly deferential to Southern whites. He adjusted to the caste system merely to survive. He later explained: ". . . I was taught to learn to give and learn to take: 'Don't learn to give so much, but learn to take more, as you go through life.'

". . . There have been times that I have been so badly intruded on that in case I hadn't been taught this caution along the line of early life, I might have been penalized or been in penitentiary. Or perhaps of got killed.

"From the earliest time of my life I was always afraid of bein' incarcerated . . . I would ruther be a 'Zulu' than to be incarcerated. A Zulu is used for convenience. You can put a lots on him that he will have to take."

When his newly-acquired stepfather Walter Harris (a man from Satartia) and Henry Stuckey were drafted and sent to France, James longed for combat. "I was a fool enough to want to get caught in it," he said of the First World War. "I was young and wild and didn't care about nothin'.'" Although too young to be eligible for the draft under the Selective Service Acts of May, 1917 and August, 1918, which set the draft age at 21, he sought to enlist by misrepresenting his age. This effort was thwarted because his mother persuaded "Kirk" Whitehead, who administered the local draft board, to reject him.

During this period he attended high school in Yazoo City, where he lived with his mother near the home of her new employer, Dr. McCormack. McCormack was wedded to "Kirk" Whitehead's sister Dotsie, and in his free time James dry-nursed their children. Each morning, before proceeding to his office on Commerce Street, McCormack carted James to school in his horse and buggy. On weekends Skip commuted on horseback to Bentonia, where he held a part-time job at the Gooching Brothers sawmill, seven or eight miles out of town. He also split rails from timber. He was able to carve a hundred rails (representing the dismemberment of two trees) per day, and sell them for five cents apiece. "At that time, five dollars was great money," he recalled. None of his subsequent manual jobs, in fact, would pay as well.

His pony, a two-year-old colt named Luisa, had been given to him by his grandmother, who had selected it from a shipment of horses to *Woodbine*. James was enamored of the animal. "I'd ride that horse around Satartia, Flora, Pocahantas, and Yazoo City," he recalled. "You know that Satartia is about twelve miles from Bentonia; well, that horse could gallop from Bentonia to Satartia without catchin' a rest...

"I'd be pickin' the guitar on him, too. Have that guitar on the horn of the saddle and me sittin' up in the saddle playin'. And then he be just bear-walkin' or runnin'-walkin'. It looked to me that his feet were just hittin' right with that music.

"... That horse was so well trained that I could just drop the rein and he'd feed right around where I was until I got ready to get him again. Then I'd get drunk at that time and fall down anywhere. Well, I could get drunk on him and lay down in the road somewhere. He wouldn't leave.

"I'd have girls on that horse—they'd really fall for him. They loved to ride him 'cause it's just like a rockin' chair."

One of the girls who fell for James' horse was R.K. White-head's own fiancee. After he had borrowed the horse several times to squire her, Whitehead began to have designs on it, and boldly hinted as much to Skip's mother. "He just nagged her and nagged her till she decided she just let him have it," James said. The transaction netted James' mother $250.

"In a way I was glad she got rid of Luisa 'cause that horse made a lot of enemies for me," James later said. "I saw lots of people get pretty mad at that horse. Then at that time some of the other musicians got kind of jealous since I had superseded so many that had been playin' so long... There's no telling but that some of those people mighta wanted to see that horse dead, too."

Though local musicians might have been jealous of his teenage prowess, James had no professional aspirations. "I didn't ever have no idea when I first started playin' to be a professional musician," he recalled. ". . . I wanted to learn it so I could entertain myself and maybe a few friends." At weekend house parties he serenaded as a teenager, he said, "sometimes they'd give me a dollar, dollar and a half; expenses; get me what I wanted to eat, what I wanted to drink."

Unlike most religious parents of budding blues singers, his mother did not chide him for performing secular music. Her admiring references to "star pianists" in the Delta like Dixie Kid and Papa Crump helped foster James' own desire to learn the instrument. She arranged for him to take piano lessons from his cousin Alma Williams, who taught music at a black elementary school in Yazoo City. In the hour he spent under his cousin's tutelage he learned to play some scales, but dissuaded his mother from sponsoring any further lessons, which he thought were overpriced at $1.50. Because pianos were spaced ten or fifteen miles apart in Yazoo County, he rarely had the opportunity to practice. Around 1918, he quit playing music for the sake of "contemplation." At that age, James' interest in girls exceeded his interest in music, but was more difficult to gratify. "It wasn't till I was about nineteen that I could see them alone or even whisper to them," he recalled. "At that time, they believed in courtship, and you couldn't get a date at any time. I don't care how eager or egotistic you were to meet her: there were visitin' hours. You couldn't take her out past nine o'clock.

"In those times, a girl would have to be at least seventeen or eighteen years of age before she could leave the house alone. When you walked out, her parents would be with her. If you would go to church on Sunday, you had to get permission from the parents to walk out of the church with her.

"Lots of times the parents would be in your presence, and you couldn't talk this old stuff they're puttin' out now. You had to talk stuff that you'd studied in school: stuff that was logical. . . . In case you got any kind of vulgarity in your idea, you better not manifest it. I don't care what kind of secret you had up your sleeve; you couldn't dispose of it. If anything in your line of promotion would put any flaw on her integrity, you were expelled from that house.

"A boy would have to get twenty one to get married. I courted one girl from the time I was twelve years old, up to about nineteen years of age. After those seven years, I still didn't get her."

Despite the chaste nature of his teenage courtships, one of them almost cost him his life. The girl in question was a neighbor who "liked to fool around with me 'cause she was a pretty good dancer, and she liked my music since I seemed at the time to be improvin' pretty fast. She wanted to go around with me at these parties, see?"

A local man twice his age was also interested in her. "Since this kid and I started goin' around together, she told me once or twice that he had been 'bukin' her about me. He was knockin' around with her himself, and then he was right smart older than she was, too. You take an old woman attached to a young man or boy, and an old man with a young girl: they're tryin' to gain time by makin' away with these youngsters, and they're apt to get very jealous. . . .

"She told me that he had been beefin' about me, sayin': 'I don't like for you to associate with Skip. You're all gettin' too close together.' She told him and I told him that we weren't doin' anything together. But yet and still he wanted to get me outta the way in case if I would. . . .

"And he got some doped whiskey and give it to this girl, and told her to give it to me."

Instead, the girl advised James not to drink it. "You could smell that whiskey and see it wasn't right," he said.

This episode only taught James to be "watchful and precautious," as he put it. Most of all, he was precautious of women. Despite the fact that his dangerous adversaries were invariably male, he came to regard women as insidious creatures against whom it was necessary to protect oneself by cauterizing feeling. "Every woman that I have come in contact with is seekin' for advantage in one way or the other," he insisted. His blues reflected this sour outlook. ". . . Every song that I composed had reference to some glameo, or some contentious woman, or someone that I was in love with," he said. He believed that love was simply desire. For the most part, it was a charade. The sole object of women, he believed, was to acquire power over men. Their means of doing so was to exploit men's "weak

spot" —sexual desire. It was possible for a man to turn the tables
on such women by governing them through sex. Otherwise, his
only recourse from enslavement was wariness. "You have to
watch women," he said.

While his misogynistic views probably had psychological origins, they were hastened if not triggered by the five turbulent
years he spent as a laborer between 1919-1924. When James
generalized about the sinister nature of women, he was gen-
eralizing from the limited sample of women—invariably prostitutes—who patronized the lawless lumber and levee camps that
were his home during these years. "On these jobs, they're rough
women," he said of them. "You better not trick 'em and don't
pay 'em. They'll cut your heart out, or shoot it out."

In part, James' scornful view of women served to rationalize
and perpetuate the predatory conduct he adopted as an itinerant blues singer:

> I'm a stranger here, I just blowed in your town
> And I'm lookin' every minute, for some teaser brown.
> *(What Am I To Do Blues)*

As often as not his consorts were married or attached to other
men. The men who were outraged by his encroachments were
fools who cherished their women out of weakness. They lacked
his sense of sport:

> The woman I'm lovin', took her from my best friend
> But he got lucky, stole her back again.
> *(Devil Got My Woman)*

At the same time, his misogyny prevented him from committing acts of violence against real or imagined rivals. He
reasoned that women were not worth fighting over. Yet as
a consequence of his abiding distrust of the opposite sex,
James became incapable of feeling genuine love. "My love
was like ice water," he once said. "I could turn it off and
on." At most, his emotional temperature became lukewarm:
"I never allowed a girl to get so close to me that I would
miss her presence," he said. Women existed primarily to grat-
ify his sexual appetites. "Once you fuck 'em, it's like you never
knew 'em," he said of the opposite sex.

Instead of expressing sentiment, his songs delineated power struggles with female companions:

> I would rather be buried in some cypress grove
> Than to have some woman that I can't control.
>
> *(Cypress Grove Blues)*

"A blues gives a person ideas about women," he once said. To James, the warped ideas he transmitted in song gave blues educational value.

8. *The Young Sport*

Had James never left Bentonia, he might not have become an emotionally stunted person. On the other hand, he would have remained a stunted musician who would have been barely distinguishable from the plantation guitarists who played run-of-the-mill songs like *Drunken Spree*. Referring to the effect of his travels on his music, he said: "I guess that's why I advanced as fast as I did, 'cause I go around them music cats and get ideas; they take a liking to me; they see I was kinda apt in a way. . . . So I kept goin'."

A desire for headier pleasures than chaste courtship contributed' to his departure from Bentonia around 1919. "I wanted to be a 'man' and get some experience," he recalled. He was also doubtless aware of the dismal future that awaited him in Bentonia, where he had no foreseeable alternative to sharecropping. Dropping out of high school, he joined a road construction camp situated near the Delta town of Ruleville. The camp was one of the numerous projects funded from 1916 to 1921 under the Shackleford Good Roads Bill, a Federal highway improvement program, and for that reason was called a "Good Roads camp."

"I had done nothin' stout then," he said. Although James had no difficulty adjusting to manual labor, he could not abide the toughs who were his fellow workers. "I was just from a refined family . . . They was all Christian, and I was reared up in a Christian home and atmosphere." None of his colleagues, he claimed, had comparably genteel backgrounds. "Most of the guys wanted to be bullies," he said. "There was so many nasty songs [sung there] it'd be just a breach of intelligence to mention them."

The conversation of the laborers was comparably obscene and belligerent. "Those guys on those camps would even get to squabblin' and fightin' at the dinner table ... The guys at the table wouldn't say: 'Pass me such and such a thing' if they wanted a big pan of meat or biscuits, or rice and stuff like that. They said: 'Let such-and-such a thing *walk* up that motherfuckin' table.' If you didn't just pass it right on to him, he'd jump on that table and walk the table to get it. Right over the plates and everything."

James soon left the camp to work as a dynamite blaster in the surrounding hamlets of Drew and Doddsville. On Saturdays, he would offer blues in Delta towns like Louise and Belzoni, often playing in front of crossroads country stores to drum up customers.

At the same time, he felt leery of the Delta, because he had heard stories of bodies vanishing in its backwoods bayous. Returning to Yazoo County, he cut logs for a local sawmill. Then he was offered a timber-cutting job by a family friend named Yank Griffin, who operated a lumber camp on the outskirts of Flora. Once he learned his trade from Griffin he joined a competitor's camp run by a man named Bob White.

A welcoming party of rattlesnakes forced White's outfit to retreat from the woods between Valley and Tinsley to Pelahatchee in Rankin County. The new camp was set on a sloping bluff. James nicknamed it "Bangling" (a misnomer for "dangling") and composed a song about it. It was sung from the standpoint of a laborer.

> If you go to Banglin', tell my boys (2)
> What a time I'm having, up in Illinois.
> Up in Illinois; up in Illinois.
> What a time I'm having, up in Illinois.
>
> You get there before I do (2)
> Tell my boys I'm comin' too.
> Comin' too; comin' too.
> Tell my boys I'm comin' too.
>
> Tell me where you stay last night (2)
> You come home this mornin', the sun was bright.

Shinin' bright'; shinin' bright.
Come home this mornin', sun was bright.

I gin my cotton and sell my seed (2)
Done give my baby, everything she need.
Everything she need; everything she need.
Done give my baby, everything she need.

Sewed a hole in my pocket so my change won't loose (2)
Gonna buy my baby, some brogan shoes.
Brogan shoes; brogan shoes.
Gonna buy my baby, some brogan shoes.

You can tear the big road down (2)
But you can't raise the mornin' gown.
Mornin' gown'; mornin' gown.
You can't raise the mornin' gown.

This song, *Illinois Blues*, was probably the first song that James
ever devised. Although James' presentation of *Illinois Blues* in
a recording studio over a decade later was replete with masterful
touches, it nevertheless bore the mark of the unfinished musician
who had originated it. The accompaniment consisted of one
chord, and had an erratic accenting pattern that made it a poor
vehicle for dancing. Its originality lay chiefly in its six-note melody
and structure. Although its intervals (1-2-minor 3-4-5-minor 7-1)
were standard blues fare, its use of the minor seventh as a prominent melody note was exotic in blues song. Its unusual tonal
ingredients and extended vocal range (nearly an octave plus a
fourth) would become basic to James, and recur in his later compositions *Cypress Grove* and *Hard Times Killin' Floor*.

Although *Illinois Blues* used the three-line rhyme scheme associated with blues, it did not take on a blues phrasing pattern.
The two measure phrases of its first six bars were cut in the
mold of conventional "rag" ditties like *Make Me A Pallet On
The Floor*, with six beats of singing followed by half-bar instrumental fills. Each verse concluded with a four-bar repeat of
its final line, phrased in single measures, which gave the song
an unusual ten bar structure.

The most significant aspect of *Illinois Blues* was that it was
the work of a musician who did not have a clear notion of

what blues represented. Working within a phrasing pattern that was foreign to blues, he imposed a blues ambience upon it by embroidering his vocal line with single-string glissandos and playing heavily-bent bass notes on the second and third beats of the seventh bar. It was as if the performer understood blues to represent a sound rather than a structure. Later works by James would reflect this unusual tendency to convert foreign musical matter into pieces that sounded like blues.

The sexual posessiveness that the final verse of *Illinois Blues* alluded to would involve him in his first known shooting scrape. This episode began when a mule-driver discovered that James had loaned his wife eight dollars during a Georgia Skin game. Reasoning that the loan concealed sexual designs, he opened James' tent. Inside, James was sitting in a cast-iron bath tub. He listened stoically to the man's tirade, and then volunteered the claim that he had loaned the money with the intention of receiving it back. The driver, however, was unmollified. "He started performin', cussin', and goin' on; see, he was one of those tough ones, too. . . . He started sayin' that he wasn't gonna pay me a damn thing, and she wasn't, neither, and that he was gonna beat the hell out of me."

"I say: 'Well, you have your privilege; you got the advantage over me.'"

". . . He stepped over inside the tent. When he made the step, I was lookin' for it in a way . . . He ought not to have done it."

In a moment James was aiming the .38 he kept concealed beneath his pillow on the bed beside his wash-tub. "I kept a gun all the time," he recalled. At point-blank range, he pumped six bullets into the man. "Could you blame me?" he later asked. "Man wanna beat me up, and I'm buck-naked?"

Knowing that there is no statute of limitations on murder, James would not admit to having killed the driver when he recounted the shooting decades later. When asked if the driver had died from his wounds, he replied archly: "I don't know what happened, but he was still there when somebody come and got him. Like I said, he ought not to have done it."

Quite possibly, he had been guilty of committing adultery with the driver's wife. In his own mind, however, he was an innocent victim of aggression. For that reason, he had felt no fear during their confrontation. "I didn't have a right to be afraid," he said, as though it were a matter of principle, " 'cause I was right and he was wrong."

To his poisonous sense of affronted rectitude, he had added another deadly twist. Throughout his life he would remain a mild-mannered creature of cunning, using a disarming outward calmness to his advantage in confrontations. As he put it: "I let the errors of others be my success." The characteristic error of his violent contemporaries was blustering or being demonstrative. He never displayed his violent intentions in advance, or forewarned his adversaries.

What was chilling about James' style in the above-recounted situation was that he had actually drawn his victim in by affecting helplessness. His behavior could only have encouraged the driver's belligerence. He could have scared the man off simply by brandishing his gun. Instead, James killed as if he had been playing poker, first lulling his victim into overconfidence, and then displaying his trump card. Instead of flourishing his winning card, he fired it: "I never draw a gun unless'n I pull the trigger," he was to say somberly.

It is impossible to even guess how many times in his life as a roustabout James pulled the trigger on someone as a matter of principle, pride, or pathology. He only discussed specific incidents of violence, and only then in the context of telling stories about his past. For the most part, he preferred not to discuss his past. The fact that James habitually carried a pistol and could kill someone with aplomb indicated that he was likely involved in several shooting episodes, considering the life he led.

When James became a prestigious blues rediscovery in the 1960s his homicidal propensities remained unknown to his fans. In the fashion of many gangsters, he sought to give the impression of himself as a refined, civilized individual, and it is likely that he used this deceptive persona in the sordid environments of his youth as a means of disarming others. In spite of his image of gentility, his songs would project an acute relish for violence, to the extent of actually celebrating murder in his greatest musical masterpiece, *22-20 Blues*. Two of the blues he frequently performed in the 1960s similarly invoked homicidal gunplay:

> I'm gonna buy me a pistol, shoot me forty rounds of ball
> Shoot crow jane, just to see her fall.
>
> (*Crow Jane*)

> I'm gonna find her, I'm gonna find her
> With my smokin' .44
> And when I find that woman,
> I'll bet her head won't nappy no more.
>
> (*Black Gal*)

Although blues specialists invariably celebrated the blues lyric for its supposed realism, James' lyrical paeans to homicide failed to draw a single comment during his comeback. Violence was simply taken as a blues conceit, of no psychological significance. It was only by passing prolonged period in James' company and becoming privy to his thoughts that one appreciated how enamored he was of this conceit, and how violence permeated his personality. The singer was less concerned with the adroitness of his picking finger than with the capabilities of his trigger finger, and he prided himself on his willingness to exercise it without hesitation in any confrontation.

Living in the midst of social anarchy, James had been provided with the equivalent of a shooting license, so long as he aimed his bullets at other blacks. Two generations earlier, a Northern journalist had been shocked by the sight of fourteen-year-old black youths openly carrying pistols in Jackson. He reported:

> . . . the great fault of the State is, that the courts do not punish murder, either of white or black . . . Everybody goes armed, and every trifling dispute is ended with a pistol. Nearly all the disorder and crime is caused by the lower order of whites and by negroes; for these latter have, it seems, generally taken up the fashion of carrying arms, and in their quarrels among themselves, use the pistol or knife freely. The respect-

able people of the State do not discourage the practice of carrying arms as they should. . . .*

Blacks still openly carried pistols in the Mississippi of the 1920s,
and just as routinely resorted to them. When he lived in Pela-
hatchie, James was already familar with a white proverb that
sanctioned intraracial murder: "Kill a mule, I'll buy another:
kill a nigger, I'll hire another." It was said that mules cost $400,
and were therefore worth more than "niggers."

Even in the 1950s, at which time Mississippi whites were given
to remark "the nigger went out with the mule," a general climate
of lawlessness still prevailed on Southern plantations. "Many Negroes are never brought to court for offenses . . . such as drunkeness, theft, or even knife-fights within their own group," a cultural anthropologist reported. **

But even had James lived in a more stringent society, he would
not have buckled under its laws, had they interfered with his
impulses. "I've been in everything you can imagine, except jail,"
he said once, before correcting himself to allow that he had
been behind bars. He had no fear of the police, even on occasions when he stood in jeopardy of arrest. "I'll tell you a little
somethin' about handlin' these laws [police]," he once said. "You
take it: a law that has any experience at all, he's gonna see how
you present yourself 'fore he does anything. He's gonna watch
you. . . .

"Sometimes he may approach you: 'Hey guy! Hey, com'ere!'
And you may have a bag of whiskey or a gun on you or somethin': you cannot look at him, and you show guilt . . . Then that
law's gonna feel a little bit superstitious [suspicious] about you
'cause it looks like you'se shaky.

" 'All right, get in here! You're the very one I'm lookin' for!'

"But you look him direct in his face and in his eyes, and
you turn him a direct answer when he walk up to you. He'll
more than apt tell you: 'Oh, go ahead guy; you're not the one
I want.' "

*Charles Norhoff, *The Cotton States In The Spring And Summer of 1875* (D. Appleton
and Co., New York), p. 78. Mississippi's state motto was "By valor and arms."

**Mortin Rubin, *Plantation County* (College and University Press, New Haven,
1951), p. 101.

There were no "laws" intruding in the affairs of lumber and levee camp workers, and it was not necessary for James to face any inquiry after shooting a co-worker. His own explanation of the event sufficed to acquit him with his colleagues. "He was wrong and everybody knew he was wrong. And his wife knowed he was wrong herself; she was glad of it." Nevertheless, James left the camp a few weeks afterwards.

He wound up at another camp in northeastern Mississippi that that was laying down the macadam road between Tupelo and Pontotoc. Working as a loader, he drew wages ranging from $1.50 to $2.00 per day. Once again, he found occasion to use his gun.

"When I was a loader," he recalled, "one guy came in drivin', and I asked him to go a certain way. He wanted to go his way, but as I was the loader, it was his duty to go as I directed him. He got offended about it.

"And he went on to the dump [levee] and picked him up a club. When he came back, he . . . made an effort to hit me. . . . He meant to hit me in the head. I dodged it, and he hit my shoulder. That is where me and him had a little tangle then.

"Quite naturally, I had to shoot him. I shot him in the neck, and then twice in the shoulder. I just wounded him enough to let him know what I would do if he made another attempt. . . .

"Of course I could *have* killed him, and after which my foreman told me I *should* have killed him . . . But I passed it up."

This was blatant double-talk, for shooting someone in the neck could hardly have been James' idea of a warning shot. Most likely, his aim had been off.

Later, James looked on as the same foreman, Les Darton, attempted to separate two laborers during a fight. "I think it started from that 'dozen' stuff," he said. When the men ignored his interference, Darton picked up a "single-tree" oxen yoke and swung it at the head of one of the laborers, a man named George Haliburton, in the fashion of a baseball bat. "He knocked his brains out; they came runnin' through his nostrils," James recalled. To James, Haliburton's murder was no more lamentable than the loss of a mule, actually less so, since it indirectly justified his own violence: "See, the foreman had to kill him because the

guy was kind of reprobrated, and everybody was kinda fearin'
him . . . he was always seekin' the advantage of other people."

When two weeks of rain brought the camp to a standstill, a
clique of professional gamblers from Tupelo descended on it.
Already an accomplished gambler, James took his earnings to
a Georgia Skin game and walked off with three hundred dollars.

He then quit the job and joined a levee camp some 25 miles
away, at New Albany. There he earned three dollars a day for
driving a mule that carried dirt to the levee. "That levee camp
was pretty hard, too," he recalled. "Lotta old dangerous and
notoriety Negroes out there on it." Miscalculations on the part
of dumpers often caused their mule-teams to skid over the levee
embankment, which rose 75 feet above the Tallahatchie River.
"The dumper sometimes would make you drive so close to the
edge of the levee that the mules would get contrary," James
said. "The dirt was soft around there and the mules would start
to slippin' offa that bank-bump on that levee.

" . . . We had three bossmen. One was named Charlie Moran,
one named Pres Moran, and one named Tate Lorraine. Tate
Lorraine was a bear: he'd kill a man in a minute. And he'd
tell you: 'Now if that mule-team go in that river, go behind
it.' And a lot of them (drivers) did do it: they didn't wanna
have some trouble or get killed. Sometimes they would get
drowned. Now he'd shoot you off in there if you didn't go behind the mules, unless you beat him to it.

"I didn't wanna get killed, and I didn't wanna kill nobody.
I was gonna try to shoot first before I got killed, if I could.
But they was gettin' a little too rough on me, so I just said:
'The best thing for me to do is pull on the string.' So I left
that place."

James was thoroughly disgusted by the lumber and levee camp
atmosphere. "The people were *no good* in jobs like levee camps
and Good Roads, and in log camps," he insisted. "You never
hear anything worthwhile other than this old vulgar stuff, and
it's from a 'damn' to 'mother talk'. . . . They got on these nasty
jobs 'cause they didn't want nothin' else. But I did."

Most of the songs he heard at such camps were as coarse
as his fellow employees. " . . . On those jobs, those guys'd sing

all them nasty songs. I never did like to sing too much vulgar
stuff, unless'n I got half-drunk. I didn't care what come out
then." The workers enjoyed taunting each other with the pastime of "playing the dozens," or making adverse reflections on
another person's mother:

> Your mama don't wear no drawers
> I seen her when she take 'em off.

In response to this diversion, which he detested, James sang
a song that began:

> I don't play the dozen and neither the ten
> I don't want nobody to ease me in.

"I didn't say 'nobody' at that time; I say 'I don't want no . . .
'mollydodger' [motherfucker] . . . to ease me in. See, they'd start
with that . . . stuff in ten verses, and if you take that, then they
ease you in to the dozens . . . . Well, I let 'em know it's gonna
be something—some trouble—if they try to ease me in. I'd tie
tails [fight] with 'em like a possum."

Another levee camp product was a worker's complaint.

> I been a twelve-day roller, and I will be,
>   if it just don't rain
> All I want you to do is pay me just the same.
>
> You know I work for the free good will
> If you don't pay me me, you're gonna have me killed.

"See, we'd work for six days a week and two weeks at a time
before payday," he recalled. "And sometimes on those jobs they
had a habit of not paying you all what they promise∴ you. They'd
pay you some and then promise you some." The rest of the
song was devoted to annoying working conditions:

> Before I'd drive old Sue and Nell
> I'd walk the levee till my ankles swell.
> I don't want no more molasses with the cub on the can
> Because these black molasses would kill *any* man.

"Sue" and "Nell" were popular names for mules, which James
found wearisome creatures as he loaded and dumped levee dirt

in and out of the wagon teams they led. "The mules wouldn't wanna go forward, and wouldn't wanna back up: just wouldn't wanna work." A staple food of the laborers was molasses; "black molasses that wasn't hardly fit to eat. It had a cub-bear on the can."

The prospect of high wages and the lure of gambling made the work camp, sordid as it was, attractive to James. "A loader would get two and a half dollars a day," he recalled, "and a dumper would get three." Had James worked along the Mississippi levee he could have realized even higher wages; a contemporary chronicle reported: "Contractors along the Mississippi River in the early part of 1920 paid thirty-five cents per hour for the commonest negro labor with prices ranging up to fifty cents for levelers and a dollar or more per hour for skilled labor on the gas tractors and dray lines."

His own camp abounded with what he called "smart gamblers" who gambled all night after work, and they became his mentors. "On those jobs, sometimes guys would mess up their money and go to the bossman the next morning and borrow half a payday. If he's a good worker, and the man liked his work, he would just as soon give him fifteen or twenty dollars. . . . Lots of times I seen guys get flat-broke like that and then lay around the crap game and beg a bet until they get lucky again. If he don't have any money, but somebody knows he's a good hustler, he can beg five or ten dollars. He'll take that and scratch around till sometimes he's won his money back and two or three hundred dollars more.

"They'd have what they call 'doodling books' that could get you through the week if you run short for anything. . . . You couldn't spend real money on the camp. The books could get you things like groceries . . . Some of those boys would get those books and go to the crap game on weekday nights to gamble those books off. A smart gambler would wind up with a handful of those books he could cash for money."

On a weekend visit to Memphis, he was recruited for a sawmill camp in Weona, Arkansas operated by a man named S.T. Shooters. In Weona, where he remained from 1921-1923, he was known as "James" or "Jay" by his co-workers.

Shooters' 300-man labor force included timber cutters, log haulers and lumber graders of both races. The owner maintained peace among them by deploying two armed guards to patrol the camp. Anyone who defied them risked burial in one of the two cemeteries on the premises.

James' night-time shift as a lumber grader left him free to congregate in the sawmill juke house during the day and on Saturday nights. Prior to that time, he had paid only intermittent visits to juke houses in the Bentonia region.

Most of his free time was spent standing behind the house pianist, a 6'6", 250-pound man from nearby Marked Tree named Will Crabtree. Crabtree, who was some twenty to forty years older than James, was the first professional musician James ever met. He became the leading influence on James' piano style. He played for both black and white audiences, frequently assisted by various female vocalists. "He played some of the songs that Bessie Smith used to sing," James said of Crabtree. James appropriated at least two of his tunes, *Rock Island Blues* and *Careless Love.*

Watching Crabtree play, James would mutter to himself: "Shit, I can do the same thing." When Crabtree would desert the piano for one of the gambling tables in the juke house, James would occupy his chair and try to "hold the house." Before long Crabtree began to encourage him by taking lengthier breaks.

If anything, James was less enamored of Crabtree's music than of his prestige with the "hustling women" (prostitutes) from Memphis who traveled to the camp every other week on paydays, which for James meant a mere thirty dollars. Most of them were attached to local gamblers: ". . . They'd have the women hustling for them while they're gambling, see?" James explained. "If she'd turn eight or ten tricks, man, at four or five dollars a trick, she'd make good. It'd give that cat enough stake to gamble with—those cats sometimes wouldn't work, but the woman would do the hustling."

Thanks to his musical prowess, Crabtree had a large stable of "hustling" women. "He was nothin' but a 'sport,'" James said of him. "He didn't have to work: womens workin' for him." His gigolo's garb consisted of a Stetson hat, Florsheim shoes, a gold watch and several diamond rings, most of which had been lavished upon him by "Miss Benny" Mitchell, a prostitute who ran the boarding house in which James lived. This attire greatly impressed James: "I used to say: 'Hot damn! I ain't gonna be nothin' but a "sport" like Crabtree!'"

In the meantime, James continued to toil as a lumber grader. As always, he made potentially deadly enemies. "This guy was goin' to Memphis, and as quite naturally we couldn't get no whiskey on the job, I gave him two dollars to bring me back half a pint," he recalled. "He went to a big ball in Memphis, and brought it in the mornin' 'fore day. He sat in my room for a while and he said: 'Oh James, go ahead and take a drink!'

"And then I looked at the bottle. The seal had been broken, and it was an old bottle. Looked like somethin' had been in it. And I taken the top off it, and I smelt it. It smelled just like garlic.

"I just topped it back up, I say: 'Oh, I'll take a drink after a while.'"

"And he said: 'Take a drink, man! It's okay.'

"I say: '*You* take a drink.'

"He say: 'Oh no, I done had plenty!'

"I just laid it under my pillow. When that guy left the boarding-house, he say: 'I'm going to take me a nap; I haven't had enough sleep . . . '

"He didn't stay fifteen minutes before he came back and see what I had drinked of that whiskey. He say: 'Oh, I gave you whiskey and you mean to tell me you ain't drinked none?'

"I say: 'Well, I haven't touched it yet—I don't like to drink on an empty stomach.' I say: 'I'll wait till I eat and then I may take a drink.'

"Well, there was a guy I was workin' with and he was one of them tough cats; they called him 'Louisiana.' His name was Irving Powell . . . He was nice if you let him be . . . but he would tear you up if you messed with him and he had even done beat up a couple of them bossmen.

"And I taken the whiskey to him, I said: 'Louisiana?' . . . I said: 'A guy brought me some whiskey, night before last. I was gonna let you look at that whiskey, and see what you thought about it.'

" . . . And he looked at it and smelt it . . . He say: 'That son of a gun!'—he called him what he *did* call him . . . He say: 'You set that whiskey up on your shelf. I'm gonna make *him* drink it.' "

Before this event could occur, the bottle tumbled from its resting place after James inadvertently slammed his bathroom door. "When it hit the floor, it was just like a shotgun: *boom!* . . . I don't know what was in that stuff, but it was some explosive, green-lookin' stuff. Anyway, Louisiana beat that guy up . . . He run him away from that camp. If the guy hadn't-a left, Louisiana woulda killed him. He didn't want nobody to intrude on me, since he had taken a liking to me."

He was uncertain as to why the man had wanted to kill him. "Maybe it was about a woman or somethin', 'cause I was kinda flirty," he said.

By 1923 James had become proficient enough as a gambler and blues pianist to attract his own "hustling woman," a prostitute named Mary Mitchell. She was the product of a mixed marriage, or what James termed "half-Celt," and was considered attractive by virtue of her light complexion, acqualine nose, and "mouth fulla gold" (teeth). In addition to the pistol she regularly carried, she wore a Bowie knife between her breasts.

"I know she's *bad*," James commented, "but she's a good hustler."

Together they moved to Jonesboro, a town thirty miles north of Weona. For two weeks they stayed in the home of her parents. "They know the stuff she's puttin' down, and the reason for me bein' there."

During the day James loafed at home and waited for her to return with money she collected by walking the local streets. "She come back, she better have somethin' or we'll tie tails [fight]," he reported. She taught him to feign sleep whenever Johns approached her window at night. In turn James told her:

"The same dog bit you bit me," by which he meant that he would love other women for profit. "I'd tap women like a coon taps trees," he said. "She'd get broke, I'd get another one."

Mary insisted only upon his emotional fidelity, which she claimed to reciprocate. By her lights, she performed acts of prostitution only for the sake of supporting him in style.

Nevertheless, James grew increasingly chary of her, largely on the basis of the stories he heard about her. Behind her back she was known as "Buno Mary"; James imagined that the name (which probably referred to the small town of Bono, ten miles from Jonesboro) remarked on her dangerous personality. Someone told him that Mary had once murdered a man and a woman in a fit of anger. He considered this story plausible; he had seen her impetuously confiscate the ante of card or dice games she did not manage to win. Anyone who did not call her "Miss Mary," in deference to her complexion, risked a tongue-lashing.

One day he stealthily packed his bags and took the imported blue serge suit she had bought him to the cleaners. After he returned from the cleaners he sat on the Mitchells' front porch, passing time with her parents. Soon he began to hear Mary's characteristic whistle from the street. As she approached the house she unleashed a stream of vituperation at him. When she called him a "goddamned black son of a bitch" he leapt from his chair and smashed her in the mouth with the back of his hand, dropping her like "a piece of beef." He then gave a deadly look towards her parents, who looked on as if they had seen nothing.

Instead of drawing her knife, she crawled to her feet and walked off whistling. When she came to their room that night she greeted him with a flock of effusive endearments. But as soon as his suit was cleaned, James escaped to Memphis.

There he lived in a boarding house on Hernando Street. Every Friday he played piano for a dollar an hour at a whorehouse on nearby North Nichols Street. Holding the floor for two or three hours, he learned to perform dance music.

"You used to pay to go in those places, maybe a dollar and a half, or two dollars for a couple," he recalled. "You would be served perhaps a small drink, and sandwiches. Then you had a chance to gamble, and anything else that you want to do in there. They had 'transom' rooms in there: you want to take your girl to a private room, you had the privilege. That'd cost you another dollar...

"Some few would go to the barrelhouse to listen and hear music ... The rest of the people was the dancin' type, out there to frolic," he said of his audiences. His songs were designed for "no special kind of dance. They'd do the Shimmy-She-Wobble, the Dog dance, Fall Off The Log, Fox Trot, Heel and Toe ... and Roll the Belly. Sure enough! I ain't jokin'! They had a dance called 'Roll the Belly.' They'd hug and oh, man, roll like that, see?"

The typical females who attended such clubs were floozies known as "sandfoot" or "fanfoot" women. "That's the type of women that don't have no special man and don't care whether she see him again since she can get what she got [elsewhere]."

As such women diverted him ("I'd do 'em like a goose: fuck 'em an' turn 'em loose"), other "hustling women" padded his income. On a return trip to Weona he ran into "Buno Mary" and brushed off her attempts to renew their affair. At the same time, he learned that she had added another woman to her list of victims.

PART THREE

9. *The Bootlegger*

The taste of easy and abundant money that James obtained by gambling and pimping would all but incapacitate him for the ordinary drudgery of sharecropping, which was virtually subsistence farming. Yet by 1924 he had returned to Bentonia, there to pursue plantation labor. Although James gave no reason for his departure from Arkansas, other than a desire to see his mother, it is doubtful that he willingly quit his short-lived pimping profession, the nature of which he never denounced or appeared to find any fault with.

One circumstance that would have readily curtailed his pimping career was Prohibition. His mentor Will Crabtree was actually an anachronism from a vanishing era of "sporting life" blues singers. The once-prevalent pimping blues singer would become a storied character, existing only as an allusion or memory, as in Bill Broonzy's recollection:

> ... New Orleans, Memphis, Saint Louis, Kansas City, Atlanta, Houston, Little Rock, Jackson, Vicksburg ... that's where these big town blues players started playing ...
>
> These musicians was not seen in the day. They came out at night. His meal was brought out to him from the white man's house in a pan by his woman. We called them kind of men 'sweet back papas.'
>
> Them men didn't know how cotton and corn and rice and sugar cane grows and they didn't care. They went out dressed up every night and some of them had three and four women. One fed him and the

other bought his clothes and shoes. These is the men
that wear ten-dollar Stetson hats and twenty-dollar
gold pieces at their watch and diamonds in their teeth
and on their fingers.

This kind of men caused women like Bessie Smith
. . . to sing the blues. The women get the blues from
all the trouble these men give them, but these men
don't have the blues, hell no.[*]

This passage would have been a fair description of Skip James,
circa 1923, but did not apply to any contemporary blues artists
who became known to posterity. The prostitutes who facilitated
such pandering were attached to barrelhouses situated in towns
and cities, as well as sawmills. Trafficking in bottled whiskey,
the Southern barrelhouse became a casualty of Prohibition, as
did, apparently, the northern barrelhouses that had catered to
tramps as an all-purpose "rooming-house, saloon, and house of
prostitution" and were already written off, in 1923, as "a thing
of the past."[**] None of the establishments that survived in such
places as Memphis appear to have been comparable to the af-
fluent barrelhouses associated with "sporting life": they were
simply seedy dives, no doubt because the prospect of legal closure discouraged any appreciable investment in them.

The swift decimation of bona fide barrelhouses containing
dance halls and "transom rooms" is pointed up by the fact that
James never saw any in Mississippi. All of his performances there
in the 1920s took place at private residences: "None of the times
would it be in clubs: there wasn't no clubs; they'd have their
'jukes' and parties in private homes."

A likely consequence of the decline of the barrelhouse was
the dominance of the guitar in the scheme of 1920s blues.
Whereas most barrelhouses had pianos, and (presumably) performers to play them, few "house frolics" had any provision
for the instrument. Indeed, had James not been exposed to the

---

*Big Bill Blues: Big Bill Broonzy's Story as Told to Yannick Bruynoghe (Oak Pub-
lications, New York, 1964), pp. 48-49. A "sweetback" was a pimp.

**Neils Anderson, The Hobo: The Sociology of the Homeless Man (Unversity of
Chicago Press, 1961 reprint of the 1923 edition), p. 27. The term itself was
first documented in 1883.

Arkansas and Memphis barrelhouse, it is unlikely that he would have progressed beyond the stage of piano putterer. During the six years he would remain one of *Woodbine*'s residents, he was to come of age as a blues guitarist. His guitar-playing would begin to spill over into his piano-playing, creating a unique correspondence between the two instruments. More than merely play tunes like *If You Haven't Any Hay* and *Four O'Clock Blues* on both instruments, James gave his piano work a decidely guitaristic cast by carefully following his vocal inflections on his instrument.

Perhaps because James could not work as a professional pianist on the local "house frolic" circuit and did not (in 1924) have polished skills as a guitarist, he initially gained a livelihood by sharecropping in Bentonia. "I always managed my own crops, and worked from fifteen to twenty-five acres," he recalled. "Just work from 'can to can't'—when you can see till when you can't.

"Now workin' on shares means gettin' half of everything," he explained. "On a big plantation, the landlord [planter] furnishes everything for you to work with. He'd furnish the seeds and tools; he'd start in March, and furnish you through July. I never would go to the expenses to buy mules, horses, work-things."

In principle, such an arrangement seemed equitable to James. In practice, however, he found "these landlords take the biggest end of the haul all the time."

"You find out in the fall when you go back for a settlement at the big store where the bosses' clerks and bookeepers were. See, under the agreement, the boss would get half of everything: if I did ten bales of cotton, he'd get five. I'd give him his five . . . and then he'd get what I owed him outta *my* five. Then he'd have interest on it. Guys like that, instead of ten cents on a dollar, would take fifty cents on a dollar; sometimes more. So I'd clear maybe one hundred and fifty or two hundred dollars when I oughta have cleared two thousand dollars.

"And he wouldn't give you an itemizin' account on what you owed him: in other words, sit down and figure out everything with you on the square. He's not gonna itemize it . . . He didn't wanna look at *my* figures: he looked at his.

"You better not 'spute him, neither. 'You 'spute Miss So-and-So, my bookkeeper?' There'd be a lynch right there.

". . . Well, I took all that: I didn't wanna have no trouble.

"Then again, they would still allow you some kind of change to realize a livin' because you was raisin' your livin' already if you had any kind of industrious get-up about you. I wouldn't go out on a plantation unless'n I raised hogs, chickens, sweet potatoes, peanuts; a cow or two.

"I'd raise even my molasses. I'd go strip my can and take it by the sogger mill where they grind it and convert it into syrup. Have my own milk and butter. Kill my hogs in the winter, at hog-killin' season time; have my own meat, grease it up for my lard; bank my sweet potatoes. I don't care how cold it got; if I want me a sweet potato or somethin' I'd go out and open my pump and get me a few."

James' forays into sharecropping were brief. "I never did very much hard, manual work after I got outta this log-timber work," he once recalled. He had less aversion to hard work than to the plantation taskmasters who typically tried to dictate the pattern and style of the work he performed for them. "I always like to take advantage of my work; not let the work work me," he recalled. "I work the work. If I don't learn to take the advantage of my work, it'll work hell outta me, just to do a little somethin'. I'll do it my way, not his way. Most of those old [white] folks wanted you to do it the hard way: his way . . . I wouldn't take it . . . 'cause *I* was doin' the work; he was ridin' around and sittin' on his butt. I give 'em to know that: 'Say, let me tell you somethin'. You sittin' down here in your car or on your horse or whatever, and I'm out here doin' all this hard manual work . . . You want it did, don't you? Well, you let me do it.'

". . . Anybody that I would work for will tell you: 'Skippy, he's a darn good worker, but just don't bother him. When you tell him what to do, just let him alone.'"

Most of the plantation work he performed in the 1920s consisted of day-labor cotton-picking jobs. Even at this, his experiences were bitter. During the picking season of 1925 or 1926 he hired himself out to a nearby planter named Alf Brown, who lived two miles from *Woodbine*. "My cousin had told him I could pick pretty good," he recalled. Borrowing a mule from R.K. Whitehead, he arrived at Brown's plantation with two cotton sacks. "He said: 'You don't need all these sacks,'" James recalled.

"Well, I said 'Okay,' and he carried me to the fields. Boy, at that time the cotton was just as thick as hair on a dog's back. I went out there and I picked. I started after seven and quit at five ... And I picked four hundred seventy-somethin' [pounds]; near about five hundred.

"He wouldn't let me come back. He say: 'I'm gonna pay you off now, don't you come back.'

"I say: 'What's wrong?'

"He say: 'Hell, that's too much money to pay one man.'

"I say: 'You want your cotton out, don't you?'

"I could pick a bale of cotton in two days—a bale was, around 12-1400 pounds."*

As both itinerent cotton picker and sharecropper, James was far more assertive than the ordinary plantation hand of the time. "I'd always start work this-a-way," he recalled. " 'I want your rules, bossman: you tell me your rules. And if we get together and I'll accept, it's okay. Now here's mine. When I work for you, what you promise me, will you please sir pay me? That's an agreement ... Now here's one thing: you can't call me too soon, and you can't work me too late, unless it's necessary. But if not, will you please not intrude on me?' "

"I went to one place," he reported, "and I say: 'What is your rule and your system, the custom of your labor here? How you work your folks?'

"He say: 'Oh well, all of my niggers are mostly like this: if you see anythin' goin' on the place wrong, I like for 'em always come and tell me what's goin' on. Then I give my niggers a break ... ' Well, see, he wants you to be a snitcher and drop sand and tote it to him.

"I say: 'Well, I'll tell you one thing ... I'm not like that now; I'm gonna tell you to start with. I don't know *nothin'* about

---

*This was a rank exaggeration; in truth, the average cotton-picker could pick only 200 pounds a day.

what's goin' on even if I look at it. That's *your* place: you got
a [plantation] rider?—that's *his* permanent duty . . . ' "

In James' experience, every Mississippi plantation had a resident "snitcher" who "would tell everything about everybody else
he sees in order to have somethin' to hide behind to keep the
boss from watchin' *him*."

He elaborated: "And this bossman, after he given this snitcher
his job . . . he'll let that snitcher work at his leisure . . . I could
pretty well spot those snitchers as I'd see him. He'd mostly
wanna be your boss instead of the bossman. He's gonna tell
you what to do . . . and say: 'Oh man, the bossman, he don't
like such-and-such a thing.'

"I'd say: 'Well, the bossman done told me what to do.'

" 'Oh well, I been here so long, he tells me what to tell people.'

" 'Well, I don't care if you was born here—you may *die* here.
Don't you tell me a damn thing, understand?'"

". . . I'll tell you about me," he concluded. "Whoever I'd work
for, I'd tell: 'Now don't come to me for nothin': I do not meddle
with anyone's business but Skip's. It takes me six months to
take care of that and the rest of the year to let the other fellow's
alone.' And you know what? They'd find it out.

"Sometimes they'd hear a racket or a fight goin' on a place.
'Oh hell, it ain't no use of goin' to ask old Skip for nothin';
you'd needn't ask *Skip* . . . Hell, if he sees somethin' (you know
what they gonna call you down there), that damn son-of-a-bitch
—that damn nigger, he ain't gonna tell you nothin.' "

His tight-lipped manner and his mother's favored position on
Woodbine enabled James to garnish a lucrative bootlegging fran-
chise from Kirk Whitehead shortly after his return to Mississippi.
His involvement with bootlegging largely accounted for the fact
that James, for all his hatred of the plantation system, remained
a plantation resident for the rest of the 1920s.

Alcohol had been an illegal commodity on Mississippi plantations since the late nineteenth century. A series of local option
laws passed between 1886 and 1901 made saloons illegal in
nearly every Mississippi town. In 1902, another state law forbade
the sale of whiskey except in towns of 500 or more inhabitants
that enjoyed continuous police protection. In February, 1908,

a dozen years before it became the law of the country, prohibition was formally enacted throughout Mississippi.

The state's officials paid loud lip service to Prohibition. Mississippi was the first state to ratify the Prohibition Amendment
of 1919, and the last state in the country to repeal Prohibition,
in 1967. Its zealousness in enacting such legislation was exceeded
only by its laxity in enforcing it. Three months after national
prohibition had taken effect, the state legislature had refused
to appropriate money to assist Federal revenue agents in enforcing it. Prohibition was thereby enforced by state revenue
agents who were largely tools of the planter establishment, and
by local sheriffs, who were outright tools of the planters. Thus
the laws were simply designed to vest control of bootlegging
in the planters.

In the 1920s, the plantation bootlegging industry flourished
almost as if National Prohibition had never occurred, churning
out enough corn whiskey ("white lightning") to support a vast
culture of weekend "house frolics" that in turn enfranchised
professional blues-playing. There were stills on most Mississippi
plantations — all owned by the resident white planter. "Back
in the Twenties and like that, the white people would have the
colored people makin' whiskey for 'em," James said. "It'd be
their outfit, and they'd be the backers, but they just got me
hired to run it and take care of it."

To James, bootlegging was an irresistible alternative to sharecropping. "Makin' whiskey was the biggest thing they had goin'
on down there to make somethin' 'worthwhile' [profitable]," he
explained, "'cause the day work there, choppin' and ditchin',
wasn't *nothin'*. Maybe two and a half dollars a day for battlin'
all day with a tractor; maybe a dollar and a half otherwise."
As a bootlegger, James was paid $60-70 per week. He explained:
"See, with those big outfits [stills] you could run fifty gallons
of whiskey in a day or night. You'd run it off twice a week,
and get maybe two or three hundred gallons a week. It would
come out to about sixteen barrels a day. You'd get a dollar a
barrel, and in two days' time that'd be thirty or thirty-some-odd
dollars on your first run. Then you can go home and sleep
while your next batch runs off."

Just as his father had been before him, James was now protected by his planter/patron. "If your bossman give you the
privilege to make whiskey, he's always gonna look out for you,"
James said. "He may hear of the revenue men comin' in, 'cause
these big mens, you know, keep themselves notified to that extent. They go to these state meetings and so forth, and they'll
be discussin' this stuff: 'They're goin' out for such-and-such a
man's place to search for a still.'

"So he'll come and tell you: 'Better not hit the woods today
or tomorrow: I got a notice that the revenue men, they'se out
searchin' everywhere. Just forget that stuff till everything gets
cool. While it's hot, don't even *go* that way.'

"You do like most of them tell you, brother, and you *will*
be protected. That's the way it was.

"Most of the time the revenues will go by him first. Sometimes
the bossman will come out with 'em in the car; walk around
with 'em while they're searchin'. Well, he done *told* the Negroes
about what was comin', so there ain't nothin' there for the revenues to see. The bossman will tell 'im: 'Well, he used to have
some stuff, but there ain't nothin' like that there now.'

"Of course, these 'little laws' [local police] . . . they never
would go on these plan'ations unless'n they consulted that bossman. If he tell 'im: 'Hell no, don't go on my place; I don't
allow you messin' with my Negroes,' they'd pretty much have
to keep off. But the boss couldn't do that with the *real* revenue
men—the state's men. He cannot prohibit them from comin';
they can go anywhere in the state they wanna.

"And if somebody had done reported you . . . they'd break
into your house even if you wasn't there . . . Break your lock
and tear up things. They ain't got to show you no warrant,
'cause they don't have to show it to you: just your bossman."

James' jaundiced view of revenue agents was similar to a modern-day drug dealer's assessment of law enforcement. "Sometimes they'd trail the guy that was makin' whiskey in these woods
and down in these bayous and so forth," he said of the 1920s
revenue agents. "These scoundrels would get on their knees and
stomachs and crawl through the thickets to those big outfits;
two and three at a time. Never under that. And they be's well-

armed, too: they carries high-powered rifles. Sometimes a rifle and two pistols apiece.

". . . Whenever the revenue mens come 'round and approach you like that, it's always best to give up, to surrender. 'Cause if you don't, and don't start shootin' them, they'll really kill you . . . And then a lot of times, when they *have* caught the colored man that's operatin' the still, they wasn't satisfied. They want the white man, the man that was puttin' up for it. They knowed no nigger wasn't able to put up a big still like that, especially in Mississippi or Louisiana. They knew it was a big white man backin' him up, so when they'd catch those one or two cats, they'd beat him up, you know, to try to make him tell who he belonged to and all.

"If you say: 'No, this ain't none of my still; this belongs to Mr. So-and-So,' hell! You might as well let the revenue mens kill you for not talkin', 'cause otherwise the bossman's liable to kill you. You'd better not tell on the white man! He done already told you: 'Now, whatever happens, it's yours, see?' That's understood."

It was the venality rather than the brutality of revenue agents that made James contemptuous of them. "Some of them mollydodgers would *drink* that whiskey," he recalled. "Sure! They wouldn't report it all, or take the balance of what they found to the courthouse for proof; they keep some of it for themselves. Then sometimes, if those revenues liked you pretty well, *they'll* back you up . . . Some of those scoundrels would sell those things to a colored person. Or they'll support him — buy all the sugar and chops and everything else, for a certain percentage of the retail price. See, if you was workin' for a revenue man, you could sell your whiskey retail and wouldn't have to wholesale it where you wouldn't get so much . . . And the rest of the revenues won't mess with you unless it's by his consent.

"Then sometimes it could be a trap for that colored cat; he didn't even consider that. The revenue man already knows exactly where the still is stationed at: he'll let you make whiskey a while, and that's where he got a trap in his net, understand?

"He may get tired of that Negro makin' money, or else the Negro maybe hasn't come up to his compromise. 'This nigger's

tryin' to be slick. Hell, he's supposed to give me a bigger percentage than that.' Or he may say: 'These barrels didn't turn
out so well this time'—sometimes maybe they won't. He'll get
hot; he figure that the nigger isn't doin' fair with him. Well,
that guy's automatically trapped, then."

Intermittently, James would make whiskey for corrupt revenue
agents in the mid and late 1920s. "I made whiskey for two or
three mens and I know I did very well with 'em," he said. "But
you know what? I quit that. And then I'd take chances on *Skip*:
I'd make whiskey for me, not the other fellow. I styled it in
this light: if I get caught, let me get caught doin' somethin'
for me, not for you, that right?"

Although James portrayed himself as merely an enterprising
character, whose bootlegging had no bearing on either his rectitude or respectability, his was actually a déclassé profession
that (thanks to its dangerousness) held no glamor for the ordinary sharecropper. Even the avid consumer of corn whiskey
was likely to look askance at the characters who produced and
supplied it, in the fashion of the Mississippi bluesman Booker
White: "I don't have to sell whiskey, I don't have to run no
gambling-house. No; I'll just try to get out an' *work* for mine
. . . When I get my money I ain't got to be dodgin' people, an'
lookin', and have to pay [bribe] somebody. . . . "

Even considering the bribe money he must have paid out to
planters or law enforcement officials, James' bootlegging enterprise was far more profitable than blues-singing, or any attainable occupation on the part of a Mississippi black in the 1920s.
His financial circumstances, vis-à-vis his pauperized plantation
peers, must have been comparable to those of a successful drug
dealer in a modern-day housing project. How he spent the proceeds of his profession is anyone's guess. He was not a materialistic person, and had no discernable attachment to possessions when he became known to latter-day blues audiences. His
only real indulgence lay in clothes and jewelry. He was, at least
by his own lights, far from being a "fatmouth"—a man who lavished money on females. One guesses that James periodically
squandered his wealth through injudicious gambling done in
the course of drinking, à la the narrator of *Drunken Spree*. "I

wanted to be a 'man,' so quite naturally I was a habitual drunkard," he once said of his youth.

James customarily gambled during intermissions as a "house frolic" entertainer, on which occasions he probably drank freely and lost money freely. But he also had a non-recreational interest in gambling; in addition to bootlegging, he worked as a professional gambler in the mid and late 1920s. From his earliest days in road and lumber camps he had acquired a lofty view of these figures: "You can define some of these people as the most progressive people of both sexes . . . they're very shifty and esteemable." But he was loathe to portray his gambling career in any detail, no doubt because he recognized that other persons did not share this exalted view of his profession. Barrelhouse gamblers were invariably cheats who fleeced gullible patrons, and it is unlikely that James was an exception, particularly as he would ironically describe himself as "lucky" at cards. His attachment to the revolver and his preoccupation with being "precautious" were probably methods of reinforcing his ordained luck, against disgruntled victims.

To the extent it was possible in his plantation environment, James also maintained predatory relationships with a nameless succession of "hustling women." In short, he did everything within his power to perpetuate the lifestyle of his Weona and Memphis days. His recordings would contain faint but unmistakable hints of the sporting persona James bore in life:

> I'm gonna milk my heifer, milk her in a churn
> If you see my rider, tell her t'ain't a darn thing doin'.
> <div align="right">(<i>Little Cow and Calf</i>)</div>

The title couplet of *Cypress Grove* could have served as a pimp's credo:

> I would rather be buried in some cypress grove
> Than have some woman I cannot control.

There was an outright passing suggestion of pimping on *Cherry Ball Blues*:

Sure as that spider, hangin' on the wall
I'd advise that cherry ball, keep fallin' on call.

Thanks to his involvement in bootlegging, gambling, and prostitution, he pursued music as a sideline rather than as a profession. How incidental music actually was to him is indicated by his failure to buy a piano, which he could have easily afforded in the mid-1920s. His independence from the dictates of a blues career enabled him to play music on his own terms, rather than function as a request performer in the fashion of the typical Mississippi blues entertainer of the period.

10. *The Musician*

The original audience for James' music had no concern with either its sources or its originality. Like other blues singers, James was simply a performer, either hired to provide a dance beat or working as self-employed street singer, out to tease nickels and dimes from passersby. When he ventured beyond Bentonia and its surrounding orbit of small plantation towns, he recalled, he would not even be known by name to his audiences.

It was not until his 1964 rediscovery that James would be congratulated for his creativity, and formally appreciated as a blues great. Because James quickly became aware that both his stature and his employability were dependent on a perception of himself as a unique musician, his appraisals of his music emphasized its maverick qualities. "I did my own composin'," he was to state four months after his rediscovery. ". . . I composed my own—never has copycatted after someone else. If I get a little idea about someone else's music, their version, I'd rearrange it and put it in Skip's. In case if I used it like they play it, that wouldn't be Skip; it'd be somebody else. And most of my music you hear is my own, an' every song you hear me sing is my own composin'. An' all the music, I rearranged it and put it to my verses." The gist of this statement was that he freely adapted various blues melodies, setting them to his own style and giving them original verses.

In this regard, James' rhetoric was conventional for a blues singer, whether the singer was a derivative or eclectic performer. Few of the songs James sang consisted of original verses. What set him apart from other musicians was his vocal and instrumental sound.

How he had developed his guitar style, he told the author in the 1960s, was "for you to figure out." Some of James' development as a guitarist was facilitated by his original mentor Henry (Son) Stuckey, with whom he joined forces around 1924. Stuckey was often known as "Sport" Stuckey because, James said, "he'd do anything to get out of work"—a comment Stuckey likewise made about James decades later.

In later years, James would never credit Stuckey with showing him anything specific, or acknowledge any general influence. "I get my music from God," he said haughtily, making a statement also attributed to Blind Lemon Jefferson. He dismissed Stuckey as "the rudiment guy"—someone from whom he had learned only rudiments of music. Aside from *Drunken Spree*, the pieces he reported learning from Stuckey were all peripheral in his repertoire, never to be resurrected in the 1960s: *Sliding Delta*, *Salty Dog* and *Stack O'Lee*. These were commonplace pieces played in standard tuning. "After my teacher learnt me—the rudiment guy—then I jumped through that," he said of conventional guitar tuning. Without expressly saying so, he implied that Stuckey had been one of the typical guitarists of his time: "Most of the people played in common C, natural C [i.e., standard tuning]," he was to say. "And I wanted to be kind of different—always have been like that." The product of this desire, he said, was his basic guitar tuning, open E minor, which he claimed to have hit upon by himself.* "... I just liked it," he stated four months after his rediscovery. "I mean, I just fished around until I started findin' it, and I just kept it up ... everybody can't play in minor ... minor music is the most difficult music to play ... " When asked how this music had originated, he replied: "Well, I'll tell you: I haven't seeked for it, but I know this little thing: I played in minor before I could start to playin' pretty good."

Reflecting the appreciative comments of blues specialists, he would say: "... that seems to be a complicated tunin' to the majority of musicianers, that 'crossin'.' " While it was easy to

---

*Assuming a guitar to be at concert pitch, it involved tuning the D string to E, and the A (fifth) string to B. The G string (left as in standard tuning) created an E minor chord when the open strings (E-B-G-E-B-E) were sounded.

play in any open tuning, it was too complicated for James, an unlettered musician, to explain intelligibly. "When you mix it, you got your 'cross,' " he said nonsensically of the tuning, "It's all the way in minor, or even in major, you don't have a cross." With the exception of *Devil Got My Woman* and *Hard Times*, all of the songs he played in the tuning had a major tonality.

It was probably because James had been rediscovered by three budding guitarists who were openly taken with his unusual tuning that he was loathe to let this sudden prestige fall upon Henry Stuckey. While stationed in France during World War One, Stuckey had acquired the tuning from a group of black soldiers whom he took to be from the Bahamas. Following his discharge in 1919, Stuckey had returned to Sartartia and begun applying it to his own songs. By the time he showed James the tuning in 1924 he had already showed the same tuning to several musicians he met in the Delta, where he played every fall.

Both Booker White and St. Louis' Henry Townsend independently acquired the same tuning, achieving sounds that were far afield from those of James (and presumably Stuckey), White with a bottleneck presentation and Townsend in a one-chord context. Any blues guitarist who tuned his instrument to a familiar open E chord, in fact, was likely to stumble upon it, for the only difference between the major and minor E tunings lay in the fact that the G string of the guitar, in minor tuning, remained as it was in standard tuning, instead of being raised to G#. A guitarist who raised his G string to play in open E was likely to find it periodically going flat, and thus inadvertently creating an E minor tuning.

According to Stuckey, James soon converted most of his guitar pieces to the new tuning, which would come to permeate his guitar playing. Eleven of the thirteen guitar songs he would record in 1931 made use of it. In most instances, the songs he recorded in "cross" appear to have originated in that tuning. Others, like *Four O'Clock Blues*, were transposed from the key of E in standard tuning. Such transpositions were easy to effect because blues guitarists working in that key customarily played a melody line in thirds, involving the first and third strings being simultaneously plucked. James would play similar melody lines in pinched octaves on the first and fourth strings.

No less important to James' development than Stuckey's tuning was his early counsel to spurn fingerpicks. By following this advice James was able to play expressively. Instead of striking strings with the flesh of his finger in the fashion of other blues guitarists who did not use picks, he plucked with his nails in the fashion of classical guitarists. This unique technique gave his notes a vibrant, crisp sound.

What Stuckey contributed to James' basic repertoire is uncertain. Like most blues singers of his era, James made no distinction between composing and arranging. Stuckey seems to have performed the parent version of James' piano piece, *If You Haven't Any Hay, Get On Down The Road*. His equivalent, a guitar song in standard tuning called *All Night Long*, used the same melody, played at a slower tempo. "Boy, it sounded good back then!" James said of Stuckey's piece, which he did not expressly attribute to him but failed to claim credit for. After learning *All Night Long* as a guitar piece, he transposed it to piano, greatly embellishing its accompaniment in the process. Its melody was simply a blues makeover of *Alabama Bound*, a standard dating to the turn of the century, with the pentatonic melodic scale of the original given a bluesified sound by the addition of minor thirds.

Stuckey also knew a version of *Devil Got My Woman*, which became James' signature song after he began playing it in 1925 or 1926. Whether or not Stuckey's version preceded James' is impossible to say: in a 1966 interview, he would not expressly claim credit for it.

James originally sang *Devil Got My Woman*, Stuckey said, as *Devil's Dream*. (There was no resemblance between James' *Devil* and the instrumental fiddle tune *Devil's Dream*, which Lafcadio Hearn had described in 1876 as a "wild, lively air.") The song was a non-generic piece that James was unlikely to have single-handedly invented, all the more so as he had a general distaste for slow songs.

Regardless of what Stuckey actually contributed to James' repertoire, his playing must have been crude by comparison, for he was basically a guitar strummer rather than a finger-picker. Booker Miller, a Delta bluesman who would know him in the early 1930s, said of Stuckey's guitar-playing: "He always played it 'complement': he 'frailed' all the time. He never did too much pickin'." Jack Owens, a Bentonia bluesman who knew Stuckey in the 1940s, also recalled him as a guitar strummer: "He could play good, but he'd 'rap' along . . . He could do more rappin' than he could anything else." Indeed, it is doubtful that Stuckey was at heart a blues guitarist. The tunes he recalled playing, such as *Pallet On The Floor*, were "rag" songs, while the ensemble work he performed in a string band when Miller became acquainted with him was not characteristic of simon-pure blues guitarists. It would seem that Stuckey began playing before blues songs as such were locally popular, and that his early genesis as a performer prevented him from becoming a straightforward blues artist in the fashion of James.

The four or five years James had passed outside of Bentonia were as critical to his development as the material he acquired from Henry Stuckey, for it prevented him from simply assimilating Stuckey's techniques, which were likely tinctured with the heavy-textured approach of the plantation dance musician. James' earliest pieces, such as *Drunken Spree* and *Sliding Delta*, had reflected this approach, presenting a combination of picking and strumming. Most Mississippi bluesmen of the 1920s achieved a similar full sound, and appeared to perform pieces that were modifications of tunes that had originally been "rapped." Heavy intermittent strumming would abound in pieces by artists like Booker White, who began his career as a square dance musician. Typically, a blues accompaniment in the A, C, or G position would find the artist picking notes within or adjacent to the chord, and within or adjacent to the IV and V7 chords that followed. It was in this fashion that James played *Drunken Spree*, a non-blues song.

James' open tuning efforts, however, were played without such chordal reference points. Instead of taking the vertical approach to the guitar neck that a chordally-oriented player did, his approach was horizontal, sweeping back and forth along the top strings to pick out melodic notes, the way a bottleneck guitarist would. In part, this way of playing reflected his piano work.

Primarily, James was a single-note picker who scarcely knew full chords. His chordal repertoire was limited to bedrock progressions in E major. He had little ability to fret with his fifth finger, and thus play either barre chords, or to attain facility in the C position (a favorite key of "rag" songs). Although James played a version of *Salty Dog* in C, he had only a tenuous grip of that piece in the 1960s. Even *Drunken Spree* was a piece he played awkwardly.

James' limitations as a "note" player were partly attributable to his infatuation with Stuckey's tuning, which simplified the presentation of works in the key of E. Although James played *Devil Got My Woman* as a song in D, "cross note" was designed to effect songs in the E position. Its net effect was to convert the guitar into a four stringed instrument, with two strings "doubled." Had James worked more extensively in standard tuning, instead of lazily exploiting the easy sonorities of "cross note," he would have become a more technically accomplished guitarist. But in all likelihood, James did not, until the late 1920s, take guitar-playing seriously enough to have any aspirations more exalted than an ability to outplay the likes of Stuckey, or any local rivals.

What enabled him to outplay rivals was his development of a three-finger picking technique, itself unusual in the realm of blues guitar. Whereas James used his index and middle fingers to pick the top three strings, most blues guitarists used only an index finger. As Blind Lemon Jefferson's protégé Tom Shaw would remark: "You seldom ever see a colored guy play with anything but these two fingers [thumb and index finger], pickin' a guitar . . . I don't know n'ar a one that was playin' with three fingers." Among Mississippi musicians, only Charlie Patton, Bo Carter, and Mississippi John Hurt appear to have played with three fingers. James' approach would facilitate smoothness and speed, and enable him to sound simultaneous treble tones by means of pinches. The fluency it afforded was ultimately responsible for *I'm So Glad*, a tour de force of fingerpicking that could not have been emulated by a one-digit treble picker.

In itself, James' determination to pick (to the extent of almost excising the strum) resulted from an apparent desire to achieve the idealized blues effect of making his instrument "talk," or mirror his vocal inflections. Although James never called attention to this aspect of his playing, his adroitness at following the changing nuances of his vocal line was one of the most remarkable features of *Devil Got My Woman* and *Special Rider*. It was this ability that would have certified him as a top-flight guitarist among blues musicians of his day. In later decades, the attention of white blues listeners would be focused on the (typically six- or eight-beat) riffs that followed each vocal phrase, and when James became a white concert performer he was to concentrate on impressing his audience with gaudy filler riffs, to the virtual exclusion of a "talking" guitar technique.

James' preoccupation with picking all but removed his music from the sphere of the plantation dance that was probably Stuckey's forte, and that of most Mississippi bluesmen. Only three of his tunes—one of them his rendition of Stuckey's *Drunken Spree*—bear a steady dance beat. His music clearly demonstrates that he most often performed on street corners, in which setting he would function as a a soloist.

When paired with James, Stuckey functioned primarily as a back-up musician, accompanying both his guitar and piano pieces. In addition to playing grizzled standards like *Salty Dog, Pallet On The Floor*, and *Stack O'Lee*, all of which James learned from Stuckey, they sometimes copied blues records, with the aim (Stuckey said) of outplaying the originals. Stuckey recalled that they performed tunes by Blind Lemon Jefferson, the Texas street singer who became the best-selling male blues artist of the decade after his recording debut in 1926. One such number was Jefferson's popular *One Dime Blues*; decades later, James would resurrect its melody to create *Sick Bed Blues*. Another Jefferson song James played was *Jack O' Diamonds*. James' high-pitched singing made his Jefferson emulations more authentic-sounding than those of the lower-registered singers who tried to capitalize on the latter's singular popularity in the 1920s.

Most blues musicians of the period trafficked heavily in blues "hits," which were in heavy demand as request pieces. A blues singer could not spurn such a request without virtually losing musical face, or ceding his position to any singer who could imitate the latest blues success. The audience of the period was responsive to songs, not styles or (with rare exceptions) particular singers. The impression of a blues singer that would be left by his recording legacy was likely to be deceptive: whereas "race" recording impresarios induced blues artists to perform original or novel-sounding material in the studio, the same singer was likely to traffic in standards or hits, unless he had somehow managed to spark a demand for one of his own songs. For the most part he functioned as a request musician.

What distinguished James from his contemporaries was his disaffection for such music. "I can play most some of everything I hear," he once explained, "but still I don't like to do that: I don't like to make that a practice," he said. "I like to play somethin' from Skip. Why? So it'll be strange to the people, to the rest of the musicians." This was almost a suicidal approach for a professional blues musician of the age to take.

James developed an unmatched facility for rearranging songs. Instead of doing a straightforward rendition of Leroy Carr's 1928 recording of *How Long Blues*, the most popular piano blues of all time, he would give the song a complete facelift, transforming it from a slow, placid ditty into a fast, frantic madcap performance. No other bluesman took such liberties with a famous original. A piece that he could not remold would take a back seat in his repertoire: though he performed a note-perfect rendition of the standard *Cow Cow Blues*, he would not (in the 1960s) perform it without considerable prodding. "That's common," he remarked, uttering his favorite term of musical disparagement.

James' uncommoness was manifest not only in individual songs, but also in his general approach to his music. He was one of the few blues guitarists of the 1920s to adorn his tunes with introductions and codas. He would become the only Southern blues guitarist of the era to create bona fide instrumental breaks on the guitar, as opposed to instrumental reprises of his vocal accompaniment. The carefully plotted instrumental flights of fancy on *Special Rider*, *I'm So Glad* and *Hard-Luck Child* would have no counterpart in blues, which were basically a vocal medium.

Perhaps James' greatest contribution to the blues idiom was his inadvertent dismantling of the distinction between blues and other idioms, such as "rag" songs. Whereas James' Stuckey-inspired *Drunken Spree* followed the conventions of the "rag" song, his *Illinois Blues* and *Hard Times Killin' Floor* used stark-sounding blues tonalities within "rag" phrasing patterns. Moreover, they were picked in the fashion of blues pieces, with single melody notes. His *Devil Got My Woman* and *I'm So Glad* were similarly rooted in non-blues material, but were played in the fashion of blues songs.

James' preoccupation with achieving musical uniqueness complemented his general distaste for musical associates. "I never did want to play in no group or no band or no nothin'," he said. "I just wanna be me, Skip." Henry Stuckey was the only musician with whom he had anything resembling an ongoing partnership.* "We were just like two brothers," he said of Stuckey. "They always styled us as brothers if we'd go somewhere we wasn't known." Decades later, the Yazoo City blues singer Arthur (Big Boy) Spires (b. 1912) was to recall "Nemiah" (whose last name he did not know) as the piano-playing brother of Henry Stuckey.

The pair dressed alike and pursued the same jaded interests: Stuckey supplemented his income as a gambler and pimp, and James did likewise. "We had some good times; we had some bad times, too—an' some hustlin' women, too!" James would recall of their adventures, or misadventures. At local "house frolics," Stuckey would invariably increase his income by gambling during intermission. "That scoundrel, he sure could shoot craps!" James said of him. Knowing Stuckey to be a crooked dice-shooter, James never played against him.

When performing together at plantation "house frolics" the pair played back to back, each keeping a wary eye on their audi-

---

*He also played with Stuckey's brother "Shug," who was two or three years younger than himself. "Shug," whom he considered a better guitarist than Henry, moved to Chicago around 1935 and was said to have become a minister.

ence. "He could sure enough fight, and he could *shoot*, too," James said appreciatively of Stuckey.

Even with the Colt revolver he habitually tucked in the waistband of his trousers, James was reluctant to perform alone at what he disparagingly called "these country balls." He recalled: "You get on these plantations, some of these guys had a pretty good influence with 'ole boss,' they called him, and they'd just as soon kill you as not ... And you had to be very careful, playin' at these places. Or had someone to kinda look out for you ... because a few country peoples that was around a guitar player had just common jealousy."

Lacking even a semblance of supervision, the plantation "frolic" was likely to erupt at any time in violent pandomonium: "... At these country balls, they'd have shootin' scrapes and things: people'd be runnin' and hollerin'." According to Son House, patrons actually looked forward to the opportunity to indulge in Saturday night gunplay: "They'd figure they *oughta* ball then. They wanna see some runnin' done." Because gambling generally took place beyond the premises, the usual fracas that resulted in a scramble for safety arose from the inveterate reaction of a male patron to a perceived encroachment upon his female escort. "Somebody there was liable to have some girlfriend there and some other man could be startin' to talk with her," Booker White recalled, "get half-drunk off that white lightnin' whiskey, you know, anything was liable to jump off ... An' they get to shootin'." Though Skip James liked to give the impression in later years that "house frolic" denizens were uncouth and uncivilized, they were in fact his own clients, out to stupify themselves with the corn liquor he provided.

11. *The Performer*

James encountered similar perils when he played for white parties in the 1920s. "I played lots of times for white parties, man," he recalled. "Man, I played organ, I played guitar, and I played piano at white parties . . . " He had a word-of-mouth reputation among local whites: "They'd come at me, askin' for me to go these different places, just like it was Flora or Yazoo, maybe, somewhere like that. They had relatives, and want to give a big party; dance. Well, they done heard about Skippy James; some of their kin say: 'How 'bout gettin' Skip?' So one of them would hunt for me and find me." It was in the interests of making himself employable for whites that he learned such pieces as *Carolina Moon*, a 1928 hit popularized by Morton Downey, which he played on the piano, and *Am I Blue?* which Ethel Waters had featured in the 1929 film *On With The Show*. He also played guitar renditions of two Uncle Dave Macon pieces: *Get Along Mule* and *See The Line*.

Most blues performers who played for white dances were chiefly impressed by the high pay they garnished in the process. Already accustomed to making easy money through illicit enterprises, James was chiefly impressed by the oppressive atmosphere he encountered at white frolics. "You go play at places like that, regardless of how well you are known . . . you create enemies, through some of these young, fancy white gals.

"They wanna come and flirt around like that with you . . . Them white gals may come up and request a song . . . And then another one the next time around, so, there'd be two or three around me, see? Well, their men don't know what them girls is talkin' about and sayin', and they don't know what I'm sayin', see?

"I may just be sayin': 'Yes ma'am' . . . 'No, ma'am. I can't play that,' or 'I will play it. Give me time,' or somethin' like that.

"But see, the men don't know that. In other words, they don't like to see 'em (white women) in my face no way. 'Cause I'm a darkie. Negro . . . And at that time, they's bad on you. They'd lynch you in a minute.

"Sometime, you know, the girls would flirt on purpose to get the men after you . . . And sometimes, some of them women wouldn't mind doin' somethin' like that [consorting with a black]. Yet most of the time, some of them will take a likin' to a . . . famous musician or somethin'.

"Then you would say somethin' back *if you were ignorant enough*, understand?"

No matter how much diplomacy he exercised at white dances, James still ran the danger of affronting white women. "Sometimes they'd get nasty because I wouldn't do her request right then, because somebody else was ahead of her," he said. "Well, she would go off and . . . tell somebody, 'Oh, that old nigger' (you know what they're gonna call us down there); 'Well, that old nigger, he tryin' to be smart.'

". . . There's a lot of them do tell a lie, and I ain't said shit to her."

When James encountered a problem of this sort he would approach the white person who had hired him to play. "I'd just tell my man, my white guardeen, I say: 'That girl, there, that white lady there, come ask me somethin' and I didn't play it for her right then . . . she got kinda nasty . . . went over there and told that cat over yonder. He say some kinda smart words about me or somethin'.'

"Over there my protector's gonna go, and say: 'What's wrong?' Say: 'What has Skip did? . . . Didn't he have any more requests ahead of you? Didn't he tell you he would play yours when he had a chance to? . . . Well, you shouldn't have gotten nasty . . . I don't want that, no how. I ain't gonna have that.' And then my man say to that ol' white cat: 'You take it quiet, brother.' That's right. He'll do it. And that cat knows what'll be next . . .

"My guardian had pretty good influence, and they [the party-goers] knew what he would do for me, too. That's another important thing: if he spoke and said, 'This is Skippy James, I

want him to be treated nice, he gonna play for us, and I don't
want nobody to even touch him. Whatever Skip wants, I want
him to have it,' that settled that. Yeah. If if didn't, they'se liable
to get a bullet upside the head, see? Right quick. Oh yeah. He'd
do it, and they knew it. I wouldn't go playin' at those places
with nobody who didn't have no more power than I did, understand?"

Characteristically, James' "guardian" was armed, as was James.
"I got some protection on *myself*," he said. "And then another
thing: you know I'll use it, too, don't you? Yeah, that's right."

Although the image of a white Mississippian taking up the
cudgels for a blues entertainer may seem incongruous, W.C.
Handy would similarly report that upon being physically attacked by a white party-goer in Batesville, another patron
thrashed his assailant and "low-rated the local boys for not pro-
tecting me after bringing me there to play for them."[*]

His main performance pieces among black audiences were
Devil Got My Woman and *Cypress Grove*, a song Stuckey credited
him with composing. The latter was a conventionally-phrased
twelve-bar blues played at a One-Step tempo and set to a solid
1-2 beat. Like the typical dance blues, it featured little variation.
Its melody was common Mississippi blues fare.

Whereas Stuckey's career was largely limited to Satartia, Bentonia, and Yazoo City, James also played in Canton, Meridian,
and Hattiesburg, where he lodged with relatives. In Yazoo City,
he worked briefly with a *Rabbit Foot Minstrel* troupe. He often
traveled with a girlfriend, Nettie ("Net") Owens (no relation to
Jack Owens), an accomplished dancer who had formerly been
a consort of Stuckey's. They sang a duet version of *Devil Got
My Woman*.

Occasionally James visited Jackson, some 25 miles and six rail
stops below Bentonia. Acquaintances there, he said, gave him
the nickname "Skippy." James was never certain what the nickname connoted. He thought it might have remarked on his pro-
clivity for dancing: "I loved that fast Two-Step," he said. But
neither the Two-Step nor any other popular dances of the period

[*]See Handy, *Father Of The Blues* (Collier Books, New York, 1970 reprint of
the 1941 edition), p. 188.

involving skipping, and the verb never appears in blues descriptive phrases applied to dancing.

At other times, he indicated that his footloose existence brought on the nickname. Were this so, it is likely that "Skippy" hinted at something darker than simple elusiveness. Most blues singers, after all, were itinerants or "rolling stones." In common usage, someone who "skips" town flees from the law, or for some other compelling reason.

The most curious aspect of James' musical development in the 1920s was his determination to become a top-flight pianist. Although numerous blues musicians played both piano and guitar (Blind Blake, Richard Harney, Peetie Wheatstraw, Henry Townsend, Booker White, Lonnie Johnson), those who did essentially dabbled in one instrument and specialized in the other. James would become a unique figure in bluesdom by acquiring remarkable facility on both instruments. His progress as a pianist was all the more remarkable because he never owned a piano, and the few pianos he had access to in Yazoo County were spaced ten or fifteen miles apart. The lack of a ready piano probably prevented him from developing an outright piano style. He rather contrived a series of distinctive arrangements; on his 1931 recordings he was to sound like several different pianists. His freewheeling approach on *22-20* and *Little Cow and Calf* would bear nothing in common with the austere twelve-bar accompaniment of *What Am I To Do?*, which had probably been one of his early efforts, or with his melodic renditions of *If You Haven't Any Hay* or *How Long*. The only unifying characteristic of his piano titles lay in their vocals, which were rendered in a soft tenor, instead of his false soprano.

It is unlikely that James harbored any momentous artistic aspirations on piano when he began as Will Crabtree's understudy. What seems to have goaded him to excel on the instrument was encountering Little Brother Montgomery, the most famous blues pianist in Mississippi. James was so determined to equal Montgomery that he told him, after initially listening to him, "If you stay where you are I'm gonna catch up to you."

He first met Montgomery around 1927 in Yazoo City. "He and I used to play together around Jackson," he said. "At that time, why he's supposed to have been my superior: he's playin' before I was." Though four years younger than James, Montgomery had played professionally since around 1917. He had begun playing in childhood, with the same *Coonshine* that had been James' earliest piece.

Early in his career, Montgomery had suffered a nervous break-down while performing *Vicksburg Blues* in a Vicksburg barrel-house called *Zach's Place*. On that occasion, Sam Chatmon had begun playing with him, only to find that Montgomery would not stop performing the song.

> Me and him started together, look like close to two hours: he stayed on steady-playin' . . . I quit and left him sittin' there playin' 'cause I could see he wasn't gonna quit, so I just got up and quit myself. When the man [owner] seed he wasn't gonna quit, well, he called the law, and the law come in there and went there to try to talk to him and he just never didn't stop, he didn't pay this law no attention: just kept right on playin'. He just actin' crazy: I got outta the way.

Montgomery was dragged off to Whitfield, the state insane asy-lum near Jackson.

His subsequent reputation rested largely on the fact that he had a theme song, as James did not: *Vicksburg Blues*, a slow tune designed for Shimmy-She-Wobble dancing, had become a standard among pianists. This song had an unusual phrasing pattern, with Montgomery doubling the length of the usual blues vocal and instrumental phrases to create a 24-bar work. Instead of featuring the usual rhythmically regular single-note bass of the blues pianist, it used unpredictable, episodic bass glissandos to create counter rhythms against the treble figures, which were often imitative of his singing.

"He didn't show me nothin'," James said of Montgomery. "He ain't showed me one thing." James had used the melody of *Vicksburg Blues* as the basis of his *Special Rider*, commenting: "I just listened to a few of his notes . . . I don't play it like he does." Yet Montgomery was to exert a subtle but significant influence on James' piano playing, facilitated by the latter's sense of musical discrimination. Most barrelhouse pianists of the period, such as Helena's Roosevelt Sykes and Charley ("44 Charley") Taylor of Sumner, Mississippi, were given to showy but unmusical displays of dexterity with riffs consisting of treble note clusters played as rapidly as possible. In the process, their rhythms became diffuse and their notes difficult to distinguish. Perhaps because *Vicksburg Blues* was a vocal vehicle, Montgomery rendered it at a slow, stately tempo that enabled him to emphasize every note and employ subtle dynamic contrasts while driving home a heavy beat. Although the content of James' piano pieces bore no similarity to Montgomery's, he appears to have absorbed these lessons, even as he played his most rapid runs.

Yet it was in keeping with James' adamant spirit of musical independence that he would not hazard his own version of *Vicksburg Blues*, even though it was a staple of pianists from Memphis to New Orleans, and an almost mandatory part of the Mississippi blues piano repertoire.

While James would assimilate underlying characteristics of Montgomery's musicianship, he rarely ventured in that pianist's native Louisiana, where Montgomery had established himself as a popular sawmill pianist. The reason, he claimed, was its virulent racism: "In some places in Louisiana up in the Twenties," James recalled, "a Negro go down there . . . in one of these stores and want a can of Prince Albert tobacco . . .

" 'All right, what you want, nigger?' . . .

" 'I want a can of Prince Albert.'

" 'Of *what*?'

". . . If you didn't say: 'Mister Prince Albert,' shit; they'd mobilize you, beat you right there . . . And sometimes those bastards didn't want to sell it to you, and *didn't* sell it to you: beat your butt and then kick you outta there." He believed that blacks were forced to pull ploughs on some Louisiana plantations. "That was long about in 1910 or 1912; I was just a kid when I heard all that kinda stuff. I was big enough to understand what they were sayin', and a lots of folks said after I got up some size, it was really true."

In response to this story, he said, he devised the couplet:

> I'm goin' I'm goin'
> Comin' here no more,

If I go to Louisiana mama lord they'll,
They'll hang me sho'.

(If You Haven't Any Hay)

Whether or not a noose awaited him in any particular place, James was typically leery of treading there, at least long enough to leave tracks. Whereas Montgomery would move to Chicago in 1928, there to join a jazz band, James' single visit to that city (the following year) lasted a week. He returned to Mississippi convinced that Chicago—a virtual city of refuge for blacks who chafed under Jim Crow—was an "underground" [underworld] city, unfit for decent persons.

At no point in the 1920s did James become a conventional blues itinerant, wandering about from place to place. He was too purposeful a person to take the common blues career path of becoming a drifting nomad facing uncertain returns in strange areas, and too fond of dressing "dudey" to take to life on the dusty road. Only once in his career did he make a pass at hoboing: "I got broke once in Jackson, and had to come to Bentonia, home. That was thirty-two miles ... I said to my mind: 'I'm broke, I ain't got no money, so what I'm gonna do?' ... I say: 'I know what I'll do. I'm goin' to the railroad track.'

"And the conductor's out in the caboose, you know. He says: 'Hey, boy!'

" 'Yas-sir.'

" 'You play that thing?'

"I says: 'I dunno; I try.'

"He say: 'Where you goin'?'

"I say: 'I wanna go to Bentonia but I ain't got no money ... ' He takes me up in the caboose with him ... sits me there and talks to me a little while. Then he says: 'All right, play me a piece.'

"The engineer, he comes back in, sits down ... And then after a while the flagman come walkin' down the boxcars ... and the conductor went over and climbed on top and called him. The flagman come right in the caboose there ...

"And oh, man—you're talkin' about how Skip did some *fiddlin'* [vigorous playing] then. Them guys give me a good drink of liquor, and gimme a dollar apiece."

At the same time, he preferred Jackson, then a city of 48,000, to his native Bentonia. During one mid-Twenties Jackson foray, James played piano behind an itinerant harmonica player from Sun, Louisiana known as "Sonny Boy Williams." Williams used any number of harmonicas, all set in different keys, and was able to produce shreiking sounds by blowing the instrument through his nostrils. Williams would soon leave Jackson with the intention of pursuing a musical career up North; James declined an invitation to accompany him.

Thanks partly to Bentonia's location on the Yazoo and Mississippi Valley rail line between Jackson and Yazoo City, James actually met as many musicians in Bentonia as he did in Jackson. He saw Jackson's most famous bluesman, Tommy Johnson, in Bentonia, Pocahantas, and Flora (as well as Redwood, Mississippi) in the early 1920s. Although James was not particularly impressed by Johnson, whom he considered only a "good songster" (vocalist), the latter's *Coal-Black Mare* interested him enough to learn:

> I got a coal-black mare, how that horse can run
> How she win every race, I don't see how it's done.
>
> I put a three gold teeth in her face, earring in her ear
> Ain't no use a-talkin' boys, 'cause the stuff is here.

These lyrics brought a chuckle to James, who had seen Delta levee camp drivers adorn their favorite mules with gold teeth.

One day between 1927 and 1929, he was amazed by the arrival of a one-armed blues guitarist in Bentonia. Chording with the middle and index fingers of his left hand and picking with his ring finger and pinky, the man produced a close copy of *Cypress Grove*. "That guy was just a miracle!" James later enthused. "He'd skip about on those strings like a squirrel on a limb."

He knew the man only as "Chief" or "One Armed Chief." Rather than sing, Chief played a kazoo. Although James only passed a month in his company, they became instant friends: "I taken much liking to that boy—man, ruther; he's up in his late forties or fifties when I played with him. He was an old dark fellow, a kind of heavy, chunky, fellow. He wasn't quite as tall as I, but he probably weighed about one hundred and sixty or seventy pounds." James knew nothing of his background except that he hailed from Louisiana.

After a few nights' practice they struck out for the Delta, an area with which Chief was already familiar. For two weeks they played at a different party each night. Their itinerary included towns like Louise, Belzoni, Isola, Bellwood, Greenwood, Indianola, Doddsville, and Clarksdale. "We would get five dollars apiece, all we could eat and drink, and a place to sleep. Then sometimes we'd get extra tips for requests; maybe fifty cents or a dollar apiece."

Their performances in Flora and Pocohantas were witnessed by Big Joe Williams, who recalled Chief as an exceptional musician. His abilities could not have measured up to James' extravagant appraisal: "Blind Lemon didn't have nothin' on *him*... If you would hear him pick some pieces that we had practiced together, you couldn't hardly tell him from me...

"Yeah, man, he could play the devil outta *Cypress Grove*; he could play all them things... In fact, I would rather play with him than play with Henry Stuckey, and Stuckey had two *good* hands."

Like Stuckey, Chief was an adept dancer. "He could really flat-foot dance. Sometimes he'd tell me, say: 'Ol' buddy, I wanna dance around, so keep the music goin'...' He'd get out there on the dance floor, put that one arm around a girl. When he'd hear those notes I played, he'd shake that nub. Boy, he's cuttin' up hard, too!"

James' veneration of Chief led him to indulge in uncharacteristic bragging about his popularity. "Oh man, we tore that Delta up! We put a chunk on that fire and left it smokin'! Chief was the 'worst' guy people had ever seen through that country. Those guys would holler: 'Come back, Chief! No, no! Don't leave! Come back, Skip! Come back, come back, Chief! When you-all comin' back?'

"I'd say: 'Don't know' and then never *would* go back there again."

A by-product of their Delta tour was James' acquisition of "Spanish" (open G) tuning. He would add two songs to his repertoire: *Pearlee* (a shopworn knife guitar staple he never played frequently) and *Special Rider Blues*, which was to become one of his basic showpieces.

After James headed back to Bentonia, Chief returned to Louisiana. In the early 1930s, Skip heard a report of his death. "Chief had come up pretty rough," he mused, "and he had been a habitual drinker practically all his life. I don't know whether that took some effect on him or not... Then in some places he took a lot of exposure, too. I heard somebody say once that a woman had doped him, and I wouldn't be surprised if he hadn'ta been trapped like that."

James, who was distinctly unfriendly towards other musicians, was so taken with Chief that he avidly reminisced about him with Big Joe Williams when the two musicians met each other at a New York engagement in 1965. Williams, who thought that Chief died in Slidell, Louisiana (a New Orleans suburb he identified as Chief's hometown), also heard that he had died from a poisoning. As the two exchanged nostalgic notes on their mutual acquaintance, James was so engrossed that he paid scant attention to Williams' admiring reminder of a now-forgotten piano piece he had played as Chief's companion, *Wild Cow*. He had been similarly enamored of Will Crabtree, who was likewise old enough to have been his father, and it was probably less the musical abilities of his handicapped companion than James' feeling of being a "forsaken child" that had created his attachment.

12. *The Devil Woman*

In the late 1920s, James married Oscella Robinson, the sixteen-year-old daughter of a local clergyman. "Some of my relatives thought she was a nice kid, bein' a nice girl, come from a nice family, and goin' to school." It was James' first significant relationship with a woman who was not a barrelhouse floozie or prostitute.

James soon educated her in the fine points of organizing Bentonia "house frolics," at which he performed and sold his own whiskey. On one occasion, her cool wits prevented the arrest of her husband for whiskey possession. "The law come in the house on us in Bentonia one night," James recalled. "When those guys come in (them's revenue men, and they'se supposed to search), she was back there in the kitchen, fryin' fish and washin' dishes and so forth in the sink. And she had a half a gallon of whiskey there, too. We'd been havin' a big fish-fry there; a party. It wasn't nothin' but a little old home party—lotta guys sittin' there in the front room playin' cards for a drink or somethin' like that.

"Some of the boys got so nervous when they saw what was happenin' they couldn't even look at a hand of cards. I was just standin' at the door with the revenues, and my wife, she heard 'em talkin' with me out in the front room. She just took that whiskey and poured it in that tub where all the soap suds and stuff was.

"Those guys come in and they're smellin' around. They smell the fish and they say: 'Oooh! Oh, that fish look might good over there, how 'bout a sandwich? . . . Oh, I smell whiskey! Oh yeah, we got it! *We* got 'em.'

"And then they start to searchin' all the different rooms. She's walkin' right along with 'em. And they got to one place there where she had poured not quite a pint of whiskey in a big glass. It was still sittin' there. They went in and smelled that big glass.

"Say: 'Oh, *this* is whiskey! Oh yeah, this is it! That's some of it. Where's the rest of it?'

"She say: 'You think that's whiskey? Taste it.'

" 'No, I ain't gonna taste it.'

"Say: 'Taste it! You know, you might *think* it's whiskey and it could *not* be whiskey.' And so he taken a drink. That's what he ought not to did.

"She say: 'Hand it to him and let him taste it, too!' The other law taken that whiskey, and *he* taken a drink of it.

"And so after them two laws taken a drink, then they wanted to smell her, say: 'Oh, you been *drinkin'*, too.'

"She say: 'How in the hell can you smell *my* whiskey for the whiskey *you* done drink-ed? And if you knowed it was whiskey, why did you take a drink of it? You'se a law and it's your place, if you knew it was whiskey, to *take* that whiskey to the city court-house, city hall or somethin'.' Say: 'you're just as guilty as I am—'

"He say: 'Oh, Goddamn, you mighty smart! You're smart, ain't you? Well, you can take a drink now.' So she took a drink and poured the rest of it out.

"She say: 'Now we'll go to jail together. You're just as drunk as I am.' Ha, that broke *that* up."

" . . . He just pat her on the shoulder and say: 'You're smart.'

"See, she wasn't even scared of them to start with. You couldn't scare that woman *nothin'*."

In 1928 or 1929 James and Oscella, accompanied by a friend, moved to Dallas. While there, he briefly joined a local three-piece group known as "Whistling Joe's Kazoo Band." It featured a washboard player in addition to Skip's own guitar and kazoo.

It was probably during his stay in Dallas that he was exposed to *So Tired*, the pop song that he was to convert into his greatest and most enduring guitar vehicle, *I'm So Glad*. The inspired version that James was to record was so firmly set in his own style that it never occurred to interviewers of the 1960s to search out its origins. Only after James died did the original model of the song came to light, a 1928 Tin Pan Alley vehicle popularized by Gene Austin on Victor and recorded by several dance bands of the day. Had James (who scarcely listened to records) first heard this song in its original 32-bar form, or apprehended it as a pop tune, he would probably have been loathe to take such extravagant liberties with it, particularly as they rendered it all but unsuitable for white consumption. He may have been exposed to the banal version of it performed by the Dallas String Band, which recorded it as *I'm Tired* in 1928.

James' musical experiences in Texas were far overshadowed by the unexpected dissolution of his marriage when Oscella became romantically involved with their traveling companion, a World War One veteran, whom James (accentuating the betrayal) would later idealize as "a dear friend of mine that I would entrust very much with my companion." Instead of confronting the couple, James let matters take their course. "After I saw the way that she wanted to go, there wasn't nothin' for me to do," he said, "I couldn't prohibit her unless'n it was gonna cause some trouble. She wasn't worth it and he wasn't either, and I wouldn't incarcerate myself for either her or for him by tanglin' up with 'em, unless he pushed for it. He stayed his distance, and so did I, and then I gave her the rope and the rein. I threw it over her head, and she could run off or do anything she wanted to do." The pair remained in Texas; James returned alone to Bentonia. Afterwards, he would have nothing but sour words for World War One veterans, whom he termed "Johnnies off the front." His friend's ego, he believed, had gotten out of hand because he had been a soldier.

Oscella's desertion was a catastrophic blow to his own outsized ego, which had never suffered a rejection. In its wake he wrestled with thoughts of suicide, and with the idea of killing the ex-friend. Although he finally decided "she wasn't worth it—worth gettin' in trouble for," he never fully recovered from the episode. Another twenty years would pass before he would marry; to the end of his life, he considered women untrustworthy.

Bentonians would later associate her with the evil persona of *Devil Got My Woman*:

> I'd rather be the devil, than to be that woman's man
> Was nothin' but the devil, changed my baby's mind.

Although James had been singing this lyric before his marriage to Oscella, in his own mind she took on the characteristics of a "devil woman." "After she and I separated, I just give that title—*Devil Got My Woman*—to that song," he once said. An acerbic comment about Oscella was voiced on *Hard-Luck Child*:

> She used to be mine, but look who's got her now
> But he sure can't keep her, she don't mean him no
>   good nohow.

The consoling belief that his rival would meet with the same duplicity that he met with helped deter James from exacting revenge against him.

Forgetting the fact that his wife was a minister's daughter, James attempted to explain her desertion as the inevitable outcome of defective genetics: "If you not 'gened to some certain effect—in other words, if you don't have the foundation to build on—your character can't be built offa nothin'. It's got to be built on somethin'. An' old people always said: 'A chip off the old block is taste of the timber.'" In Oscella's case, James claimed, "that chip is from a bad block to start with . . . just a bad attitude in life . . . bad everything . . . You couldn't tell her nothin'; couldn't learn her nothin', because that was in her . . . for her to be like that."

This view of his wife conveniently omitted his own misbehavior as a husband. Henry Stuckey later said of their marriage: "She never had any kind of husband, so you couldn't blame her. He was too wild to be a husband to any woman. He drank and gambled so much she near about had to leave him."

13. *The Songwriter*

Although *Devil Got My Woman* was considered an autobiographical song by his neighbors, its lyrics did not portray James' actual experiences or attitudes regarding Oscella Robinson. It was rather the general condemnation of a "devil woman" that, coupled with James' bitterness over his broken marriage, created this association, both in the minds of other Bentonians and in his own. No one appears to have grasped the ultimate, inadvertent implication of the phrase "I'd rather be the devil, than be that woman's man"—which was that James had metaphysically and cold-bloodedly positioned himself beyond the pale of virtue, just as he did in life.

James himself seems to have made only a rhetorical correlation between Oscella and the woman of his theme song: "I came in contact with a companion, and she was so contentious, unruly, and hard to get along with, I just compared her to the devil—one of his agencies. Since doin' that, I just turned her over to him, and I just give her to know that I would rather *be* the devil than to be her man, because she was so contentious and I couldn't get along with her in no way . . . I just decided I would quit worryin' with her so much."

But any number of James' consorts would have fit the role of the demonic woman, particularly since, by his lights, Satanic posession was little more than a figure of speech. His Satan simply made women grouchy: " . . . You can lay down happy at night. You and your companion will be in harmony. Everything goin' well. Satan'll creep in that house overnight. She may get up the next mornin' and you can't get a good word

out of her. Why? Because Satan has got the bill of sale
over her ... "

It was actually when James sang couplets that spoke of his
own inner pain that he was reminded of his marriage:

> The blues is on my brain, and it hurts my tongue to talk
> The blues is on my feet, and it hurts my feet to walk.

"When you get in that attitude, that's where people gets ready
to commit suicide ... " he said. "See, I like to get in that mood
one time ... I guess ... Like to got in trouble hurtin' somebody
else about a no-good woman; she wasn't worth it; worth gettin'
in trouble for. But the way that I was treated, that was what
made me feel like that."

James was too emotionally guarded to make his songs a direct
medium of self-expression. The driving force of his emotional
life, at least after he was abandoned by Oscella Robinson, was
an attempt to build an impregnable fortress against feeling. To
expose any vulnerability was to allow himself to be taken advantage of. His horror of displaying emotion made him more
akin to a Victorian or stoical New England personage than a
product of his own era. He became a man of immense inner
anger who was given to vent it in a quiet voice, with no display
of emotion. "I never knowed Skip to get mad," Jack Owens
was to say of his demeanor in the 1940s. In the only situations
where James appeared to be angry to Owens, he did not even
argue with the person who had provoked it, by not paying him
for his Bentonia "house frolic" performances. " ... He'd get his
guitar and leave there," Owens told Edd Hurt.

Although James' temperament suited the somber tenor of
blues lyrics, it could not abide the primary blues conceit—the
reversal of fortune. He could not endure the idea of anyone,
particularly a female companion, getting the better of him. His
songs were paeans to his illusory sense of power or control.
In song situations, he would perpetually grant himself the upper
hand:

> If I send for my baby, and she don't come
> All the doctors in Wisconsin, they won't help her none.

> Cherry ball quit me, quit me in a calm good way
> But what it take to get her, I carries it every day.

After indicating that his ex-wife was the subject of the above *Cherry Ball* couplet, which no doubt meant that he sometimes thought about her while singing it, he felt constrained to add: "'What it take to get her back I carries it every day'—*if I should want her back*. That's where I hit it."

He would say: "... that 'cherry ball' was referrin' to a damsel, that's right. In every song that I compose, I had refeerence to some glameo, or some contentious woman, or someone that I was in love with." But love or his own emotions scarcely figured in James' tunes, which were largely taken up with the same fleeting depictions of actions that saturated the pre-1930s Southern blues song.

James' songs revealed nothing directly about himself, and the oblique personal references that occasionally emerged in them were tidbits that had passed through his elaborate mechanicism of inner censorship. They were safe, and for the most part, inconsequential revelations, set forth by a secretive individual who did not like to disclose any facts about himself to anyone else, or let anyone actually get to know him. Yet James considered blues lyrics as a kind of autobiography. This was largely because they were cast in the first person. He viewed blues as a depiction of "experience"; a product of one's imagination was, in his mind, worthless. "See, what you hear me sing is not just what you hear somebody else sing; I done experienced those things," he commented.

Shortly after his rediscovery, James listened to a white blues singer at a Newport Folk Festival "work shop" declaim:

> Hitch up my pony, saddle up my black mare
> I'll find a rider, in the world somewhere.

Turning to the author, he sniggered: "There's no reality in that statement." What was faulty about the couplet, James found, was that the singer had obviously never owned a horse.

Pedantically, James justified his most commonplace blues couplets on the basis of their "reality." Thirty years earlier, he had sung the then-popular "pony" couplet as part of *If You Haven't*

Any Hay. ". . . This verse in that song particular referrin' to the horse: I used to ride horses and have had horses, an' raised horses."

Likewise, James considered it valid for him to sing *22-20* because he had owned a gun, although there was actually no such weapon as a 22-20. "I had experienced some guns, boyhood days, an' . . . Well, quite natural when I was comin' up I always did wanna own a gun . . . "

Despite the absurd lengths to which he carried this literal-mindedness, James was nevertheless willing to sing couplets involving experiences he never had:

> I been to the Nation, from there to the Territo'.
> *(Hard-Luck Child)*

Indian Territory had ceased to exist in 1906, when it was incorporated into Oklahoma as part of the latter area's statehood status. But James did not know that the "Territory" was an actual place: in his mind "the 'nation' is just a heap of people; a nation of people. When you go through the 'territory' you're just tourin' the countryside, like through New York or the rurals."

In spite of James' keen interest in vocabulary-building and his precocious intellectual curiosity, he never bothered to inquire into the meanings of song expressions he acquired. Indeed, he did not necessarily understand his own lyrics, when they were acquired from another source. The song phrase "cherry ball" had been the subject of several blues before he employed it on one of his own records. In June of 1930, Joe McCoy had recorded a *Cherry Ball*, using the phrase as a vague double-entendre as he cast himself in the role of gigolo:

> I ain't gonna give you none a my cherry ball
> Well you'll not get mine now, till you buy me clothes.

The term actually referred to cherry wine, "ball" being a slang term for a drink of liquor. In this sense it had been used by Caldwell Bracey, a Bolton blues singer:

> Ain't gonna give you no more cherry ball
> 'Cause you may get drunk and show your Santa Claus.
> *(No More Cherry Ball:* 1930)

Without much thinking about the matter, James applied the phrase to a female. As a recent blues rediscovery he gave a gibberish account of its origin in the interests of obscuring the sexual connotations he thought it had: " ... some cherries are kinda sour, they when they get ready, ripe; they are sweet.. . I just give it a 'ball' in that song because it's a round little old ball that grows on trees." A revised account that likened it to female breasts also reflected his own misunderstanding of the term; seeing a "nice-lookin' girl" in the recording studio as he prepared to record the song, he said, "I just dedicated the song to her ... she had those cherries, holdin' them over her shoulder ... I was interested in that kind of stuff back then."

Cypress grove, likewise, was a hackneyed figurative expression for a graveyard, to such an extent that Flaubert's *Dictionary of Platitudes* had stated of cypress: "grows only in graveyards." This conventional association had emerged on Blind Lemon Jefferson's 1927 best-seller, *See That My Grave Is Kept Clean*.

> My heart stopped beatin' and my hands got cold
> It ain't no more for you but the cypress grove.

When James sang *Cypress Grove*, he appeared to envision an actual cypress grove, for in discussing the song, he never alluded to a graveyard. In this respect he was typical of the rustic blues artists of his time, being generally unable to observe a distinction between a figurative and literal expression. He would compare "crow jane" to a bird, and construe "salty dog" (a phrase derived from the 18th century term, "salt bitch") to mean a bulldog, with a "tenacity that is unlooseable."

For the most part, James' lyrics either replicated or paraphrased conventional blues couplets around him. In this respect he was little different from most Mississippi blues singers. In part, James' largely undeveloped ability to compose rhymes for blues couplets arose from the fact that his original interest in song had a musical basis. When he first attempted to learn guitar and play songs like *Drunken Spree*, he was too young for the words of its tunes to have great significance for him. When he came of age, he learned that singers were not employed for their songwriting ability. It would have been impossible for blues singers of James' time to put a premium on their lyrics because the usual length of their songs greatly exceeded the three minute span of the 78 record. An ordinary James song might run to something like ten minutes, a span of time that would involve the use of perhaps twenty couplets. What James and other blues singers of his era appear to have done was to attempt to make the first two or three verses of their songs memorable; most of their subsequent couplets were used as padding.

His Mississippi audiences, he was to remark, characteristically paid little attention to the words of his songs, unless they were off-color, in which event they were heartily appreciated. When James sang in the 1920s, his couplets were laced with profanity:

> The woman I love, I took her from my best friend
> But that bastard got lucky, stole her back again.

> Crow jane crow jane crow janie, don't hold your ass so
>   high . . .

However, James seems to have made little or no attempt to pander to his audience's relish for songs about sexual activities. This was likely because sexual references were regarded as intrinsically humorous, and James was basically a humorless person. His only gesture of frivolity as a performer was to point upwards when his guitar sounded a pitch his voice could not match: "Sometimes I'd get high; have fun around those cats that we tryin' to copy . . . I'd make those high notes on a guitar . . . run them high slurs . . . I'd just point up—let 'em know there's another note I couldn't quite reach it . . . "

In later years he would carry his sense of decorum to absurd lengths of prudery. At the height of the "free love" era, James decided to bowlderize *Special Rider Blues*, lest "students" be exposed to untoward vulgarity. "Rider" was a common term in blues song rhetoric (though not in black speech), meaning simply, in the words of one informant, "a fuck." In keeping with his determination to keep his lyrics firmly on the footing of bare experience, James would remark: "When I composed *Special Rider Blues*, I was a little wild and rough myself and didn't have no 'special.' You know how it was: youngsters are the same now." He altered its title lyric and sang:

> I ain't got no special lover here

In the company of students, James would try to excise both his memories and his songs: "I just tell 'em now, 'Oh, I forget such-and-such a verse,' or 'such and such a place I was in.' And for these teahouses and concerts, I can sit down and start to playin', and if I'm comin' to one of those verse about this 'social' [sexual] life stuff, I can think of another one 'fore I get to it."

On the same grounds he resisted discussing life on levee camps: ". . . evil can poison the mind of a kid quicker than anything that has any significance or value to it. That's why you have to be continually approaching kids to look forward to somethin' worthwhile instead of catching hold to this no-good stuff."

James' moralism was tinctured with self-interest. One of the most significant differences between blacks and whites, he thought, was that the former were too preoccupied with sex. By making his performances relatively chaste he was better able to present himself as the figurative white person he aspired to be. Thirty years earlier, before James had any pretensions of being a do-gooder, the tenor of his songs would also reflect his social position as the product of a "refined" family. The son of a pastor and a plantation cook would not sully his blues with references to alcohol, even though he was, by his own description, "a habitual drunkard" during his blues-singing days. His respectability was such that he became indignant when he discovered that record collectors had thought (thanks to his slurring of words) that the expression "killin' floor" had been sung as "shit ass floor." This misinterpretation, in his mind, represented a complete misunderstanding of himself: he would never use such an expression on a record. On the other hand, shooting an unruly woman via *22-20* was not what James considered (to use one of his pet phrases) "a breach of etiquette." Nor was expressing his admiration of a legendary criminal in his society:

> Hey that .38 special, buddy it's most too light
> But my .22-.20, Mister Cress all right.

"In olden times Mister Cress was an outlaw," he explained, "just like Jesse James and all those . . . I wanted to let him know that I was just as 'bad' as he was."

James once remarked enigmatically: "There's a cure for the blues within the blues, if you only study the lyrics." He probably meant that the blues postures of disaffection and detachment—often, sheer sour grapes—worked to overcome any sorrow for the females who occasioned "blues." When James was to listen to the last couplet of his recording of *Four O'Clock Blues*, which repeated the line, "Goodbye my darling, honey and fare thee well," he laughed and said: "I should have said: 'You don't mean me no good and you can go to hell.' " The subtext of *Devil* and most of his other songs was simply *Good riddance!*, and this was a posture he likely assumed in the interests of steeling himself so that his experience with Oscella Robinson would never be repeated.

James was capable of writing a first-rate blues song when he turned his energy towards producing one. His *Hard Times*, for 1931, was an exceptional composition, its dark depiction of the Depression perfectly complementing its dirge-like melody:

> Hard times here an' everywhere you go
> Times is harder than ever been before.
>
> An' the people are driftin' from door to door
> Can't find no heaven I don't care where they go . . .
>
> Let me tell you people, just before I go
> These hard times will kill you just "dry long so"
> [without cause].

James was far more verbally adriot than most Mississippi blues singers. Yet he could never have churned out dozens of blues compositions in the wholesale fashion of his protégé Johnnie Temple, who became a popular recording artist in the 1930s less on his singing ability than on his facility with blues rhymes. One of reasons that James did not develop any sustained song-writing gifts is that he was constrained by religious attitudes. Intellectually, he considered blues the product of Satan. Of spirituals, James would say, in a tone of marked significance, "That's a true song." In his mind, blues songs told literal truths about passing events, but were compounded of figurative lies about what life was actually about. In this belief he was no different from the ignorant "plantation Negroes" he was fond of disparaging.

It was thanks to his conviction that the Bible contained the ultimate answers to every subject that James did not concern himself with such matters as the origin of blues. In later years, he would set forth an account of the origin of music. It did not begin in Bentonia, or Africa, but in the Old Testament: "Jephthah was the first one that could read a note . . . He taken a cow hide and stretched it over a hollow log. After he got that hide tight—I presume, that's the onliest way I could see he'd get a tune out of it—he perhaps may have thumped on it or hit on it with a stick . . . And then from that, he decided he'd make him an instrument. He taken a cane, like they use for fishin' poles, and I imagine he must have cut a couple of holes in it. Then he bore holes at the end of it, for his mouth, so he could blow through it . . . I think that's the origin of music." Blues song, he thought, originated with spirituals.

Despite the premium he put on portraying his "experiences," none of his original recordings expressly depicted autobiographical events or even episodes. Most of them were random collections of fleeting happenstances, or expressions of attitude. Only three of his fifteen secular recordings of 1931 would have a full-dress theme, and these (*22-20 Blues, Hard Time Killin' Floor Blues*, and *Cherry Ball*) were at least partly created at his recording session. But the real subject of his songs was always himself: what James portrayed as a song about a gun (*22-20*) was really a song about what he intended to do with it, and what he portrayed as a song about a "glameo" (*Cherry Ball*) was not a depiction of a female, but of his relationship with one. In this regard, James was a typical blues singer. Only an immense catastrophe like the Depression could enable James to move from center stage, and sing as a chronicler or observer.

It was the tunnel nature of the blues singer's vision that would lead writers of future decades to construe blues as a reflection of black society, remarking on experiences attainable only by blacks. This interpetation of blues largely reflected the fact that blues songs did not have a broad dimension, or provide anything with which a listener who did not directly partake of the blues life could personally identify. But the blues did not reflect the

agitation of a race: the songs of Skip James represented the
life style of a professional blues singer—and reflected the
crabbed, flinty vision that ensued from it. The prominence of
the first person in the blues couplet ultimately reflected the
fact that the blues singer was cut off from his own society, and
unconcerned with anything beyond his immediate welfare,
which was the underlying subject of most blues song.

James' artistry partly consists of an ability to ennoble shabby
sentiments in stirring song. Above all else the singer doesn't
want anyone to make a fool of him. If this requires him to
pull the trigger on a disobedient girlfriend, so be it:

> If she gets unruly, gets so she don't wanna "do"
> I'll take my 22-20, I'll cut her half in two.

"If she don't wanna 'do' she don't wanna be ruled or governed
by me, understand?" he would explain. His imaginary retaliation
was was not posturing or play-acting, but a projection of the
pimping identity that James had assumed at the outset of his
professional musical career.

His songs were the expression of his determination to fire
the final shot in his war with a world of lowlifes who were his
only associates. They were tactical documents, riddled with warning shots to females who might otherwise imagine him a sucker,
what he and other blues singers termed "a monkey man," always
(in James' words) "grateful to touch the hem of a woman's garment."

James felt that blues represented the expression of "a dissatisfied mind." His understanding of the idiom arose from the
familiar blues catchphrase: "Got the blues, can't be satisfied."
To the original blues audience, this statement signified ungod-
liness, for the God of Psalms was said to "satisfieth the longing
soul" (Psalm 107:9). Though James was steeped in Fundamentalism, a sense of perpetual frustration represented a natural
and even desirable state of human mental affairs for him. "A
fool is mostly satisfied in life with what he gets . . . If he's halfway
there . . . he's satisfied . . . Now you take a wise man, son, child,
or adult: they have an object in view. They're never content:
they're never satisfied. A person that is inclined or gened to

this effect always has an intensity for higher things in life." To James, the person who even sought inner satisfaction or happiness was "building on sinking sand." He was someone to avoid; his quest for fulfillment would make him intolerant of reversals. "If he wants everything to go his way, he's liable to make *sure* that it does by tryin' to cheat you."

Indeed, dissatisfaction was James' perennial mental state. He was also dissatisfied with the status quo of his music, and kept attempting to improve it during the 1920s.

14. *The Murderous Music Cat*

It was no doubt because of his unbridled lifestyle that on returning to Bentonia from Dallas around 1929 James met with local reports attesting to his violent death. The same stories had greeted him, he reported, when he had returned from Arkansas five years earlier.

In 1929 he acquired his first real protégé, a Jackson musician named Johnnie Temple. Though only four years younger than James, the 23-year-old Temple was virtually a novice when he met James while performing at a house party in Pocohantas (twelve miles below Bentonia) or Flora (eight miles below Bentonia) with his future stepfather Lucien "Slim" Duckett. "Skippy and Stuckey came in," he later recalled. "And so everybody was beggin' Skippy to play a number, and I and Slim was wailin' on the *Big Road Blues* and the *Cool Water Blues*." The latter songs were Tommy Johnson staples that James never played, dismissing them as "draggy" (slow and lifeless). Recalling James' appearance, Temple said: "Boy, he rocked the house, old Skippy!" Then James performed some duets with Stuckey, who did not have a guitar. "I let Henry play my guitar . . . They both picked it—trottin'!"

Temple said of him: "Skippy was a *born* musician; a natural-born musician." His agile picking greatly impressed Temple: " . . . he got a terrible-movin' finger." Later he was to discover that James could "play most any string instrument he pick up."

The young blues singer would next meet James in Jackson when "he came into town to (see) a friend of his . . . call him Luckett." The friend, Horse Luckett, lived near Temple on Savage Street and had known James from their boyhood in Ben-

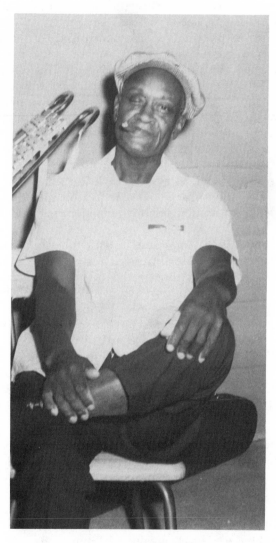

Johnnie Temple a year before James' death
(Courtesy Gayle Dean Wardlow)

tonia. James often visited Luckett (who did not play music) to gain access to his piano.

"He's playin' piano there," Temple recalled, "an' so he heard me playin' a little bit on the guitar. And so he told me he could make a good guitar-player outta me, see?" This offer was extended, Temple thought, because James needed an accompanist, and local musicians were incapable of following his music. James claimed that Temple insincerely extended the hand of friendship by inviting him to board with him in Jackson: "I spent a couple of weeks at his house. And that was specifically for him to catch ideas—I know what it was for."

As a result of James' tutelege, Temple learned to play in "cross note" tuning, which was unknown to Jackson musicians. He also attempted to copy his high falsetto until James admonished him to sing in his natural voice.

The single piece James later recalled showing Temple was *Devil Got My Woman*. He disparaged Temple as a "dummy" who would require two or three nights of practice to master any song and was unable to learn *Special Rider*. Whereas James was accustomed to learning by ear, Temple lacked this ability. "Sometimes I just sit down and just almost had to put my finger on the strings to show him a chord," James said.

James' experience with Temple led him to generalize: "I can sit right here with a guitar . . . and I can show you, day in and day out, but if you're not musically inclined, you'll never get no further than when you first started . . . "

Using Temple as an assistant, James pocketed extra money by operating a music school for would-be blues singers in Jackson, dispensing lessons on guitar, piano, and even violin. His pupils, whom he later dismissed as "thick-headed Negroes," tended to drop out after a few perfunctory lessons. "I didn't give a shit," he said perversely. "That's all I wanted 'em to do. I didn't want 'em to learn." Perhaps for this reason he remained friends with the relatively untalented Temple, often visiting him for two or three weeks on end. "He wanted me with him all the time," he said of Temple.

Despite his frequent visits to Temple and Luckett, James never became part of Jackson's thriving "house frolic" circuit. Instead,

he worked locally as a solitary street singer. Perched on a curb-
side, he cut a forlorn figure. Passersby, Temple thought, were
as interested in silencing him as in rewarding his music: "They
say: 'Well!,' say: 'We got to give this boy somethin'!' ... And
man, they'd pay him, too!"

James would say of his own street singing: "If I played on
the streets, like on a corner somewhere, the people that'd heard
me playin', if they liked my music, they'd come out of their
house ... Then they'd drop fifty cents, or, they may drop a quarter, may drop a dime in my hand or hat ... Sometime I could
make as high as ten or twelve dollars sittin' on a corner like
that, in the afternoon if I ain't doin' nothin', and I wanna pick
up some quick money ... I'd play there about half an hour;
go to the next corner ... then afterwich, all the people come
'round and say: 'Skip, where you gonna play tonight?'

"I say: 'I'm gonna play at such-and-such a place.' Well, that
place'd be packed when the time comes for me to play."

In Temple's company, James passed entire days in a state of
catatonic drunkeness, brooding about Oscella Robinson. His
general mental state in this period is probably reflected in his
recollection of himself as an unhappy "house frolic" performer
after the dissolution of his marriage:

"... I take me a little drink ... and maybe say a few words
and play a little tune ... Well, quite naturally that would kind
of revive you a bit ... people givin' you drinks and laughin' an'
goin' on. Heap of time you see some nice-lookin' girls comin'
in to entertain you ... Heap of times, long as you have been
in kind of a merry bunch, and so perhaps playin' for an' en-
tertainin' yourself and other people you feel lots better.

"Just to be alone a heap of time when you [feel] mistreated;
that make the blues *bad* on ya—make you have different ideas,
too. A personality will do most anything if he's not at hisself
an' not, you know, to thinkin'."

Temple's fear that James was headed for a nervous breakdown
lingered until a local girl named Mary began to distract him.
She lived across town near West Caplin Street. "... We'd leave
from over on Savage Street about nine, ten o'clock, and walk
all the way out there," Temple recalled. "He carried his guitar.

It'd be rainin', but he'd carry his guitar and put it off in his raincoat . . . We'd get near about to the house, he'd start to pick it, so she'd hear him come. You'd see doors openin' everywhere, man!"

Another woman who put herself at Skip's disposal was Temple's wife, Mattie, or so James was to claim. To preserve Temple's friendship and hospitality, James discouraged her advances. On one occasion the trio made a trip to Pocohantas, where James and Temple serenaded a "house frolic." Mattie was openly dismayed by their forward manner towards the women who attended the affair. After explaining their behavior as a tactic to garnish tips, James concluded that Temple was "hen-pecked," and decided not to travel with him again.

"Before I got to Jackson," James remarked, "I never was strong enough to be a professional; just make some chords, play for 'jukes,' frolics, and so forth. But after I got to Jackson, around a city, quite naturally I take more interest in my music." Jackson boasted of a large stable of professional musicians, local and transient. Blues performers had been gravitating there long before James arrived there; as early as 1910, the city served as the residence of Memphis Minnie, then a thirteen-year old runaway who supported herself as a street singer. "She was what I call a burr-head woman," Sam Chatmon recalled, " . . . young, but she was out hustlin' for herself . . . I knowed Minnie long about 1910 . . . she could pick a guitar then. I used to look at her and say to myself: 'That gal with that short hair sure can pick a guitar! . . . She had so much nerve, to be as little as she was, and she'd pick everywhere!'"

To James, such figures were professional enemies.

In "places like Jackson, Yazoo City, Vicksburg, and Memphis," he would reminisce, "I run into lots of 'music philosophers.' I call 'em 'cats'—'music cats'—they call themselves professional musicians . . . You can spot those music cats. They gonna come in, sit together, and if there's any criticism to be made [of your playing], they gonna touch one another. And then you make some . . . kinda 'bad,' out-of-sight chords, they look at one another; hunch one another. 'Did you see that?' 'Um hum.' If you was close enough to 'em, you'd hear 'em say that. They gonna watch nothin' but your fingers and your feet: that's your time.

". . . They'll stare and stare, gettin' upset: 'Hey, where you playin' that?' 'What key you playin' this in?,' if it's on the piano. Playing guitar, [they] say: 'Say, what tune you got that in?'

"But they don't come up to you. That's givin' me too much honor or consideration. If they can steal it, they would . . . They won't gimme the consideration because they were playin' before I was. Since they've been in the racket so long, they just feel ashamed of themselves."

A determination to thwart would-be copyists led him to rearrange his music constantly and to accelerate his tempos whenever he noticed another musician watching his fingers. It was thus that Ishmon Bracey, a popular local bluesman who saw him play in Jackson, recalled that his fingers moved "like lightning" on the guitar.

James' antipathy for "music cats" was partly occasioned by the fact that he was one himself. He imagined that other musicians eyed him with the same unfriendly opportunism that he applied to their performances. He once said: "If I go to a place where musicians are . . . I listens attentively, an' if he [the musician he saw] should make an error in his playin', I let his error be my success . . . I won't say nothin' . . . And heap of time, people be playin' and I be sittin' there, and they don't think I be payin' them no attention. I be listenin' attentively . . . " It went without saying that he listened "attentively" enough to absorb whatever music he cared to incorporate. For example, there were subtle overtones of Little Brother Montgomery in his own piano playing. Yet he never socialized with Montgomery, or expressed the slightest appreciation of his music, though Montgomery had congratulated him in Memphis for his *Little Cow and Calf* after hearing the record.

Towards the neophyte musician he was more fraternal. In 1930 he met the teenage Lightnin' Hopkins, who was to become one of the most commercially successful post-war bluesmen. A native of Texas, Hopkins spent a week in Jackson. While Hopkins later said that the pair only gambled together, James claimed to have given him some guitar pointers. He considered

Hopkins a kindred spirit: "Lightnin's kinda like myself," he would say approvingly. "On the pimpy side."

By comparison to his bootlegging proceeds, the money James made as a musician was small change. Once an intense bidding war broke out between two Bentonians for his services: one proprietor, a man named Ben Tell, offered him three dollars to play, while another, Bessie Owens, offered him five dollars, along with his expenses and drinks. At the same time, he was able to wholesale kegs of moonshine on a weekly basis to such "house frolic" organizers for thirty or forty dollars.

Not surprisingly, he decided to open his own jukehouse in Bentonia and retail his whiskey there, while offering himself as its leading attraction. This event took place in 1929.

His profits from selling food, drink, and his music averaged nearly one hundred dollars a night. Like other "house frolic" entrepreneurs of his area, he stashed his proceeds in glass jars. James had observed frequent "frolic" robberies that were staged by a patron who blew out the kerosene lamp that illuminated the establishment, and then attempted to make off with the money jar. For this reason, he tried to position himself next to the kerosene lamp.

Like other "house frolic" organizers, however, he did not frisk patrons for weapons. The club was only a few nights old when a gunfight broke out between two patrons as he played piano. Quickly it became "like a war." Stray bullets shattered the club's kerosene lamp and windows, and whizzed past James, nicking his piano.

Enraged, he flung his piano stool at one of the shooters. It caught him on the back of the head, pole-axing him on the spot. By then several other patrons had drawn their own guns.

James retreated into his kitchen. In a moment he appeared with a shotgun. He looked fruitlessly for the customer he had cold-cocked with his piano stool, but someone had already dragged the man outside. In a murderous rage, he then levelled the gun on the dance floor. He did not stop firing until the club was empty.

No one will ever know how many people were injured or slain by James—a deadly shooter with a deadly weapon—that night. No one much cared what happened to black partygoers on Mississippi plantations of the period, least of all James' boss, who would sometimes mildly chide James after an eruption of gunfire from one of the "frolics" his bootlegging tenant threw had disturbed the sleep of himself and his wife. Nor did James care about the casualties he inflicted during his rampage. Believing that the shooting had been staged by rival bootleggers to put him out of business, he grimly closed his club the following day.

When James recounted this episode decades afterwards, it was to illustrate how other people attempted to thwart him. The concentrated coldness in his eyes and voice indicated that the shooting had not dissolved his anger, any more than his previous shootings had. If anything, his reenactment spoke of his dissatisfaction with not having killed everyone in sight; his resentful tone of voice left no doubt that his revenge was incomplete, and that he had never adequately gotten even with his enemies.

PART FOUR

15. *Recording*

It was probably because he enjoyed a significant non-musical income that the idea of recording did not particularly interest James in the 1920s. In 1927 he was approached in Bentonia by an itinerant OKeh talent scout whom, he thought, hailed from Sun, Louisiana. Although the man scheduled a recording session for James, it never came about. Henry Stuckey later said that illness prevented James from consummating the session; James recalled being hospitalized in Yazoo City with influenza and balking at the scout's offer of $15 or $20 per side. He once remarked that he did not feel confident enough as a pianist to record during that period.

Most blues singers of the period had no qualms about recording. Some of them were outright pests, like Ishmon Bracey, who paid frequent visits to the record store of his discoverer to tout himself as a recording prospect. Around February of 1930, Bracey began a tour of the Delta with his recent recording partners, "Kid" Ernest Mitchell and "44 Charley" Taylor, a pianist from the Delta town of Sumner. At a "house frolic" in Pocohantas, they encountered James. According to Bracey, Taylor upended him in an impromptu blues piano-playing contest.

Following this event, the musicians talked of their recent recording session for Paramount Records, and urged James to audition for H.C. Speir, the Jackson record dealer who had sent them to the company. But James took no action on their advice.

Speir had been a major supplier of blues talent to record companies since the fall of 1927, when he had discovered Jim Jackson in Memphis. Since then he had turned up such artists as Bracey, Tommy Johnson, Charlie Patton, Blind Roosevelt

Graves, Blind Joe Reynolds, and Bo Carter. With the exception of Patton, none of his Mississippi discoveries had generated any stir within the record industry. Thanks to the speculative nature of the "race" record business ("they always told me, they figure they got one hit in ten," Speir recalled), his failures did not diminish his influence among the five record companies with whom he periodically placed blues and gospel talent.

By February of 1931, a year after meeting up with Taylor, James was the only notable musician hanging around Jackson who still remained unknown to Speir. While visiting Johnnie Temple that month, James met "One-Legged Sam" Norwood, a popular local back-up guitarist who had earned $250 for recording four spiritual duets with Slim Duckett at a local OKeh session supervised by Speir the previous December. After recounting his success, Norwood urged James to audition for Speir. Further encouragement was given by Horse Luckett, who was hoping (Temple thought) to recoup some forty or fifty dollars in board and moonshine bills James had accumulated as his house guest.

"I wasn't positive about it 'cause I didn't have no idea of makin' any records at the time," James recalled. On the morning after this discussion, however, he set out for Speir's store at 111 Farish Street in the company of Temple, Luckett, and another friend from Bentonia, Doodle Mitchell. "In the music store, it was a pretty good-sized office," he recalled. "It was seats for a dozen people or perhaps more, at the time that I went through the test, that little place was just about crowded, 'cause some of the people had to sit down on the hallway, for people to take their test. Some had two-three instruments; some had a light band. Myself and some other fellow, I don't know who he was, were the only ones alone."

Later, Temple spoke of himself as being the only other aspirant in the store. In any event, Temple was rejected, while James' music quickly impressed Speir as desirable to record. By James' doubtless gilded account, "I didn't have to play but two verses for my examination before he told me I made a terrific hit."

H.C. Speir's music store two years before James' audition, with Speir at right
(Courtesy Gayle Dean Wardlow)

Although the Depression had completely gutted the "race" record business, Speir had a ready client in Arthur Laibly of Paramount Records, the only recording director who would accept his recommendations without so much as an audition record. Thanks to Laibly's passivity, Paramount was the logical place for Speir to place James.

The company had been producing "race" records for black customers for over nine years. In that time it had issued over a thousand such records and had garnished some of the industry's biggest hit-makers, including Ma Rainey and Blind Lemon Jefferson, whose 1926 recordings had produced the commercial vogue for solo blues guitarists. Yet Paramount had not had a modestly successful record in over eight months. While the company's Grafton, Wisconsin studio had been recording about fifty titles per month during the previous six months, few of these items were blues.

Whereas Paramount once sold between 10,000 and 100,000 of its "race" hits, it was now hard put to sell over 500 copies of any particular record. The loss of its leading distributor in 1930, who had defected to sell radios, had left it without direct access to Mississippi retailers.* Speir, who had been one of Paramount's three major suppliers of talent in the late 1920s, had not sent any artists there for the previous six months.

After evaluating James, Speir told him to return the next day to sign a contract and pick up his ticket. "I told him 'Yes' 'cause I figured that I was prepared," James recalled, "that I was strong enough to protect myself."

A session for James was apparently arranged on the basis of a wire sent to Laibly in Wisconsin. On the morning after his audition, James left Speir's office with a train ticket to Milwau-

---

*According to record industry rhetoric of the day, there was no Depression underway; nothing but the laziness and intractability of record dealers prevented the industry from attaining its earlier profits. To account for the dismal year of 1931, Brunswick's sales manager claimed: "Customers had to fight to get records and the general lack of co-operation on record selling brought about a dropping of the record volume . . . " The *Talking Machine Journal* claimed in its review of the year: "The dwindling of retail sales effort with records has been more responsible for lowered sales than any other one factor . . . "

kee. Temple and Duckett accompanied him to the Jackson depot to wish him well.

Beyond asking James how many records he thought he could make, there had been little contact between the scout and his discovery. Having auditioned him as a guitarist, Speir had no idea that James so much as played piano. In presenting him to Laibly, he would inadvertently shorten his nickname from "Skippy" to "Skip" James. For his part, James would know Speir as "H.C. Speirs" and Laibly as "Art Laible."

James left for Wisconsin only with the idea of garnishing some money and playing well enough to "protect" himself against musical competitors. He had no inkling that his records would become classics, creating a reputation that would outlast his life.

16. *Greatness At Grafton*

To H.C. Speir, the discoverer of many legendary blues singers, the idiom was essentially a panhandling device on the part of alcoholics: "A blues singer, what he's doing is trying to make nickels and dimes, get him a little something to drink."

Regardless of who is playing it, the blues remain an open-and-shut musical form, offering (thanks to the brevity of its phrases) little scope for significant invention. To achieve real instrumental artistry requires a performer to go against the grain of the blues idiom.

Skip James' own remarkableness was largely expressed within the forbidding territory of the blues idiom. He was not a ground-breaking revolutionary. He prided himself on acquiring a professionalism that he associated with the reigning blues singers of his days in Weona. When he first met the author he pronounced himself "a blues singer, like Clara Smith, Mamie Smith, Bessie Smith . . . all those sisters." He even claimed to have accompanied Bessie Smith on piano during the early 1920s, when he was situated in Memphis.

When he spoke of his determination to be "different all the way" from his peers, he was primarily referring to his desire to sound different from musical acquaintances like Henry Stuckey—performers who could directly compete with him for jobs or adversely affect his local reputation. He wanted others to credit him for his musicianship, and he recognized that being imitative would detract from his musical credit ledger. It was no doubt for this reason that he would transpose a guitar tune of Stuckey's (*All Night Long*) to piano, and adapt Little Brother Montgomery's *Vicksburg Blues* to guitar. The sources of most

of his inspirations, he said, were obscure to him: "I don't know—
the songs come to me like dreams."

How different he sounded from Stuckey is illustrated by
Booker Miller's reaction to his recording of *Cypress Grove*, which
both Bentonia bluesmen performed in the 1920s. Rather than
think to compare it to Stuckey, whom he knew in the Delta,
Miller likened James' recording to his own playing: "Now that's
my style of playin', the way I picked . . . They say I liked to play
guitar the hard way." Primarily, James' performance is distinguished by uncommonly crisp picking that makes his notes ring
out with an almost bell-like clarity, even as he plays a half step
below concert pitch, which would tend to blunt the vibrance
of his tones. On other pieces—*Special Rider* and *I'm So Glad*—
James' guitar has an altogether different sound, unlike that of
any other known instrumentalist, so staccato-like and strange
in its marshalling of tones that it almost doesn't sound like a
guitar.

The common thread that runs through his guitar playing (beyond *Drunken Spree*) and gives it such an unusual quality is its
overall isolation of treble and bass tones, which are heard distinctly as he plays octave pitches that join two registers. His
single-note work (like the six-beat riff of *Cypress Grove*) is invariably performed in one register. He does little blending of
tones by means of strums, and his horror of chordal sounds
("mighty seldom you'll hear me 'rap,' " he was to say) is so great
that he attempts unlikely chord arpeggiations in *Drunken Spree*
and *Special Rider*. This mannerism gives James' guitar the aura
of bottleneck playing, which (because it involves one finger fretting) involves a similar division of treble/bass tones. James appears to have acquired this sense of sound from his piano-playing, which involves a similar unconventional separation of tones,
his hands often working independently of each other to produce
purely treble or purely bass runs.

For the most part, James expressed his musical nonconformity
by negation, steering clear of familiar songs and sounds. It was
in keeping with this determination that he would record
Stuckey's *Drunken Spree*, which occupied such an insignificant
part of the latter's repertoire that he could not even recall ever
playing it when interviewed in the 1960s. Although James played

140   I'D RATHER BE THE DEVIL

Catfish Blues in the late 1920s, he did not think to record it, no doubt because it was common enough to result in negligible prestige or recognition.

But working up a distinctive repertoire or distinctive arrangements did not make James qualitatively different from most professional blues players. As he said of his peers: "They have their version of playin' music, and I have mine." There is nothing to indicate that James basically approached blues differently from other performers, except to play "rag" songs exactly as he played blues. Only a handful of exceptional tinkerers were to make any significant structural alterations to the blues, and their creative contributions were so irrelevant to the thrust of the genre that they remain completely unrecognized.*

Every artistic improvement that individual singers made to the blues mold as it existed in the early twentieth century fell completely by the wayside, as if on deaf ears. Most blues players had neither the ability nor the desire to change the prevailing characteristics of blues. Blues was a performing medium, the point of which was to show off one's wares before a paying audience. Clarence Williams, a pianist James knew in Memphis in the early 1920s and respected as a real musician of stature, was lionized by the *Talking Machine Journal* in February of 1924: " . . . with a repertoire of two songs, he secured a job as a piano player and after eight lessons had mastered the fundamentals of music." James began performing in Weona with a similar lack of experience, and had, even before that, offered his wares in Mississippi as a novice guitar player.

Where James differed from his peers was that he did not reach

---

*Only two singer/guitarists made any notable improvements on the unwieldy blues phrasing pattern: Henry Spaulding and Scrapper Blackwell. Instead of rendering the typical six-beat blues instrumental phrase as a single measure riff with a superfluous two-beat tonic strum tacked onto it, Spaulding arrived at a genuine six-beat instrumental phrase (cadencing to the tonic chord only on the final beat) in *Cairo Blues* (1929). In songs like *Kokomo Blues* (1928), Blackwell smoothed out the inherently unbalanced blues phrase by pairing two vocal measures with two instrumental measures. The only performers who significantly altered the blues' typical melodic presentation (AAB, or ABC) were Sam Butler and Charlie Patton, Butler by creating a continuous set of melodically complementary stanzas in *You Can't Keep No Brown* (1926), and Patton by singing successive variations on a basic theme on *Screamin' And Hollerin' The Blues* (1929).

a certain level and simply arrest his development. He kept attempting to improve his skills even as he was able to profit from his playing. The level of musicianship he displays on *Special Rider*, a tune he began playing only two years before his session, is far afield from that of *Drunken Spree*, one of his original works. In all likelihood, James was still developing at the time of his recording session, and his most brilliant pieces appear to have been relatively recent works.

James' exalted skills did not mean that he occupied an exalted position among audiences of his time. Had he never recorded and acquired a legendary name among blues researchers, he would have become known only as a passing reference in the remiscences of fellow musicians. None of the assorted bluesmen who recalled him singled him out as a popular or unequalled performer. It was the sound rather than the substance of blues music that attracted (and still attracts) listeners, and in James' age the size of a singer's sound was basic to his appeal. Although James had one of the finest voices found in blues, it lacked the volume and fullness to garnish him the prestige of a Tommy Johnson or Son House. In a performing medium without microphones, his relatively thin sound relegated him to the status of a virtual also-ran, and it was probably for this reason that James was so apt to dwell on his penchant for being "different." He employed this word almost as a euphemism for "less appealing," and as a substitute for popular success. In this respect, he made a virtue out of necessity.

It was doubtless because James did not have any great audience impact in his day that his entire reference point was other musicians, and that he rarely spoke of himself as a vocalist. He rated himself in terms of his ability to stand up against competing "music cats," not singers. His only real boast was that no one he heard could cow him, Little Brother Montgomery included: " . . . he started playin' first," James said of his arch piano rival. "But I'm not ashamed of him now; ain't afraid today." (Though at one point he must have been daunted by Montgomery, in general, he claimed, "I didn't care nothin' about those old cats that had been playin' for years.") However he prided himself on his playing ability, he knew that playing skill, in the pre-microphone age, was a decidely secondary consid-

eration in blues presentation. It was not until white enthusiasts
of the 1960s created the cult of the blues guitar that James'
talents were truly appreciated.

James' stature would increase immediately as he sat before
a microphone in 1931. The genuine greatness he manifested
at Grafton was a momentary greatness, achieved in certain
songs, and resting upon his ability to impart real depth and
feeling to his idiom. He was one of the few blues singers of
his time who knowingly and self-consciously attempted to play
real music (as he understood it) through the medium of blues,
rather than simply perform songs or show off his skill as an
instrumentalist. Although he lacked a cultivated vocabulary, and
could not so much as name a note he played, he had a cultivated
aesthetic sense that readily distinguished musical diamonds from
musical dross. The simple remark he made of his *Special Rider—*
"That's a deep piece"—was a statement no other blues singer
of his milieu would have made.

James was a shameless braggart about most of his routine
abilities. He considered himself a youthful sex machine because
he was able to have three orgasms in one day. He boasted of
his surpassing skill as a plantation tractor driver, and of the
boxing prowess he had once displayed in informal Weona con-
tests. "I hit as hard as Jack Johnson," he said, referring to a
storied black champion noted for his defensive rather than
punching ability, "and you know Jack Johnson broke Jim Jeffries'
neck with an uppercut." Blues singers of his age routinely
boasted of their musical triumphs and abilities with the same
brazenness. "I run into lots of 'hard' guys," the modestly talented
Ishmon Bracey said of other musicians: "I work 'em over."

By comparison with his other boasts, James' musical self-ac-
colades were surprisingly delicate. "I don't style myself as superior in the music world to anyone; I count myslf as the *least*
of all the musicianers," he was to say. What was surprising about
such false reticence, expressing the opposite of his true belief,
was that he would display it, rather than act as the familiar
blues braggart, claiming eminence by word rather than deed.
He was loath to cheapen his music with crass comments, because
it had real inner value to him. As he once said: "You can't

put a price on a song." Perhaps because he had not (in his heyday as a pimp and bootlegger) found it necessary to seriously merchandise himself as a musician, his music became central to his interior identity. It held such significance for him that he would blindly approach his ministerial father as a blues singer several months after his Paramount session in the belief that his musical talent alone could move a man of the cloth.

It was this belief in his musical worth that proved to be his tragic undoing as a blues musician. Had James been the same calculating blues musician as he was a calculating bootlegger, he would have placated his father with a soothing round of spirituals. His futile attempt to communicate with his father via blues song would soon lead to the loss of his bearings in the blues field, and eventually to the complete destruction of his artistry by submission to Christian dogma and the conflicts it generated. He was never able to put the same feeling in his spirituals that he had put in his blues.

Because of his religious remoteness from the sphere of blues, the real secrets of his music lie locked in his records, or lost in time. Although he was probably the most significant blues singer of his time to become a living subject of blues research, he had nothing illuminating to say about his music, or music in general. By the 1960s he appeared to have no regard for music, and little feeling for it: when recognition finally came to him, he had soured altogether on the profession. Instead of evincing artistry, he evinced pretenses. Without directly saying so he conveyed the impression that other blues singers had been (and were) mere players, while he was a genuine musician. But by then he himself had become a player. Had he always borne the same supercilious attitude he could not have attained his own level of artistry, because one's playing capacity is invariably a reflection of one's listening acuteness. His own playing of 1931 demonstrated his lost love of music.

James appeared to have created surpassing songs not through advanced technical ability, but by having an acute awareness of the sounds he was making. He was a listener as well as a player, and he used his listening ability to improve his product. This self-consciousness is evident in the simple two chord song that is *Devil Got My Woman*, where the listener feels the impact of every note James plays, thanks to his timing, tempo, and emphatic touch. He had a similar facility for making every note emphatic as he played graceful piano pieces like *If You Haven't Any Hay*.

To this indispensable component of solid music, James was able to add a loftier ingredient that gave his greatest songs an ethereal quality: a sense of drama, all but absent elsewhere in the blues genre. In *Devil Got My Woman*, his vocal presentation added to the tension of his tempo and tonality (an ambiguous and probably accidental mixture of major and minor): its third and fourth verses had a sudden climactic effect, created by heightened volume and pitch, an effect that was to be lost when (in later years) James played lengthier versions of his signature song. His voice, already pitched to the top of his tenor, rose a third (from the major second to the dominant) and erupted in falsetto as he sang the last two verses.

James was virtually unique among blues musicians in his intuitive appreciation of the contrasts wrought by such crescendos. He used ascending instrumental breaks to create crescendo effects in *I'm So Glad*, leaping an octave above his open top string in the process, and achieved a similar effect in *Special Rider* by beginning his instrumental breaks at the same octave. To achieve a crescendo effect on *22-20*, and illustrate the onset of a fusillade of bullets as he threatened to murder a girlfriend ("I'll take my 22-20; I'll cut her half in two"), he broke out with a violent eruption of foot stomping that coincided with two measures of bass playing, the notes exceeding the volume and forcefulness of all the riffs that had preceded it.

James' relish for explosive mini-climaxes seems to have been a natural outgrowth of his musical aesthetic. His best songs create an air of apprehension. Both his timing and his inflection of tones give off the impression that he is straining; when something climactic happens, it is almost as if it had been foreshadowed, or was inherent in the music. The very way that he frequently pitches his voice—generally at the top of his tenor—creates an element of stress: the voice is unnaturally high, poised at the threshold of falsetto, as if ready to go off in another direction, upwards or downwards.

Although James' devices for generating apprehension and expressing turbulence were arrived at intuitively, he could not have exceeded them had he consciously set out to do so, in the manner of some trained composer. Like a composer, he made skillful use of two-beat rests to create an apprehensive effect on *22-20*, the piano masterpiece that probably offers the greatest instrumentation of any blues song. The violent burst of treble and bass notes he unleashes in emulation of a rapid-fire rifle is the closest thing to program music found in blues.

No blues pianist has ever displayed the arresting variety of instrumental phrases he uncorks after every vocal line of *22-20*, which is probably the most impromptu, improvised effort found in blues recording. These are zany and unpredictable punctuations, generally amounting to six or eight-beat outbursts; in one instance (following the second line of the fourth verse) he uncorks a cascading series of descending single notes that amount to the equivalent of an entire blues vocal phrase (two and a half measures) and take him from the treble to bass register, smoothly played as if with a single hand. Every interlude is completely whimsical, such as the sudden non-stop glissandos (of the type Jerry Lee Lewis was to make familiar) that erupt in the seventh and tenth bars of his thirteen-bar instrumental break. The verse that follows this break and closes out the song marks an end to James' pell-mell pyrotechnics: it would be a perfectly conventional twelve-bar stanza, but for a single slapdash vocal beat added to its initial phrase.

The completely pianistic, percussive character of James' effort is evident from its unsuccessful 1980s' transposition into a classical string quartet piece by the Kronos Quartet, which replicated his vocal and instrumental line, but could not capture the nuances of the piece. It is not even certain that James himself would have been able to replicate it, even at the same session, had Laibly called for a retake. In later years, James was to dwell on its makeshift nature; his ability to spin out such a piece, he implied, was a testament to his musical skill: ". . . This *22-20*, Art Laible asked me when I got to Grafton, Wisconsin, an' I was recordin: 'The *44 Blues* is out, rushin' pretty good, havin' a fast sale,' an' he asked me could I think of a gun that would compare to that; make a pretty fast sale. I called two or three

Arthur Laibly, four years after recording James
(Courtesy Gayle Dean Wardlow)

... '.38 Special,' he say 'No, I got that,' '.45,' say 'No, I got that,' I say: 'I don't know any real guns, but ... see I knows 22s ... How 'bout 22-20?' ... He say: 'Well you ain't got but three minutes now.' "

Since *22-20* was only the third piano piece James recorded on the second day of his session, it is doubtful that Laibly had suddenly thought to suggest a song about a gun, all the more so as *44 Blues* (a version of *Vicksburg* recorded in 1929 on OKeh by Roosevelt Sykes) was neither current nor a hit record. The likelihood is that James (who ended the song with the phrase "An' my .44, layin' up an' down my breast") began playing the tune as *44 Blues* on his own accord and was asked by the recording director to alter the caliber in the interests of avoiding duplication of *44 Blues*. Although it is absurd to suggest, as James did, that the song was the product of three minutes' reflection, there is little doubt that his was basically an off-the-cuff performance. Not only do his vocal and instrumental rests bear the mark of someone literally gathering his musical thoughts, but James renders the lyrics almost as a recitation, his inflections completely devoid of expression, as would have happened were he preoccupied with simply slinging rhymes together. Even as a completely composed number it would stand at the pinnacle of blues piano playing; in fact, it is James' *Little Cow and Calf*, a repertoire piece he used as its immediate point of departure, that sounds like the unfinished, imprecise product by comparison. His sublime piano runs on *22-20* transcend the venality of its homicidal lyrics, which paradoxically his playing was intended to augment. In no other blues piano piece (except his own *If You Haven't Any Hay*) are instrumental figures so responsive to singing, and at times they echo his vocal phrases with the finesse of a skilled blues guitarist.

In general when James sang in his lowered tenor (as on *22-20*) the result was an unexpressive product. It was probably in the interests of attaining greater emotion that he more often sang at the top of his tenor register. In the fashion of Blind Willie Johnson, who glided effortlessly between a false bass and a natural tenor in delivering spirituals, James created two voices within *Devil Got My Woman* and *Special Rider*, using the soprano for

crescendo purposes. On *I'm So Glad*, he used an even freer mixture of dual register singing, complementing his heightened
pitch with intensified volume.

James' singing and playing both bore witness to a capacity for
development that was rarely found in blues. The songs of most
blues artists are cut from a single mold, the performer applying
one overall technique or reaching a single plateau of playing skill.
Only with a few blues singer/guitarists does one see evidence that
the musician had attempted to improve or refine any particular
pieces beyond what they had apparently been when he first learned
or mastered them. It is usually the additional touches created by
tinkering that make for truly great blues pieces, and result in nuances lacking in the typical one-dimensional blues.

This facility on James' part is most evident in *Devil Got My
Woman*, a song that stands completely alone in the blues canon.
Its very existence as a blues song was the result of his ambitious
tinkering with a simple vocal phrase that he had almost certainly
heard in the form of an a cappella air, most likely in some
levee or lumber camp (if not a cottonfield). One guesses that
the non-blues phrase he was embellishing was essentially the
same one he used as its opening theme (identified below as
"A"), given two extra beats.

This initial phrase consisted of four basic notes, its steps
arranged in a minor seventh-keynote-major second-major
fourth pitch sequence. The prominence of the major second
and fourth in the melody gave it an unusual sound within
the realm of blues, which often avoids these tones altogether.
Ultimately he would double the length of the phrase, adding
minor thirds, fifths and major sixths to it. One guesses that
the five-bar theme he finally arrived at was inspired by the
elongated vocal of Little Brother Montgomery's *Vicksburg
Blues*, where the ordinary ten-beat blues phrase was similarly
doubled.

Out of simple, unprepossessing melodic material, James
was to create a flowing, almost majestic dirge consisting
largely of two line stanzas, with each of its four verses taking a different, unpredictable phrasing pattern. The unusual phrases set forth below illustrate that James' notion

of himself as a unique musician was not simply (to use his own expression) an "air pudding"; it had a concrete basis in his signature song:

Verse	line of verse	melodic theme	number of vocal-guitar beats	resulting measures
1	1	A	10-8	4½
	2	A	12-6	4½
2	1	A	11-8	4¾
	2	A	12-8	5
3	1	B	20-8	7
	2	A	12-10	5½
4	1	B	20-8	7
	2	A	12-8	5
	3	A	12-4	4

What made gave the song its blues-like character was not its phrasing pattern (which resulted in off-beat stanzas of 9, 9¾, 12½, and 16 measures), but the keynote ending of each vocal phrase and the brief instrumental section appended to each vocal line. What made it a masterpiece of blues-playing was the fact that James could overcome the intrinsic awkwardness of his material, singing and playing with such finesse and smoothness that the basically disheveled structure of the song is not even noticeable to a listener. He used a simple but remarkable device to give each vocal line an overall coherence: a two-measure guitar motif (based on an A7 configuration), sounded at different points within each phrase:

Verse	line	number of vocal beats in line	placement of riff
1	line 1	10	beats 2-9
	line 2	12	beats 3-10
2	line 1	11	beats 2-9
	line 2	12	beats 3-10
3	line 1	20	beats 11-18
	line 2	12	beats 3-10

There are almost no comparable instances of such an interior riff, able to stand by itself, played within a blues vocal line, and none whatsoever of a portable riff being shifted around in this fashion. The way that James deploys this portable riff reveals his embroidery of the bedrock vocal phrase it accompanies. The expansion of the first line of the third and fourth stanzas into a unique five-bar vocal phrase is effected by adding a two-bar snippet to the beginning of the phrase: upon completing this enhancement, James returns to his basic *Devil* theme and begins sounding his guitar motif.

The vocal embellishments are effected so smoothly and are so complementary with the theme they embroider that James' musical hemstiching is all but invisible. Their purpose is to heighten the emotional impact of his performance: they involve dramatic rises in pitch and volume. No other blues singer seems to have elongated a vocal phrase in the same fashion, and James plainly did so not simply to improve it but to suggest turmoil—the turmoil he undoubtedly felt in the wake of his broken marriage. Complementing the heightened tension he introduced at the onset of the third verse was a reference (in the form of an acquired blues couplet) to the turmoil his singing simultaneously suggested:

I lay down last night; lay down last night, I
Lay down last night
Tried to take my rest.

My mind got to ramblin'
Like a wild geese in the West;
In the West.

James said the verse portrayed *"feelings.* 'You know that man
has gone plumb insane?' 'Where's his mind at?' 'He got a feelin'
for such-and-such a thing.' See, that feeling has caused your
mind to be rambling or ramshackled." It was probably to placate
listeners who would (he assumed) wonder what brought him
to this pass (the brink of insanity, apparently) that he offered
the concluding couplet:

The woman I loved
Woman I loved; woman I loved
Stoled her from my best friend.

But he got lucky;
Stole her back again.

James attached no autobiographical significance to this derivative couplet, but the reference to a "friend" was obviously a
means of indirectly portraying his situation with Oscella Robinson.

Just as *Devil Got My Woman* was one of the most extraordinary
feats of vocalizing found in blues song, *I'm So Glad* was one
of the most extraordinary examples of fingerpicking found in
the realm of guitar music, one that is virtually impossible to
improve upon. It is apparent that James had passed considerable
time running through the piece as though it were a picking
exercise, attempting to play it as rapidly and fluently as possible.
The result is astounding, thanks to his juxtaposition of a discreetly practiced picking pattern with the emotiveness of his
singing, and the way he picks up momentum during the piece,
expanding its $4^1/_2$-bar breaks to $9^1/_2$-bar breaks in the process.
James was able to arrive at his uncanny playing speed by all
but foregoing his usual practice of following his voice on

Sheet music for *So Tired*
(Courtesy Dave Jasen)

guitar: instead, he propelled the song with forcefully thumbed single notes on the fourth string, which accompanied an eccentric vocal phrasing pattern consisting of $3^{1}/4$ measures. An unexpected, frantic-sounding three-beat treble figure completed the measure, and foreshadowed the two basic breaks he used in the song. The leaping dynamics that accompany his eruptions into falsetto singing, augmented by his explosive fingerpicking, give it an almost unwordly sound.

The truly inspired musicianship James displays on *I'm So Glad* is even more impressive in light of its underlying source, which contains all of the essential melodic ingredients of James' version but bears no resemblance to its spirit. No other blues singer besides James could have wrought such magic from the original *So Tired*, a happy-go-lucky tune with a decided Twenties' cuteness. Indeed, the version recorded by Lonnie Johnson (*I'm Tired Of Livin' All Alone*), who was a far more accomplished guitarist than James, is completely undistinguished by comparison.

James' conversion of this pleasant-sounding, ingratiating period piece into an enduring classic that sounds like blues (and was even played like blues, with a twelve-bar opening stanza consisting of a single four-bar phrase, twice repeated) establishes his real musical credo, which ran directly counter to the proclamation "I'm so glad." His musical motto was the equivalent of the Steve Martin quip, "comedy ain't pretty," James telling listeners, in effect: "Life ain't pleasant." He did everything within his means, tonally, to give his music a mordant, acrid edge: the sudden break he unleashes on *Special Rider*, beginning an octave above the keynote of his verse accompaniment, almost sounds like a shreik. Unable to distort pitches on piano, he gives his playing an air of turbulence and truculence by unusual dynamic contrasts, virtually pounding the instrument on *How Long* and sounding the musical equivalent of thudding bullets on *22-20*. At the same time, James always played with a certain elegance that took the mean edge off his music and added a paradoxical touch to its basic ambience, as though he were somehow out to express ugliness and beauty simultaneously.

In giving his music its turbulent character, he was conveying the meaning of blues, as he took it to be: the expression of a "dissatisfied mind." But there was nothing intellectual about this expression: as James understood the word, "mind" was a component of the human soul, along with the breath. His entire being was invested in the blues ethos. He was so consumed by this ethos that he would offer a stilted rendition of the placid *Drunken Spree*, which was actually easier to play than most of his songs. His falsetto rendition of the standard *Four O'Clock*, while melodically exact, is pitched at such a high vocal register as to replace the ordinary placidity of the piece with an almost shrill sound, and he gives a similar aura to *Drunken Spree* by pitching it at the top of his tenor. Of his sixteen surviving Grafton blues recordings, it is only a title that he had completely forgotten about—*What Am I To Do Blues*—that offers a relaxed, peaceful instrumental sound. This abandonment to a vinegary musical ethos precluded the possibility of his ever becoming a popular blues performer. The blues recording hits of the period consisted almost entirely of the kind of catchy, placid ditties that ran completely counter to his own sensibility: *Kansas City Blues* (1927), *How Long Blues* (1928), *Tight Like That*, and *Sittin' On Top Of The World* (a melody he was to replicate in the 1960s, as *D.C. Hospital Blues*).

Just as the music of most blues artists was not painstaking, so was most of James' own music not painstaking. There is a marked discrepancy between his surpassing and ordinary pieces, even though their musical ingredients overlap. At the pinnacle of his majestic musical pyramid lie *22-20*, *I'm So Glad*, *Special Rider*, and *Devil Got My Woman*, all of which were (with the exception of *Special Rider*) first-take efforts. These are works of real majesty. The rest of James' canon attests largely to craftsmanship. At the next plateau of accomplishment lie *If You Haven't Any Hay*, *Hard Time Killin' Floor*, and *How Long "Buck"*, works that are too rigid and repetitive by virtue of their flimsy construction as simple eight-bar ditties to equal his supreme efforts. Yet James adds impressive touches to these performances: the rhythmic foot-tapping that sounds continuously in the background of *If You Haven't Any Hay* is unparalleled in recorded blues, and more complicated than most blues washboard playing. Only a musician with a great ability to concentrate could have made a true second instrument out of his feet. The skill with which James welds the separate single measure phrases of his song by means of various boogie-like figures serves to provide a real bridge between the vocal and instrumental sections that is absent from other variants of *Alabama Bound*, such as Charlie Patton's *Elder Greene Blues* and his own guitar version of the same piece. *Hard Times* is distinguished for its off-beat instrumental voicing, James rendering the melody with single bass notes (in contrast to his soprano voice), and *How Long* for its stop-time effects, as well as for its frantic tempo.

His other 1931 works, amounting to two piano blues (*Little Cow and Calf Is Gonna Die Blues* and *What Am I To Do Blues*) and seven secular guitar songs (*Cypress Grove Blues, Cherry Ball Blues, Illinois Blues, Four O'Clock, Hard-Luck Child, Yola My Blues Away*, and *Drunken Spree*) are basically stylized genre pieces. Although James displays a striking guitar sound, especially considering the fact that he tuned his guitar a half-step below concert pitch, his guitar songs are stylistically constricted: his fondness for picking out a melody line by means of a pinched first and fourth string octave in open tuning eventually becomes a pat mannerism, indulged on every one of his open tuning pieces. Yet even as he purveys what is essentially a lazy player's gimmick in these songs, James generates an undercurrent of excitement: except on the cut-and-dried *Cypress Grove*, he gives the impression of chafing under the blues formula, and of almost straining to cut loose in the crazed fashion of *I'm So Glad*. Indeed, the instrumental breaks he ventures in *Hard-Luck Child, Yola, Illinois* and *Drunken Spree* are imperfect expressions of this urge. One senses that James wanted to do more with such pieces.

The longing for expression that makes James an arresting and at times brilliant blues performer was basically a handicap in his own profession. He had little interest in performing what was his real function at a "house frolic": supplying a steady dance beat. The sing-song nature of the recurring 1-2 beat of *Cypress Grove, Hard Time Killin' Floor*, and *What Am I To Do Blues* (a song for which he had difficulty concocting lyrics) demonstrates that James had no real flair for dance music. His indifference to accenting patterns is announced at the outset of *Devil Got*

My Woman. Its seven-bar instrumental introduction offers one of the most random succession of accenting patterns found in blues: a single unaccented measure, two 1-2-3-4 measures, a 1-2-3-4 measure, a 1-2-3-4 measure, and two 1-2-3-4 measures. The last two measures, using a square dance accenting pattern, regularly recur after each stanza. His early exposure to square dance music in the form of *Drunken Spree* was also evident in the accenting he used to play the recurring six-beat bass riff of *Cherry Ball.* On the fourteen-bar *Special Rider Blues,* he created a unique clash of a 1-2 and 1-2 accent, using the former to float his vocal phrases and the latter to facilitate his one-measure instrumental riffs. One guesses that without the presence of Henry Stuckey, James would have been an outright liability on the Bentonia "house frolic" circuit.

The impression he ultimately gives off is that of a musician who would have broken free of his restrictive genre, had he the musical means to do so, and who would have become a notable musician in whatever culture he might have occupied. His greatest guitar piece (*I'm So Glad*) lay outside the blues idiom.* The lasting enigma of James' musicianship remains the question of why he should have displayed the level of ambitiousness that gave rise to the exalted likes of *I'm So Glad* and *22-20,* both truly inspired works of music. It was as if James was determined to leave his mark beyond what he termed "the music world"—a world he did not enjoy.

Most blues players were basically complacent, as was James himself, in his ordinary efforts, and as he was to become in the 1960s. One apparent personality difference between James and his blues-singing peers of the latter period lay in his self-consciousness and reflectiveness. That he would apply himself so feverishly towards scaling the highest heights of which he was capable, was, one guesses, a result of this reflectiveness. The James who recorded in 1931 was, within the context of his own society, a profoundly worthless person. Simply becom-

*Although James had a keen sense of his lack of formal education, he never evinced any regret over not having had musical training. This was probably because none of the musicians he had contact with had such training, or were able to accomplish anything that lay beyond him, musically.

ing a blues player had placed him in the category of social trash, and his other pastimes were not calculated to improve his negative image, or inspire respect. The point is impossible to prove, but bears considering: in extending himself well beyond the musical expectations anyone of his time had of a blues singer, James was groping for some inner vindication.

On his very deathbed James had nothing to fall back upon except his claim to have achieved musical excellence. He had raised no family. He had virtually no friends. He had nothing to substantiate his grandiose claim to have been "one of the best men that ever walked," or even his song refrain, "I'm a poor man, but I'm a good man, you understand." Eminence, except in a ludicrously limited sense, had escaped him. As he lay writhing in agony, he proclaimed his belief that no one would ever equal his *I'm So Glad*, and that his rendition of it was better than the recent rock version. It became, for lack of something better, his life's legacy.

17. *Releasin's*

By James' count, he recorded twenty-six sides at Grafton. Besides his known output of eighteen titles, he recalled recording an *I'm So Glad, Part Two*, on which he sang one verse, performing the rest as a guitar and kazoo instrumental. (Improbably, he claimed that this version was faster than the one Paramount released.) He also recorded a piano version of Bessie Smith's *Backwater Blues*.

Neither title was ever issued, and it is unlikely that James recorded the additional six sides he believed he had. In the late 1920s he played a version of *Crow Jane*, an eight-bar standard that was related to *Slidin' Delta*. He also played *Catfish Blues*, a percussive one-chord tune that would become a Mississippi standard in the 1940s, thanks largely to its recording by Muddy Waters. His failure to record either tune (both staples of his 1960s' performances) is a likely indication that he did not actually produce the twenty-six sides he recalled recording.

Nonetheless, the unusual length of his session indicated both Art Laibly's enthusiasm for James' music and the prominence of H.C. Speir in the scheme of dwindling company dealers. Whereas Little Brother Montgomery had been allotted only two sides after driving to Grafton from Chicago six months earlier and presenting himself as a ready-to-record blues act, James produced more sides than any Paramount artist besides Charlie Patton had recorded in a single session.

James left Grafton with eight dollars in expense money given him by Laibly, along with an undetermined pay-off. The financial arrangements he had made with Laibly would remain murky, thanks to James' later insistence that Paramount had short-changed him. He once stated that he had asked for $1000 to record, and that Laibly had offered him $250 instead, along with a royalty. The likely accuracy of this account is indicated by Johnnie Temple's recollection that James returned to Jackson with $200 or $300, some of which went to square accounts with his friend Horse Luckett.

Soon after recording, James saw posters bearing cartoon depictions of himself plastered on various telephone poles in Jackson. These advertisements must have been posted by H.C. Speir, whose store James was to visit some three weeks after his session to obtain copies of his first record. They made a vivid impression on him. A cartoon depiction of a figure (himself, he thought) with a horn and tail and pitchfork illustrated *Devil. Illinois* was represented by a drawing of James with a red handkerchief and a cowboy hat, standing near a depot; *Cherry Ball*, by a woman holding bowl of cherries. *Cow and Calf* bore a picture of a running cow. Although Paramount had previously used a similar style of advertising to generate mail order sales in the *Chicago Defender*, James' pictures were likely conceived by Speir independently of the company, which was to assign *Cow and Calf* as an unfeatured "B" side. Unless Speir was attempting to simulate orders for records, James must have seen these advertisements over an extended period of time.

His first Paramount was not issued until the spring of 1931. A run-of-the-mill Columbia "race" record issued in April of 1931 received a pressing run of 650 copies, and it is likely that James' first record was issued in lesser numbers. At that time, Paramount was steadily sinking towards oblivion: only 88 records remained for it to issue before it folded its operations. Of these titles, nine would be Skip James items; considering the straitened market of the time, it is doubtful that the final ones were pressed in quantities exceeding 300.

None of his tunes would be copyrighted, but all but one (*Jesus Is A Mighty Good Leader*, which he actually called *Let Jesus Lead You*) would bear his name as the composer in parenthesis beneath the title of each records These attributions had been made by Laibly on the basis of James' affirmative responses when he asked him he had composed or wrote the song he was recording.

Like other contemporary Southern blues singers, James did not actually understand what constituted an original composition; as long as he had figured out the song himself, he was, by his lights, its author. Thus he would be credited with a spiritual (*Be Ready When He Comes*) that was obviously acquired from church sources, for *Drunken Spree* (a Bentonia acquisition) and for *I'm So Glad*, the melody of which he had only an original arrangement. It was only in later years that his copyrights had any ramifications, and the attribution of his songs was, for Paramount, merely a formality to forestall the unlikely possibility that someone would demand payment from the company by declaring himself the author of a James tune. How casually and carelessly the company worked is indicated by Laibly's billing of him as "Skip James" rather than "Skippy James," as he was then known, and by his labeling *How Long Blues* as *How Long "Buck"*, either in the mistaken belief that James had played a buckdance accompaniment or simply as a ploy so the copyright owners of *How Long Blues* would not see an opportunity to dun Paramount for royalties. Although James considered *I'm So Glad* a Two Step song on the basis of its fast tempo, it was designated an example of "novelty singing"; as was always the case with contemporary "race" records, none of his songs were labelled as dance pieces, even when they merited such designation.

The order of their release indicates the relative favor they found with company officials. *Hard Time Killin' Floor Blues* (backed with *Cherry Ball Blues*) and *22-20 Blues* (backed with *If You Haven't Any Hay, Get On Down The Road*), pieces that had obviously impressed Laibly on the basis of their thematic lyrics, were the first items the company issued. Perhaps because of its bleak title, the topical *Hard Times* sold poorly even by Depression standards; to date only two copies exist of the record. *22-20*, on the other hand, was among the most successful James releases: over five copies have been retrieved by collectors. *Illinois Blues* (backed with *Yola My Blues Away*) and *How Long "Buck"* (backed with *Little Cow And Calf*) marked the third and fourth James issues. Only two known copies exist of each work.

It is likely that none of the six remaining records Paramount issued struck company officials as being particularly commercial.

Despite its position as the centerpiece in his repertoire, *Devil Got My Woman* was only the fifth James record released by Paramount; moreover, it was backed with his other guitar repertoire staple, *Cypress Grove*. As something like a half a dozen copies have surfaced since it was recorded, this work sold well by Depression standards, and probably exceeded the sales of his other records.

I'm So Glad and *Special Rider* merited sixth on Paramount's list, and were not issued until the fall of 1931. Two scratchy copies remain of this classic, which was probably the greatest double-sided blues 78 ever issued. It was followed by *4 O'Clock Blues* (backed with *Hard-Luck Child*), of which four copies are thought to exist. Three copies still exist of Paramount's eighth James release, *Jesus Is A Mighty Good Leader* (backed with *Be Ready When He Comes*), songs James had recorded in reponse to Laibly's request for spirituals. The final James side, *Drunken Spree* (backed with *What Am I To Do Blues*) was not issued until January of 1932. The single existing copy of this record would not surface for fifty years. It probably merited its low position in Paramount's scheme of issues because the featured side was perceived to be a hillbilly melody (as it may have been, originally) and thus not appealing "race" fare, while James sings in an undertone (sometimes sputtering out completely) on *What Am I To Do* as he gropes for suitable lyrics. The fact that Laibly did not call for a retake of the latter piece shows how casually he operated James' session. For that matter, neither the musician nor the recording director apparently noticed that James' guitar was out of tune on *Four O'Clock Blues*. In later years, he was to make the equivocal boast: "If a guitar's not substantially in tune, I won't hit the stage with it."

In general, James could have rightly claimed to have greatly exceeded his self-proclaimed general credo of correctness: "Everything I do, I do decently and in order." His playing was all the more enhanced by his use of a studio guitar, and had James been strapped with his own customary cheap instrument the legacy of his recordings would have been considerably lessened.[*]

[*]James' session probably involved two guitars, the guitar of *Drunken Spree* tuned at concert pitch, that of his other titles tuned below concert pitch.

James' records were for the most part purchased by dealers who decided to order them by mail, presumably on the basis of a monthly company flier that likely listed his titles (along with other current releases), without any attempt to pitch them. The primary customer for his records was no doubt H.C. Speir, whose significance in the Paramount dealer hierarchy was the reason he had been recorded in the first place. The orders Speir placed for the records of his various discoveries were based on his reactions to each record he sampled. When Gayle Wardlow was to play James' *If You Haven't Any Hay* for him decades later, he would remark dourly: "Sure wouldn't sell . . . the harmony; the feelin' . . . [it's] no good."

But no records issued in the period had any sales potential: national record sales of 1931 amounted to $17.6 million, a drop of over fifty percent from the previous year. It was not until 1937 that industry sales even reached this depleted total again. In practical terms, the mandated scarcity of James' Depression records prevents a historian from acquiring any real sense of his contemporary commercial appeal. By Paramount's diminished standards, he was successful enough to merit a follow-up session, sometime after Laibly was fired in the spring or summer of 1931.

James recalled receiving a Bentonia visit from another company official who attempted to record him several months after his first session. The man was probably Henry Stephany, who had replaced Laibly as recording director and might have been paying a sales call to H.C. Speir's store. On this occasion, James planned to record with his fifteen or sixteen year-old cousin Willie Mae Polk (later, Wallace) who was his frequent vocal duet partner of the period. "She could sing like a mockingbird," he recalled. James recalled that the two of them signed a contract for a Paramount session, but that her mother (his aunt Martha) balked at the idea, causing him to cancel his plans to record.

Had James consummated the session, his records would have been even rarer than his previous ones, for Paramount was rapidly becoming a virtually defunct label. H.C. Speir recalled attempting to order four hundred copies of a James record, only to learn that there were none to be had. The company had sold out its initial pressing, and had no plans to press another batch.

James himself never heard most of his records. He claimed to have had an arrangement whereby Paramount was to pay him $20 per record issued: "That was set up like this . . . I was supposed to get twenty dollars per record. As a releasin' . . . depends on how many they sent out. If they sent out three, I'se supposed to get sixty dollars. Sent five, I was supposed to get a hundred dollars." He reported: ". . . I got one releasin', that's all. One releasin' did I get. Out of all those records." The check he received amounted to a lump sum payment of forty dollars, "about two or three months after I recorded," he reported. This check was sent to H.C. Speir.

On another occasion James spoke of having received two royalty checks, and cashing them at the general store operated by D.C. Sigles, "the biggest Jew in Bentonia . . ." The small talk Sigles made when he brought his first check there remained etched in his memory: " . . . He said: 'I think if you will continue to keep on with this [music],' says: 'someday you'll be a worthwhile man.'

"Now you know what that means, don't ya? . . . That I would come in possession of somethin' beyond makin' a strainy livin'; I wouldn't have to do a whole lotta hard manual work . . . That's what he had reference to."

But it was Sigles rather than James who prospered: " . . . he got so rich he decided he'd go back to his home, that's over in them foreign countries where them Jewish towns are." When James' trickle of meager royalty checks came to a halt (perhaps in early 1932), he wrote to Paramount to ask what had happened to his anticipated releases. When he learned that the company was going out of business, he said, he wrote and threatened legal action, to no avail.

It is likely that James received a form letter simply claiming that the label was out of business. The company had actually been misrepresenting itself to the State of Wisconsin as a non-existent business enterprise since 1924, for the sake of evading taxes and (it would seem) discouraging lawsuits. It would formally ended its operations at the end of 1933, after having been all but inert since mid-1932. In James' lurid view, the reason for the company's demise had nothing to do with the Depression, which made the already luxurious and overpriced 75¢ record an unthinkable consumer commodity, particularly for blacks. He fancied that Arthur Laibly had swindled it out of existence, and had gone into hiding with an embezzled cache of money representing its profits from himself and other artists.

Despite his later claims, the fate of his records probably had little or nothing to do with his retreat from blues-singing.

18. *The Convert*

Late one night in the latter part of 1931, a short, bull-necked pastor found himself at a deserted railroad depot on an umarked country road in central Mississippi. He was en route from Dallas to Birmingham with his wife, a school teacher from Tuscaloosa. An anticipated turn-off to Jackson was nowhere in sight.

The 51-year-old Eddie James stepped out of his Buick and beamed a flashlight across the depot sign, which read "Bentonia."

Some twenty-five years earlier, he had left Bentonia as a wanted man. Not long afterwards he had permanently parted company with his wife in Sidon, leaving his small son in the process. He quit the household with no possessions, but better prospects than most blacks of his time and place. A high school degree set him apart from the adults his son would come to know around Sidon and Bentonia.

The educated Southern black could then realize the "worth" of his studies in two professions: teaching or the ministry. Somehow (his family was never party to the details), Eddie James opted for the pulpit. He soon became known as the Reverend E. D. James, the operator of a Texas seminary that turned out ministers.

The spirituals he sometimes composed and hawked to local congregations attested to his literacy, if not originality. Paraphrasing the beginning of Whitman's *O Captain My Captain*, he derived a stanza for *Sea Walkin' Jesus*, his signature song. Citing every Biblical reference to water and immersion, he compiled an exhaustive dissertation entitled "Why I Am A Baptist," for which his colleagues had awarded him a Doctorate of Divinity.

Yet beneath his veneer of aloof rectitude, E.D. James was a man of primitive anger. When another minister questioned one of his assertions at a theological conference, he retorted: "Are you calling me a liar?" When the man gave a nodding shrug in reply, James promptly knocked him unconscious.

As he drove through Bentonia in 1931, Reverend James had no intention of renewing his acquaintance with his twice-remarried former wife. When he took lodgings for the night it was with his sister, Martha Polk.

While conversing with Martha Polk he learned that his 28-year-old son, who was boarding with other relatives a mile away, had become an extraordinary musician who had made records earlier that year.

A summons from his long-vanished father was relayed to Skippy James the next day. Guitar in hand, he arrived at his aunt's. His father asked politely: "What kind of music do you play? I've heard about your fame and records and am very proud of you."

Skippy replied: "Any kind of song—blues and spirituals." His father requested a spiritual, which James performed; his stepmother a blues, which he also performed. The blues James played had no effect upon his father, who sat stolidly throughout his performance. At its conclusion he commented: "Son, that's nice and I liked it, but I'd like for you to reverse this thing. In other words, go back to the church."

This appeal left James unmoved. In neighboring villages like Flora and Pocahantas he and Henry Stuckey were already wont to represent themselves as sanctified singers. Sometimes he played piano at a local Baptist church. He performed spirituals for money, not inner satisfaction. Although he believed in the literal truth of the Bible, he rarely read it.

Having failed to convert his son, the father all but lost interest in him. Soon he left to continue his journey. As he drove through Jackson, however, he convinced himself that his son was a candidate for conversion. He returned to Bentonia and approached him with a new proposal: that he accompany the father to Dallas and attend the seminary he had founded.

"I'll think it over," James replied.

To soften his resistance, Reverend James added: "I can't blame you for singing blues; I've done all that myself." This confession was no news to Skippy; while growing up he had heard numerous stories about his father's wayward days. "My daddy used to be somethin', man!" he would later recall. "Very 'skillful,' you understand?" James believed that he had inherited the same cleverness.

Yet for all his own cleverness, he was often embroiled in situations where his survival depended on his readiness to draw the Colt revolver he habitually carried. As 1931 drew to a close, he made his way from Bentonia to Arkansas. As he traveled in the Depression-ridden South, his father's offer of a few weeks earlier began to weigh on him. In hopes of gaining a patron, a protector, and a father, he decided to give up blues-singing.

19. *Devil Got Religion*

In late 1931 or early 1932 H.C. Speir attempted to record James
in Memphis, most likely for Victor Records. "He soured on me,"
the scout later recalled. "Got religion right there in Memphis."
In later years, his memory of James as a musician would be
overshadowed by his memory of him as an unwilling bluesman.
"Skip James, he's moody," Speir would tell Gayle Wardlow. "Get
religious ideas, you understand."

Speir had already witnessed numerous impulsive conversions
on the part of blues singers, who were temperamentally akin
to the slaves chronicled by an antebellum observer: "You will
find . . . one of the most striking characteristics of the negro in
the South in the religious bent of his mind. Whether a member
of the church or no, he is essentially at war with the devil."[*]
In 1899, another observer wrote of blacks: " . . . one rarely finds
among them an adult who has not gone through an emotional
experience known as conversion, after which it is considered
vanity and sinfulness to indulge in song other than that of a
sacred character."

Thanks to the relative mildness of his mother's African Methodist faith, James probably suffered fewer pricks of religious
conscience than most Mississippi blues singers of the 1920s:
Methodists lacked the fire-and-brimstone fanaticism of the more
prevalent Baptists, and it was not until 1919 that the white Methodist church got around to formally proscribing dancing. Yet,
like most blues converts to the church, James was ultimately

---

[*]Edward A. Pollard of Virginia, *Black Diamonds Gathered in the Darkey Homes
of the South* (Pudney & Russell, New York, 1859), p. 34.

motivated by fear of retribution. By Fundamentalist standards, blues-singing was the devil's work, and the performer who persisted in this calling was in for an eternity of hellfire. As James himself had sung on *Be Ready When He Comes*:

> Jesus is comin', [to] the world again
> Comin' to judge the hearts of men
> Don't let Him catch your heart filled with sin
> He's comin' again to stay.

> Don't let Him catch you like he done before
> Skippin' and dancin' on the barroom floor
> Raisin' [the devil] everywhere you go
> He's comin' again to stay.

Even in the 1860s, the term "devil-songs" had been current as a racial description of secular tunes; the first book devoted to black music (Allen, Ware, and Garrison's *Slave Songs of the United States*) referred to such unspecified tunes as "common" among blacks of the period. The Fundamentalist believed that it was the duty of every singer to devote himself to spirituals, in keeping with the injunction of the Psalm to "Praise the Lord with harp: sing unto him with the psaltery . . . Sing unto him a new song; play skillfully with a loud noise" (Psalm 33:2-3).

As the Bible was the sole book of his acquaintance, and the church the sole repository of values for him, the Mississippi blues singer was unable to mount any intellectual opposition to his own condemnation. Although the Bible said nothing about blues-singing, the fact that pastors said that God stood firmly against it was enough to cow its practitioners, particularly when they lived in a stultified plantation environment.

The prospect of death, and with it, the condemnation of God, was a real one for any blues singer of the early twentieth century. Blues-singing was, in fact, one of the most dangerous occupations in America, and James was fully cognizant of its dangers. Looking back on his career, he was to say: "It's been trouble in mostly every place that I've been playin': Texas, Arkansas, Misissippi . . . all over." In retrospect, he could only consider his survival lucky: "In some way, I'd miss any traps set for me," he was to say in the 1960s. "I'd be able to go around them or shun them."

The "traps" James personalized were in reality occupational hazards. Thanks to the anarchy of the "house frolic," his profession would sport a frightening casualty list. Aside from numerous historical nonentities who were reportedly murdered in "house frolic" carnage, their numbers included Charlie Patton, who would be almost fatally knifed in a 1933 Delta "house frolic," and Robert Johnson, murdered in 1938 in Greenwood.

Almost every Mississippi blues singer could recount at least one deadly assault attempted upon himself by a resentful male at a "house frolic" who did not like the way he acted towards his own girlfriend or wife. "At that time peoples in the South was in the country was jealous of musicians," David Edwards claimed. " ... So when a man could play the blues and had a good voice and made him a couple of numbers, recorded a couple of numbers, well he was a great man at that time, and the mens, well some of the mens down South had some pretty womens down there. And a musician could get most any of 'em he want ... But the other guy that can't do anything ... if he think you likin' his women, he turn sour in a minute ... "

Likewise, James was to say: "When I'd sometimes be playin' in places, quite naturally some old clowny woman wanna clown over you ... sometimes they'd be a little funny with you. Quite naturally their boyfriend or their husbands wouldn't like that. Sometime a clowny woman, she get a drink or two in her head, and she just wanna show herself ... She had never seed you before sometimes, just ... make people think you done fell for her ... See, that'd cause jealousy: boyfriend or husband or somethin' say: 'Get rid of that nigger; kill 'im.' Heap of times on those plantations you'd get killed. You'se close to some of those old big bayous, lakes ... you could get knocked off and throwed in there ... "

The misbehavior of blues singers seems to have largely precipitated this aggression. "All the musicians was women-chasers," Johnnie Temple said. This fact was roundly advertised in their lyrics, which were (deliberately, it would seem) calculated to arouse the envy of less successful males. From James' standpoint, which was that of a typical blues singer, if a man murdered another man for the sake of jealousy over a woman, the person inherently responsible for this violence was the female. She had converted the male assailant into a "monkey man"—a female's dupe who was "grateful to touch the hem of a woman's garment." This contemptible fraternity included virtually everyone who wasn't a blues singer, or a pimp.

In later years James did not enumerate any violent confrontations with males as a performer, and it is possible that he rarely or never experienced them. He claimed to have generally avoided plantation "house frolics" as performing outlets, and his meager dance repertoire attests to this likelihood. The precautionary measure of appearing with Henry Stuckey or "Chief" would have buffeted him from the kind of assault to which a lone blues singer was subject. So would James' aversion to playing popular request pieces, which was the surest way to galvanize a tipping female patron, and arouse the emnity of her male companion in the process. Ishmon Bracey's avidity for such coin almost resulted in his murder at an Elton, Mississippi frolic in the 1920s; as he told Gayle Wardlow:

> That *Vicksburg Blues* was popular then an' they want to hear it . . . He [a male customer] had done got a four hundred dollar bonus . . . He had done cashed his check and she [his female companion] had the biggest of the money, see, and she was a nice-lookin' little woman, too.
>
> And so she come over to where I was and she asked me to play the *Vicksburg Blues*, say: "Here's a dollar, play it again." And, I played it and so she came back over there, and say: "Here's another dollar, play that again." I played and she came over there the third time . . .
>
> After she left, he came over there, say: "You see that woman over there? In that corner?"
>
> I say: "Sho'! I see her!"—I'se tryin' to be lively and friendly.

And so he say: "That's my wife!"

I say: "Yeah!" I said: "That's the first time I ever seen her . . . You have a nice-lookin' wife."

He say: "Well, listen: don't you let her come over here all up in your face no more."

I said: "Okay!" I say: "She just asked me to play a piece . . . wasn't nothin' to it . . ."

He say: "I done told you!"

. . . She come back, she said: "Here's a dollar . . . Play the *Vicksburg Blues* for me 'gain." I taken the dollar . . . I say: "See that man, the tall old dark bastard? . . . Isn't that your husband?"

She say: "Yeah, how you know?"

I say: "He come over here an' told me . . . for you not to come up in my face no more." I say: "Now I play that *Vicksburg Blues* till day, long as you give me money . . . You want me to play [it] now, you *send* me somethin' . . ."

Fourth time she left here he come back with a crabapple switch [switch blade knife]; draw it back at me. He said: "You so-and-so, you!"

. . . The guy I was playin' for was tough—Marshall Serge—so he come in there and got his gun, and made him beg me pardon and everything. So he got kinda quieted down, and so he went on out. 'Bout a halfhour, forty-five minutes, or somethin' like that, he brought in a little old whiskey bottle—half a pint.

Say: "Aw, let's drink it off and be merry!"

I said: "You drink; I don't want no whiskey. I ben drinkin' . . . I'm playin' for a man that sells whiskey; you know I got plenty—as much as I want."

"Oh, you have the devil in you, eh?" He broke at me that time and Marshall ran in there with his gun. And ran him home.

The proferred whiskey, Bracey discovered, had been poisoned.

By the mores of his society it was Bracey, not his antagonist, who "had the devil in him," and the murder of a blues singer was never an occasion of community lament. The nonchalant way in which a blues singer's murder (real or imagined) would be mentioned by a surviving peer is ample testatment to the negligible value assigned to his life. In James' phrase, he would be "rotten and forgotten"; not even entitled to pity, for he had taken up his calling with full knowledge of the risks it entailed.

The possibility of sudden slaughter must have weighed upon every blues singer at the outset of his career, for bloodlettings had been a perpetual part of plantation "house frolics" since their known inception in the late nineteenth century, before the vogue for blues. Booker T. Washington was to recall his 1881 visit to an Alabama plantation where, "[a]t night, during Christmas week, they usually had what is called a 'frolic', in some cabin on the plantation. This meant a kind of rough dance, where there was likely to be a good deal of whiskey used, and where there might be some shooting or cutting up with razors."[*] In 1910, a Southern observer noted: ". . . the country Negro is fond of dances, which often turn out unseemly and lead to affrays and murders."[**] Because blues performing involved singing impious words, the performer of James' era who died in a "house frolic" or barrelhouse bloodletting was in more danger of postmortem heavenly retribution than his square dance predecessors of the nineteenth century, who were likely to play instrumentals on violin or banjo. His songs were public announcements of his breach with the church, and even his seemingly innocuous lyrics contained rebellious overtones that would have been clear to himself, if not his contemporaries. As James said of the title lyric of *Cypress Grove*: "I had heard those old people sing a song about 'I don't care where the Lord bury my body,' and 'I don't care where you bury my body, since my soul's gonna be with God.' But at that time I was kinda rough, an' I . . . say: 'I'd rather be buried in a cypress grove . . .'"

His own sense of playing a daredevil game that ran counter to the values of his culture was captured in a couplet of *Cypress Grove*:

[*]*Up From Slavery* (Doubleday and Co., New York and Garden City, 1963 edition), p. 97.

[**]A.D. Hart, *The Southern South* (Appleton & Co., New York, 1910), p. 117.

> The old people told me, but I never did know:
> "The Good Book declare 'You got to reap just what
>   you sow.' "

The suggestion of this verse was that he had escaped the consequences of his impious actions.

The challenge of the blues career was to complete this escape,
by getting out alive, and getting oneself "right with God" before
the curtain closed upon an impious life. The trick was to delay
foreclosure until the last possible moment, when one had ex-
tracted all of the worldly pleasures and riches possible from
blues-playing. For many bluesmen, the onset of an illness (signifying, in their minds, a foretaste of heavenly retribution) was
a sign to stop singing blues. On his deathbed in the 1940s,
the fiddler Lonnie Chatmon would vow to end his career.
"When I'd go out to see him," his brother Sam recalled, "he
says: 'Whenever I get up, if I live to get up, me and you gonna
put out nothin' but gospel music . . . I done joined the church
and I don't wanna play no more blues.' " Tommy Johnson made
a similar pledge to Ishmon Bracey shortly before his death in
1956. But the blues singer who did not become a pastor invariably remained a blues singer, and the fact that mere church
membership counted so little with blues singers indicates that
their conversions usually had the quality of a charade. Blues
songs were completely cynical on the subject of church membership and preaching, particularly when it came to the Baptists
who constituted two-thirds of black church-goers in the mid-
1930s:

> Oh I'm gonna get me a religion, I'm gonna join the
>   Baptist church
> I'm gonna be a Baptist preacher an' I sure won't have
>   to work.
>   (Son House: *Preachin' Blues*, 1930)

Because Baptist congregations (unlike most Methodist ones)
were generally willing to support a full-time cleric, they served
as a magnet for opportunists who were basically loafers. As the
majority of Southern blues singers had a Baptist background,
they took a special relish in rhetorically reducing the sect that

condemned them to their own base level. As James' later associate Jack Owens would sing, in his own version of *Devil*: "Devil got religion, joined the Baptist church."

There was enough truth in this sideswipe to make it plausible even as its author professed his own religiosity, for no one could claim that the caliber of evangelical congregations was lofty. Of Southern black Baptist and Methodist sects in the early twentieth century, Hart wrote: "These churches do not represent an advanced type of piety. Conversions are violent and lapses frequent ... "* In 1870, a white Sunday school teacher wrote in *Putnam's Monthly* that black communicants would "go to the evening meetings, stamp, shout, have the 'power' and 'get religion,' and the next day fight, and swear and steal, as they did before. ..." Sixty years later, a Baptist preacher voiced the same complaint on a "race" record:

> Some of you church members just make me sick.
> You're always fulla religion one minute, and you're
> fulla the devil the next minute. You're shoutin' one
> minute, an' cursin' the next minute.
> (Reverend A.W. Nix: *How Long How Long*, 1930)

The Methodist and Baptist sects had originated not as theology, but as theatre, disseminated by rabble-rousing preachers who had set out to spark the hysteria of revivalism in eighteenth-century England. Constancy of conduct was not even a consideration; in keeping with their traveling circus approach to theology, the sects emphasized faith above works, and exhibitionistic euphoria above articulate faith. To "join the Baptist church" required only one's attendance in the congregation, and submission to a baptist ritual; there was no binding creed, catechism, or code of conduct that one had to ingest in the process. Thanks to the propensity of rural blacks for baptising children, it was not even necessary for the born-again Baptist to undergo the immersion ritual that gave the sect its name. As was true of all Fundamentalism, the convert was welcomed as if he were a store customer, there to purchase goods.

*Hart, p. 117.

The greatest appeal of the Southern black church was to the middle-aged or elderly, and particularly the female; to join the church in youth was almost to forego one's youth, renouncing its heady enjoyments. Had blues-singing been a more enjoyable endeavor for James, it is doubtful that he would have become a convert at the age of 30 or 31, in 1932 or 1933. Had he been strictly or even basically an entertainer, the church would have posed a dreary alternative to his career. Whether his claim that singing blues in private sometimes brought tears to his eyes was true or not, his approach to blues singing was calculated to heap misery upon himself.

Instead of coming to terms with his failed marriage, he had practically become a torch singer. His songs were littered with what could only have been reminders of his former wife, were they not indirect references to her:

> I never loved her, I hope I never will
> I never loved her, I hope I never will.
>
> It's a brownskin gal she's rollin' 'cross my mind
> An' she keeps me worried, bothered all the time.
> *(Four O'Clock Blues)*

Had James been an entertainer at heart, he would have been less susceptible to self-expression, and less trapped within a bleak and forbidding emotional range. But he was actually a musical dramatist, out to inflict his dark mood on others, believing that blues would "take more effect than any kind of music," scornful of a dance ditty like *Drunken Spree* that "wasn't deep enough suited" to move others. He was to invest his music with the virtual power of a hoodoo hex, claiming that his songs could "deaden the mind" of some female who had mistreated him, causing her to realize that "her life will be a void without my presence." These sentiments plainly indicate that he counted on his musical expressiveness to reduce Oscella Robinson to a supplicant, regretting her rash defection from him. It is even possible that this attempt to weave a musical web that would enmesh her in his own misery played a significant part in the electrifying aura of his 1931 musicianship.

Whatever his aspirations or calculations, James had nothing to show in 1932 for his exalted musical triumphs. His records had not even made him a blues celebrity in Jackson. Moreover, he had reached his peak: he could not possibly have played better than he did on such works as *I'm So Glad* and *22-20* without leaving the blues idiom.

At the same time, James had no blues career to uphold. He presented himself to his ministerial father as a musician, but this was a half-truth: his real occupations were bootlegging, card-sharping, and pimping. But these sources of income were likely to have been pinched by the time he saw his father in Bentonia, perhaps a year after his session.

In later years, as a blues rediscovery, James was to declare that the white youths who took up blues-playing could not acquire a feeling for this art because they had not lived through the Depression. But it was during the Depression that James defected from blues, and it is doubtful that his desertion would have occurred were his father (who operated a small seminary) not well situated by comparison with contemporary blues singers. Far from inspiring contemporary blues, the Depression was probably the primary cause of the relative dearth of blues singers found in the 1940s. There were uncounted numbers of blues singers who were born around the turn of the century, as James was; although the social system that had produced them had little changed in the 1930s, only a smattering of blues singers seem to have begun careers then.

The obvious reason for this decline was that the Depression blues singer cut a shabby figure, who did not tempt emulation the way a gaudy gigolo like Will Crabtree was able to impress the teenage Skip James.

A confluence of circumstances afterwards brought James to Dallas in 1932 or 1933. By blues standards, his conversion was without calculation, and the fact that James did not figuratively approach his father on his knees as the result of suffering a catastrophe partly explains the erratic nature of the conversion that followed. There had been no sign from above or warning from God; merely a summons from a man who was a virtual stranger to him.

According to James, he decided to visit his father in Texas and renounce blues completely of his own accord: "Well, he didn't persuade me to, because I'd already been informed of this desire. Nothing happened when I saw him that cause me to renew my spiritual feeling. It was no experience that drawed me back, but a conscience within. See, just like there's a 'me' within me, and when you sleep sometimes that 'me' is wondering and picking up ideas. I always had an inward intensity to be saved." However, were his father not pivotal to his reconversion, James would have joined his mother's Methodist church, in which he had been reared.

James found ample expression of his antagonisms in Fundamentalism, with its emphasis on retribution and its conviction that the world was a rotten place, infested with hell-bound sinners. The church he embraced would have held considerably less charm for him had it been more concerned with affirmation than vitriolic denunciation.

Most of James' doctrinaire religious dogmas appear to be ones that he found congenial, rather than those imposed by creed. His father had been a strict Missionary Baptist, which set him at odds with the Primitive Baptists of the period:

> The Primitive Baptists, they believe
> You can't get to heaven unless'n you wash your feet.
>
> ... Now the Missionary Baptists, they believe
> Go under the water, and not to [just] wash his feet.
> (Washington Phillips: *Denomination Train*, 1927)

In later years, James would display no interest, let alone preoccupation, in any particular ritual of baptism. The only outright Baptist notion to which he appeared to attach even casual meaning to was predestination: "Predestination is this: whatever it's in for you to get, you'll get."

James read the Bible voraciously, and he could spout or paraphrase passages of it almost reflexively. The faith that was reflected in his Biblical discourses had a strong Old Testament tinge: as in spirituals, God rather than Christ was its commanding figure.

The God James worshipped was an unforgiving strongman, out to smash His enemies in the fashion of a Mafia Don. Like such a Don, He was all-powerful. When a calamity struck somewhere in the world, His hand lay behind it. The victims of any worldly catastrophe were entitled to no mercy; as James was to say in the 1960s, after reading about a Welsh coal mine disaster that caused numerous fatalities: "People say it's a pity, but they brought it on themselves."

Even as a teenager, James had acquired this image of God as a scourge of death. In the wake of the post-World War I influenza epidemic, he had learned a spiritual, *Influenza*, which portrayed God as a killer from on high:

Influenza is a disease
Makes you weak all in your knees
Makes you weak all in your bones
In a few more days you are gone.

It was God's almighty hand
He was judging through the land
He was judging the rich and the poor
Because the rich and the poor must go.

Aside from avenging Himself upon His enemies, and giving object lessons to abject mankind, His basic function was to serve as a soul inspector on the day of death. As James envisioned it: "...You got to be judged, I don't care where you may be: in the sea, they got to give up the dead, your body's dead and sunken, you done been cremeated; them ashes got to come up and give an account. You got to take your deeds there to be weighed on an even balance..."

James believed that this process was as literal as having the cotton he picked weighed by a foreman. "...The deeds that I have done, I got to carry them up in a bag. Dirty deeds. Good deeds. I may have one bag on this shoulder, one on the other ... if that good deed outweigh the bad ... then, I'll get my crown. But if them bad deeds outweigh the good deeds, hell I'm gone."

Although James would never tire (at least in later life) of giving extended Biblical discourses, their selective nature was such as to make his professions of Christianity appear to be nothing more than a vigorous, vainglorious exercise in self-deceit. He never once referred to what for most believers would be the indispensable components of a Christian creed: the necessities of loving one's neighbors and forgiving one's enemies. The Biblical words of Jesus, insofar as they related to conduct, never entered his discourses, and the thoughts that they embodied never directed his attitudes. He never referred to a single one of his pre-conversion actions (such as shooting someone) as having been sinful, or even wrong. The Christianity he imbibed and regurgitated instilled him with an overweening sense of righteousness, while having no effect whatsoever on his feelings or outlook, save for a general sense that it was wrong to "seek the advantage of people." His moral ledger sheet consisted entirely of wrongs and injustices he had accumulated from others; although he doubtless knew better, he never so much as hinted that he was the author of any wrong-doing. He was even to state that those who felt guilt for their actions were "sick," which was the inveterate claim of the sociopath.

James' essentially nihilistic Christianity cannot be assessed merely in terms of the quirks of his own psyche. By contemporary church standards he was anything but a quack, or even an eccentric: even his pious wife of later years saw his faith as flawed principally by virtue of his smoking and drinking, not his corrosive attitudes. To a large extent, the fault line in James' Fundamentalism ran parallel with an institutional or congenital fault line in black Fundamentalism, thanks to its origin as a slave religion.

Listening to James' homilies, one formed a vivid impression of what "old-time religion" amounted to on the slave and Jim Crow plantation. James had an impressive command of Biblical naratives and references, and was never at a loss for Scripture to spout. But his recitations were on the order of a child's, devoid of any sense of their significance. He had no sense that the Gospels were supposed to supercede the Old Testament, in Christian thought, and no concept of God or Christ as having any moral component. God was essentially a plantation owner with whom one could curry favor, and thereby avoid the lash of Satan, his punitive overseer. The reward that awaited him for adherence to his planter/patron was celestial residence in a nebulous sky city containing golden gates, where he and other staunch Christians would repose, wearing white robes.

Because black Fundamentalism was the handmaiden of white slavemasters, it could scarcely rise to the level of penetrating thought. Otherwise, the reflective convert would be vexed if not tortured by the incongruity of his hypothetical heavenly and actual earthly station. A host of questions would be automatically suggested by this disparity: why were blacks singled out for slavery? How was it that blacks and whites worshipped the same God, with the same texts?

But such considerations were completely alien in James' theological world, whose concept of virtue was entirely bound up in a few observances and rituals. Its basic omission of virtue, the very lynchpin of what elsewhere passed for Christianity, could not have been accidental. Nor was the devaluation of Christ, a decidedly secondary figure in black spirituals of the plantation era, whose textual focus was on Psalms. It is likely that the image of Christ was so readily confused with that of the slavemaster that it became an impediment to slave faith; such white hymns as *When The Roll Is Called Up Yonder* (1803) would have sounded grotesque on a plantation:

> Let me labor for the Master from the dawn till the
> setting sun
> Let me talk of all His wonderous love and care...

By contrast, the Old Testament God promised to "bringeth out those which are bound with chains." (Psalms 68:6) In the context of slavery and Jim Crow, the Christian injunction to love one's neighbors could only have been an awkward if not distasteful subject to pursue on a pulpit, because it was difficult to construe whites as being anything other than the rampant enemies of Southern blacks. To raise Christ and his teachings to the fore of black Christianity was to state that white people were likeable and lovable, not simply in the abstract, but in the flesh—the flesh of louts like Mack Rollinberg, one of James' Bentonia adversaries of the Twenties or Thirties: "Mack Rollinberg his name was; he had a big store in Bentonia. I don't know whether he was a Jew or Eye-talian, but anyway; he's mixed. And he got stuck on my cousin.

"She was kinda light-skinned and attractive. He told me: 'Hey, Skip?'

"I say: 'What is it?' I say: 'Yas-sir.'

" 'I'll give you a dollar if you go in there and tell that girl I wanna see her.' See, my cousin was standin' right across the street.

"I say: 'What you think you want me to do that for?'

" 'Oh, I'd like to talk with her; I'd like to see her.' Now, I could see these white girls across the street near where my cousin was. One or two of them.

"I say: 'You give me a dollar to go down and tell my cousin you say: "Come here?" '

" 'Hell, yeah!'

" 'I'll tell you what you do: I'll give you the dollar back if you go down there and tell that white lady I say: "Come here." ' I looked him right in his eyes.

"Boy, he turned red! He turned red as hell. 'What the hell you say?'

"I say: 'What the hell did *you* say?'

"He say: 'Goddamn!'

"I say: 'Hell, I think as much of mine as you do yours. That's my cousin you're talkin' about—you didn't know that, did you? Is that *your* cousin yonder?'

". . . He didn't do *shit*! He went back into his store and closed the door. He knew goddamnit I had somethin' *for* his ass, too. Man, he was watchin' me whenever I went back to Bentonia, but he never did say nothin' else to me. *Never did.* 'Cause he just figured if I had *that much* nerve I had nerve to battle his ass, understand? He'd call me crazy to this day if he were livin'."

Blacks who did not openly express such aggression must have nonetheless wanted to on many occasions, as they felt themselves the perpetual objects of contempt and hostility on the part of Southern whites. The subject of white people was discreetly avoided in the context of black Fundamentalism of James' day, and with it, the doctrine of assuming any express attitude towards one's neighbor. So it was that James could rage

against anyone he liked and have no sense that he was con-
travening any of his Christian principles.

Had James acquired a real sense of Christian ethics he would
have been rendered almost speechless as a blues singer, and
found it necessary to rewrite his lyrics when he subsequently
performed them. As it was, his jaded, bitter, violent, and sensual
songs did not expressly controvert anything in the Baptist theology he espoused, particularly as "fornication" (a favorite subject in white churches) was all but overlooked in the rhetoric
of black ministers—themselves notorious for sexual looseness.
His father considered pastoral "love affairs" a normal course
of clerical business, cautioning him only against becoming involved with the "sisters" of his congregation, with the words:
"If you start dealing with just one, she'll spoil the whole church
... She'll tell her friends that you're associatin' with her, and
eventually the whole church will know about your secrecy and
your love affairs."

One of the reasons that James' conversion failed to penetrate
his psychic core to the extent of softening his intractability towards "enemies" was that it involved him in an ongoing struggle
against alcoholism. Drinking was the cardinal sin in his church,
and a temptation he would contend with to the end of his life.
On a practical level, the church acted as a drying-out clinic for
him; his lack of constancy as a convert was partly attributable
to a periodic lust for liquor.

However delusional James' beliefs, the practical effects of his
conversion could only have been positive in everything except
a musical sense. Joining the church kept him away from the bottle, and removed him from the dangers he had faced during
his unsavory blues period. The question remains how often it
did so.

20. The Prodigal Son

There are numerous indications that James' conversion, while foreclosing his blues career for some twenty years, was not tenacious. In the 1960s, for example, his Biblical verbiage was not adorned with an impressive number of spirituals. Had he been firmly committed to the church he would almost certainly have thought to translate *I'm So Glad* to a gospel song, the way Robert Wilkins was to convert his *That's No Way To Get Along* into *That's The Way To Get Along* following his own mid-1930s' conversion. James' song was tailor-made for gospel presentation, its title phrase actually a church catchphrase, already employed in at least two spirituals of the same title:

> I'm so glad, I'm so glad, I'm so glad there's no dying there.*

> I'm so glad trouble don't last always (3)
> Oh my Lord, Oh my Lord what shall I do?**

Another indication of his loose tie with Christendom lay in his failure to take a wife in his father's congregation, as he would doubtless have done had he been determined to settle down.

That his position in the church was relatively tenuous is further indicated by his failure to become a minister in Texas, although he spent three years there (c. 1932-1935) under his father's wing, ample time to absorb and regurgitate sufficient

---

Jubilee and Plantation Songs, Characteristic Favorites as sung by the Hampton Students, Jubilee Singers, Fisk University Students, and Other Concert Companies (Oliver Ditson Company, Boston, 1915).

**Spirituals Triumphant/Old and New*, edited and arranged by Edward Boatner (Sunday School Publishing Board, National Baptist Convention U.S.A., 1926).

Biblical text to become formally ordained. Although James did some informal preaching, his real position in his father's church was that of pianist. His father, who played such songs as *I've Got The Key To The Kingdom* on organ, was openly appreciative of his music.

Although James aspired to become a minister, there is no evidence that his father encouraged him in these efforts, or even viewed him as likely ministerial material. While James had a preacher's wordiness, and a preacher's love of airy rhetoric, he was not cut out for preaching, a mode of performing the same way blues singing was. The preacher's immediate mission was to dominate his congregation by a forceful voice and manner. The sense of his utterances was secondary to his style. James' thoughtful nature and his calm, low speaking voice were not calculated to rouse an audience. There was nothing remotely theatrical in his manner, and when he would spew out chunks of Scripture in later years, there was no recognizable rhetorical intonation in his voice. His inflections betrayed the fact that he had spent most of his time sitting on the sidelines, listening to his father.

The forbidding role model who was his father only complicated James' conversion, enmeshing it in a maze of bewildered emotion. He could not have felt especially loved by God, because he felt unloved by God's emissary, the architect of his conversion. "My daddy never did take too much interest in me," he was to say ruefully. The two remained virtual strangers, only communicating through small talk and Christian pieties. James was never comfortable enough with him to ask him questions about his past, which his father never mentioned of his own accord. The result was that his father's life was largely a mystery to him.

Although his father had greeted him like "the prodigal son" upon the son's arrival in Texas, he seems to have retreated quickly into a stiff, stodgy ministerial role that kept his son at a perpetual, uncomfortable distance. In later years, James was to display an awkward timidity whenever he attempted to move beyond polite formalities with others: a simple question about someone's personal life would be invariably prefaced with a nervous disclaimer: "Now, I don't mean to intrude or pry into your personal affairs, but . . . " It was as if James were accustomed to being put on a leash, or kept at arm's length.

The elder James was never disposed to give him any direct Biblical guidance. When the fledgling convert was first introduced to his father's congregation, as "the son of the Reverend James," he had been invited to extemporaneously explain his beliefs, without any preparation. His later requests for theological explanations as he studied the Bible were always brushed aside: "If you get it you shall, if you won't, you won't," the father would tell him.

James' native intelligence enabled him to make seemingly astute observations at his father's weekly "ministerial alliances and councils," where he sat admist "all those high-faluted mens of deep profundity." He recalled: "Sometimes I could speak some things that would paralyze their minds, and they'd have to listen: 'Oh, Doctor James, that your son?' 'Where he get those ideas?' "

He would liken his eventual accomplishments as a preacher to his musical success. "In my ministerial life and ministerial career I have been a magic to a lots of people, just like I am in the blues and music world. When I would get up to preach, I didn't think about the degrees that those big high-faluted preachers may have had. I just thought about my little bit." The subject of his first sermon, a homily from Joshua 6 and 14 he presented at his father's church, was: "If it seems evil unto you to serve the Lord, choose you this day who you will serve." He recalled: "My discussion and my topic was: 'Have you decided?' It scared a few people, I think." But it is difficult to imagine the soft-spoken James becoming a frightening Fundamentalist, or becoming the aggressive, take-charge figure who was E.D. James, a Baptist bulldog who would confront his congregation with the statement: "I've chewed up and spit out this Bible more times than you can think of."

Spouting Scripture was indispensable to his father's success, because the Baptist church, for all its rigid Fundamentalism, had no express doctrine beyond its baptismal formulas. Its policies were set by local churches, which were responsible to no governing authority; the ultimate appeal of the Baptist minister was to the Bible.

The Reverend E.D. James was an iconoclastic figure for his age in his emphasis on Scriptural study. Most Southern Baptist ministers of the early twentieth century had no formal credentials; they responded to a self-assumed "call to preach." In James' environment, there was outright prejudice against a minister who aspired to study, which was considered a weak substitute for flamboyant faith. As a spiritual of the times put it:

> There's another class of preachers that's high and sweet
> They had to go to college to learn how to preach . . .
>
> That kind of a man, he's hard to convince
> A man can't preach unless'n he's 'sent.'
> (Washington Phillips: *Denomination Train*, 1927)

Largely because of its uneducated character, the Baptist church became basically a Southern sect, after taking root in the New England colonies. The half-educated convert who was Skip James would himself refer disparagingly to "this here grandiloquentism, this here bombastic language" that the educated preacher emitted: "they use all those high-falutedism words and so forth, and people can't understand it." At the same time, he was cowed both by his father's learnedness, which he obviously attempted to mimic, as well as his outward rectitude: he never saw him smoke or drink.

All of the arrogant confidence that James projected when referring to other people (whom he considered "nothin' but meat") was to perceptibly diminish when he mentioned his father, who seems to have infected him with tentativeness. The marked tentativeness he was to display as a blues singer in the 1960s almost certainly had its origins in his dealings with his formidable father, whose memory remained alive throughout his resurrection as a blues player. Having a forceful and dogmatic father as a ministerial role model must have also made it virtually impossible for James to acquire much assurance on the pulpit.

Whatever its causes, his general theological slant was far too equivocal to translate into effective preaching. In an age of hard-sell Biblical bluster, James took a soft-sell approach: ". . . Don't you believe everything Skip say," he was to counsel a listener in the 1960s. "You study some and look some and use your decision about a lot of things. I don't believe everything I hear anybody say, regardless to who it is. I believe some portion of it, and then fathom the rest out. Now I tell 'em that when I preach: 'Now you can fall in line with me if you want to, but do as you please. Because it's mine and I'm not going to try to persuade you. Now you can consent to the truth if you hear it. And if I speak it. '" This contemplative matter-of-factness would not have played well on any Fundamentalist pulpit.

But in part, James' moderate ministerial style reflected the moderate nature of his conversion. Because no dramatic event or inner reflection had turned his thoughts to God, and caused him to renounce his past life, he had no stirring epiphany to serve up to an audience. His religious rhetoric was tempered by the fact that he had never fully vanquished temptation. His conversion was firm only in principle: although he never said so, it was obvious that he felt a strong tug towards his former life. One night in 1932, for example, he sneaked out of his father's house, driving the latter's Buick to a barrelhouse. As he played piano, he noticed a tough character standing behind him. The man told him that he did not want to see James flirting with his girlfriend Eunice, whom James had taken to be a "good gambler." James retreated from the hostilities, but made it a point to return for a one-night stand with her.

Between 1932 and 1935 he appears to have oscillated between the church and the pool hall: he worked both as a fledging minister in the Dallas suburb of Plano, under his father's wing, and as a pool shark in Dallas and Fort Worth. For a time he was even supported in Dallas by a prostitute named Willie. He also worked as a tomato picker in Plano, an onion picker in Sulphur Springs, and, when all else failed, as a bread line recipient.

His backsliding gave him the typical Baptist fascination with the Church of God in Christ, the late nineteenth-century upstart sect whose members believed that upon receiving communion with the Holy Spirit they would no longer sin:

> Now the Holiness people, when they came in
> They said: "Boys we can make it by livin' above
>   sin."

> *(Denomination Blues)*

To James, and other Baptists, these "sancts" (as he called members of the sanctified sects) were getting away with something. "They pretend to live above those things, and not to be tempted. But they'll lie," he said of them. "Yes, they do. Yeah, 'cause when I've tried it out on them, I know some of them very sancts that was dancin' by that sanctified music come and danced by some of my blues music."

Abstractly, he bore the typical Baptist view of mankind as a sin-blackened creature. "You born in sin and shaped in iniquity," he said. The idea that one could live "above sin" struck him as the ultimate blasphemy. "If you're livin' free from sin and above sin, what you got to ask God for? Huh?" he asked in later years. "You don't need His assistance, because you gonna be equalized with Him."

James' view of sin was equally extreme as that of Holiness members, but ran in the opposite direction: sin was not only inescapable, but omnipresent. "Onliest way that you'll live free from sin is when you're ready to leave here," he said. "For the few moments or seconds that you're leavin' here, you may be free from sin, because your mind ain't on nothin' else. Nothin' can contaminate you or confuse your mind . . . "

Yet for all of his hypothetical saturation in sin, James did not have the slightest understanding of what sin amounted to, in conventional Christian terms. The reason sin so readily contaminated people, he reasoned, was because it was imposed from without. "You can't think righteousness always because of the environments around; the atmosphere is poison with sin. And it's impossible for a person to live holy and righteous in this sinful world." This conclusion, no doubt, presented him with a ready rationalization to do much as he pleased in life, while maintaining his own piety.

It is tempting to view James' lurid view of sin as a reflection of his own lowly image of himself compared to his lofty father. "The best you can do," he would maintain, "is filthy rags in the sight of the Lord." But despite this self-abasement, his own Biblical outlook bore a curious underlying resemblance to that of the "sanct." He had very little contrition, or even humility. In the 1960s he persistently regarded himself as a Godly person when, by the standards of his Baptist faith, he had no religious qualifications whatsoever, and never even attended church. It was no accident that his wife would be a "sanct" who was more tolerant of him than any Baptist mate would have been, though she did not share his claim to be "one of the best men who ever walked."

21. *Limbo*

Although James' fledging ministry may have been marked by a lack of constancy, it had none of the unsavory quality of his previous careers. In an age of opportunistic preachers who were stereotyped in blues song as womanizers and charlatans, James attempted to live up to the ideals of his calling. "Now I know there are lots of preachers just for the filthy lucre sake, and also for socializin' [sex]," he would say in the 1960s. "And when they pastor churches, the best-lookin' sisters of those member-ships is his associates and concubines. In some churches, he will not be successful unless he does socialize with some of those sisters, 'cause they have the influence by bein' secretary in the church and so forth. But I never did like that ..."

As a neophyte in the church, he appears to have done little outright blues-playing. He gave up guitar altogether, and made no reference to his musical past in the company of fellow church members. For this reason he was able to astound one of the females in his father's flock who owned a copy of *22-20 Blues*; after noticing the record on a visit to her home, he took great delight in casually duplicating it on her piano.

While studying for the ministry, he played in his father's church in Plano, worked as a church piano tuner (a skill he had learned from a man in Natchez) and repairman (primarily re-felting hammers), and sang in the choir of the church. He then became the pianist and lead singer of the Dallas Jubilee Quartet, an outfit whose bookings were arranged by the deacon of his father's church. Using his father's 1927 Buick, they appeared in Tulsa, Oklahoma City, Kansas City, and Wichita. On one occasion, he played blues in Oklahoma for a white party. Since there had recently been a racial disturbance in the vicinity, he was provided with an armed guard. He was even more impressed by the fact that a white woman hugged him after he gave a performance in a white church.

James disbanded his gospel group after about a year because its married members objected to being separated from their wives. Their domesticity caused him to snort: "There's no sense wasting holy bread on dogs."

The spiritual he most doted on during this period was his father's composition, *Sea Walking Jesus*, which was sung in a sedate style. It remained one of his favorite pieces, rendered on both piano and guitar. Although James was the most gifted blues musician of the era to become a spiritual singer, he did not create any sacred songs in the fashion of his father or Thomas A. Dorsey, the ex-blues pianist who became the accredited pioneer of what became known as "gospel" music. As a blues musician, James was among the most imaginative performers of his generation; as a spiritual singer, he was a conformist. The bold departures of another Baptist quartet, the Soul Stirrers, who were to modernize black religious singing, would remain alien to him, although they were founded in 1934 in Trinity, Texas, not far from Dallas.

It was not accidental that James' spiritual performances lacked the impassioned quality of his blues. He associated exhibitionistic religious fervor with "sancts," and his prejudices against the sanctified church were amply gratified in Texas when overzealous sisters knocked him off his piano stool as he performed *I'm So Glad Jesus Followed Me* at a church function.

The sedate, bridled quality that was to permeate his religious performances was to similarly permeate his presentation of secular music. It is significant that his single blues guitar acquisition of the early 1930s, a version of Joe Pullum's 1934 hit *Black Gal What Makes Your Head So Hard?* which he transposed from piano to guitar, was slow and bland almost to the point of insipidness. Unless his original performance of the piece differed markedly from its 1960s versions (on both guitar and piano), this tune represented a musical turning point for James, providing the earliest inkling of the ordinary blues singer he was destined to become in the 1960s.

Just as any of his peers might have done, James had latched onto a tune for its popularity as a request piece, without doing anything to alter or improve it. Thanks to his church connection, he was plainly seeking the maximum return for his episodic sinful excursions, and determined to make them as effortless as possible. His days as a blues composer or striking rearranger were behind him, and his music was to become progressively tame, civilized and spiritless. He had sold his soul to the church.

A genteel style of delivery was appropriate for *Stormy Weather*, the popular ballad James probably began performing on piano not long after its appearance in 1933, when it was introduced by Ethel Waters at the Cotton Club, as well as *Lazybones*, another 1933 hit he played for whites. However, the subdued tenor of *Black Gal*, which was to become his basic mien of the 1960s, was not suitable for most of his own songs. Churchification and its consequences were to completely cripple him as a pianist, even as he was able to play that instrument with more regularity than he had in the 1920s. The full-sounding, chordal accompaniments that marked his gospel tunes became instrinsic to his piano-playing to such an extent that by the 1960s he was unable to even suggest his once powerful Paramount percussiveness, or play any arresting single note runs. It was James' anemia as a pianist that would lead Johnnie Temple, after listening to one of his piano recreations on a 1960s album, to remark: "If he had one of them old raggety pianos he could play that thing; one of them old barrelhouse pianos. See, that's a baby grand he foolin' with there . . . and he got tangled up on that. But if he had one of them old raggety pianos with about eleven keys on it — heh, heh, heh!"

Temple himself was to become one of the leading exponents of the insipid blues that enjoyed a commercial stranglehold on the "race" market of the mid-1930s. Lacking an expressive voice and an impressive vocal range, he learned to adopt the low-key delivery of Big Bill Broonzy, whose similar vocal deficiencies led him to pioneer the Chicago mode of blues presentation.

His fortunes arose less through musical ability than through his contacts. Among the various Jackson artists to whom he attached himself were two of Mississippi's most opportunistic blues-players, Charlie and Joe McCoy. Originally from Bolton, the pair had moved to Jackson around 1918, there learning to play musical instruments. "They didn't like to work in no fields," Sam Chatmon recalled. Joe, a mediocre singer and guitar player with a reputation for surliness, lacked the ability to perform as a soloist: "He's just a back-up," Sam said, "he couldn't play no blues." In the late 1920s he would latch on to Memphis Minnie, an established blues singer who had previously consorted with his brother, serving as her back-up player. His vicious treatment of her became legendary in blues circles; even James, who rarely concerned himself with other singers, reported: "I heard that he was on the jealous order and he used to beat her up pretty bad." If a man gave her a 25 or 50¢ tip, Robert Wilkins recalled, McCoy would accuse her of flirting with him, and begin abusing her physically. "He didn't want her to look at another man," Wilkins said. "That's why she got rid of him." It was probably the eventual loss of this gravy train that led McCoy to move to Chicago in the early 1930s. There he became an adjunct of his more talented brother, whose assortment of pop and ethnic tunes found a ready saloon audience in white neighborhoods. In search of a vocalist, apparently, they persuaded Temple to join them in 1935.

Their 1934 Decca recording of *Devil Got My Woman, Evil Devil Woman Blues*, was one of their earliest Chicago recording efforts. It was not released until 1940, and James was never to hear the record (or meet either McCoy). The banal ditty that the McCoys managed to make of it demonstrated how much the success of the song was due to its arrangement by James, rather than its intrinsic musical properties. While the song consisted of the same basic musical ingredients as *Devil Got My Woman*, it occupied a separate musical world, in much the same way that *I'm So Glad* and *So Tired* did. Their 11-bar treatment (consisting of two unvaried and identical phrases, each 5 ½ bars) was largely an attempt to supply the song with polish and smoothness — and, in the process, provide it with potential white audience currency. Although the melody (sung by Joe in a bland tenor) began with the same dominant James had deployed as a crescendo in the third verse of his record, it had an altogether placid feel, thanks to its treatment of tones, and its emphasis on the dominant, which was used as a phrase-ending cadence. It also had a pronounced rhythmic pulse that James' song did not, maintaining a steady 1̲-2 square dance pattern until the third (1̲-2-3-4̲) vocal bar, which was altered to end on a strong beat.

Although the McCoys' version is virtually a translation into white melody-making on its most insipid level, by most contemporary standards (including, no doubt, their own) the bleached product marked an improvement on its predecessor, modifying its quirks to produce the blues equivalent of "easy listening." In this instance, the predecessor was no doubt Johnnie Temple's version, which Joe McCoy had probably lifted without even knowing about James' original.

In keeping with the Chicago blues of the period, he attempted to convert *Devil* into a full-blown theme. The result was a classic specimen of forced blues lyricism:

> I'd rather be the devil, oh rather be the devil,
> Be that woman's man.
> Aw, she was evil, oh she was evil,
> Wouldn't work hand in hand; hand in hand.

> Oh, she's all right now, oh she's all right now
> She's all right with me; all right with me.
> But the devil is evil, oh devil is evil; as he can be . . .

> I tried to be, oh tried to be,
> Tried to treat you nice and kind
> Oh she was evil, oh she was evil, would not change
>   her mind.

> I'd give you my money, oh give my money
> To buy your shoe and clothes
> But you was evil, you was evil, kicked me out of doors.

> But that's all right baby, that's all right baby
> It's comin' home to you; home to you.
> I tried to be, oh tried to be, tried to be a man to you.

The conniving McCoy did not make for a convincing victim, and did not even sound as though he had convinced himself that he had undergone an ordeal of any sort.

Temple's debut session, occurring in Chicago nine months later, illustrated his original position as a James understudy, as well as affirming his teacher's dim assessment of his musical talents. His contemporary version of *Cypress Grove* remained un-issued, and remains inaccessible; his version of *Devil, The Evil Devil Blues*, was remarkably inept, considering the six years he had to refine it. Rendering the song in 9-bar stanzas (each consisting of two identical 4 1/2-bar phrases), Temple painstakingly copied James' melodic line, including his falsetto crescendos and his phrase-doubling extensions. That its awkward phrasing thwarted him is indicated by his meager accompaniment, a single C7 riff in standard tuning played against Charlie McCoy's lead guitar (which was miked less prominently). Even with this easy instrumental surface to glide along, Temple's vocal delivery was rhythmically erratic; to mask his weak singing, apparently, he rendered the song at twice the tempo of the original, which made its timing more precarious.

Temple had obviously taken up a tune that was designed for an accomplished singer (and should have thus had no appeal to him) in the interests of impressing other Jackson musicians (like the McCoys) with an unusual offering. This effort is indicative of James' obscurity to Jackson audiences: had the two tunes he recorded been locally associated with James, Temple (in the interests of garnishing prestige for himself) would doubt-less have passed them by, as he did with the well-known staples of another mentor, Tommy Johnson. His 1935 recording of *Devil* doubtless indicated his knowledge that James was no longer a fixture on the Jackson blues circuit, where unfavorable comparisons between himself and his mentor might occur.

Ironically, Temple did more than James to foster perform-ances of the latter's theme song. Even before James had aban-doned his career, Temple had apparently been a conduit be-tween James and Robert Johnson. In 1931 he had worked with a hoboing bluesman from Hattiesburg who introduced himself only as "R.L." Five years later, "R.L." would record as Robert

Johnson, and eventually become a blues and rock icon, leaving a storied legend that was made possible by his early murder, and subsequent historical remoteness. One of Johnson's last recordings was a version of *Devil Got My Woman* he likely acquired from Temple. Recast as *Hellhound On My Trail* and issued as the "B" side of *Four Until Late* in August, 1937, it became central to his formidable but fanciful literary legend. When blues writers would create the lurid image of the dogged, doomed singer who was to be poisoned the following year for indiscreetly taking up with a barrelhouse owner's wife, they were largely inspired by the text of *Hellhound On My Trail.*

Johnson was a musical dramatist much in the mode of James, his dramatics consisting largely of lyrics that came across as urgent proclamations. Autobiographical or not, the subject matter of *Hellhound* was likely an attempt to complement the "devil" theme of the James song. Johnson's accompaniment, performed with a bottleneck in open E major tuning, is so sketchy as to indicate that he had acquired it early in his career, discarded it in favor of other pieces, and resurrected it in the interests of prolonging his recording session. (It was the twentieth of twenty-nine pieces he recorded.) Its title verse amounted to 16 $3/4$ bars, with two eccentric thirteen-beat vocal phrases paired with another of fifteen beats. Despite its vocal nasality and lurching rhythmic quality, *Hellhound On My Trail* has a striking sound, partly because Johnson (unlike his ordinary practice) sang in full voice, while completing vocal lines with conversation:

> I got to keep movin' . . . blues fallin' down like hail
> "Blues fallin' down like hail."
> Mmmm, blues fallin' down like hail
> An' the day keeps on 'mind me, there's a hellhound
>   on my trail
> "Hellhound on my trail . . . hellhound on my trail."

Johnson must have esteemed James' records, for he never copied a similarly unsuccessful recording artist. His *32-20 Blues* (released in February, 1937) was a vocal and lyrical reprise of *22-20*, set to guitar and basically phrased in twelve bars. Owing to its rapid tempo and relatively clipped phrasing, it contained ten verses, six of which (including the first four) were copied almost

verbatim from James' original. Such wholesale lifting of lyrics
was extremely rare in blues.

Although the source of *32-20* was plainly James' record, and
the source of *Hellhound* was probably Johnnie Temple, it is altogether possible that Johnson had some incidental encounter
with James when he was associating with Temple some five years
before his recording session. Any hoboing musician who struck
out north from Jackson (as "R.L." would do when he customarily
left the city, bound for Saturday night engagements in Sun-
flower) could readily reach Bentonia. In this fashion the Louisiana bluesman Joe Holmes (who was to record as "King Solomon Hill" in 1932) had encountered James in the late 1920s
during a hoboing jaunt from Jackson to Memphis. According
to his traveling partner John Willis, they spent two or three
nights playing at "house frolics" around Bentonia, where Holmes had impulsively disembarked in search of a musical outlet.
Such random encounters were routine in blues, and generally
of no significance, unless in the process a performer added
something to his repertoire.

The tangible results of Johnson's exposure (whatever form
it took) to James were less interesting than the less tangible
resemblances between them. Like James, Johnson would largely
disdain dance music, setting only two of his songs to a discernable dance pulse. He would also grope for climactic touches
that were alien to blues-playing, beyond James' sphere; his sudden four-bar falsetto surge in *Kind-Hearted Woman* had a distinct
Jamesian ring of crescendo. James would have applauded the
humorless, ungenerous spirit that generally guided Johnson:

> If I had possession over judgment day
> The woman that I'm lovin' wouldn't have no right to pray.

But James never heard of Johnson, and was unaware that the
singer had recorded renditions of two of his songs. When the
author attempted to play Johnson's songs for him in the 1960s
he declined to listen. In his world, far removed from the fancies
of blues fans, Johnson was a rank nonentity. Similarly, he did
not care to listen to Joe McCoy's version of *Devil*. It was Johnnie
Temple who had cut a prestigious blues figure in James' day,
and Temple's 1939 band version of *Devil* (which he always called

"Devil Number Two") that aroused his competitive ire. "He put out 'Devil Number Two,'" James said. "But his *Devil* was so much different, it didn't take so well with the public." When James would make murderous pronouncements about the city of Chicago, which he regarded as the citadel of evil, he was likely assessing that city as Temple's springboard to success. For while he had only a fleeting acquaintance with Chicago from a 1920s visit, its very existence rankled him. "Chicago should be wiped off the map," he once said in the 1960s.

The enshrinement of blasé singers like Temple was largely due to the calculations of record producers like Decca's Mayo Williams. Instead of seeking a new blues brew or reacting to a perceived shift in audience tastes, Williams was merely perpetuating his decade-old notions of what made for blues hits. As a Paramount producer from 1923-1928, he had put a premium on lyrics, considering the sound of the singer to be largely irrelevant to consumers. The surprise success of Blind Lemon Jefferson had thrown record companies of the late 1920s into a largely futile search for Southern singer-guitarists who might approximate his success, and it was this attempt that had briefly enfranchised musicians like Skip James. When the 1930s arrived, it was back to business as usual, with a new cast of characters. As the black vaudeville houses from which the ranks of Bessie Smith and Ma Rainey had been plucked in the early 1920s were no longer in existence, the male blues singer — most often a carryover from the late 1920s — now occupied center stage. Improved recording quality made it possible for singers like Temple, who had no voice to speak of, to flourish as studio singers.

What came to be called the "Chicago blues" of the 1930s by later blues chroniclers was basically the studio blues song, as rendered by a variety of facile lyricists like Temple, Peetie Wheatstraw, and Kokomo Arnold. Their prototype had been Lonnie Johnson, who had used the same basic guitar accompaniment for dozens of 1920s recordings. The concern of these singers was simply to churn out a succession of blues rhymes on some subject with as little effort as possible. Performing the piece for live audiences was secondary. "I'd practice a song for about ten or fifteen minutes; then I'd go in and cut it . . ." Temple told Gayle Wardlow. So it was that scarcely one memorable blues melody emerged from the hundreds of Chicago and New York Decca recordings made between 1934 and 1941, let alone a striking instrumental accompaniment. The two rival companies that manufactured blues records in this period were scarcely better.

By Temple's lights, he achieved a professionalism lacking in artists like James. Whereas Temple became a mainstay of the newly formed Decca label, James became a kind of footnote in its recording ledger. In 1935, the company included his *If You Haven't Any Hay* among some fifteen titles it purchased from the dormant Paramount label (perhaps through an intermediary, Gennett). Reissued on a subsidiary (the Champion label), the record floundered, and soon the project itself was defunct.

Had Temple already established himself as a successful blues singer, James might have been more readily tempted to return to secular music in 1935, when he moved to Bentonia after his father moved from Texas to Birmingham. Henry Stuckey, who had recently returned to Satartia after running a jukehouse for three years in Morgan City (there making more money than he had in the 1920s, he said), was baffled to find his former running mate proclaiming his religiosity. When Stuckey first saw him and attempted to coax him to play at a schoolhouse birthday party, James refused on religious grounds.

"The next time I saw him, he had a guitar in his hand, playin' blues," said Stuckey, smugly mollifed by James' swift reversion. But he also recalled that James refused a recording session on religious grounds; his cousin Burnside likewise reported that he tried, without success, to get James to record during a blues session of the period. The session was apparently arranged by H.C. Speir, who was recruiting singers for the American Record Company for a session in October of 1935. Speir once related that James had refused to record anything but spirituals for this event, and was thus written off.

By 1936, James was not only performing blues and putting on "house frolics" but had resumed his old profession, bootlegging, as a tenant of R.K. Whitehead's plantation. ". . . Quite naturally I would sell a little whiskey to help myself along," he recalled, without explaining how he had reached this pass, after a period of supposedly devout church membership. "I wasn't makin' enough otherwise, and if a man had enough skill about him to help himself, any man that was 'worthwhile' wouldn't say nothin' about it—*if* you was doin' it right—'cause you wouldn't have to be runnin' to *him* for money all the time, see?" Apparently James was self-employed, but working with Whitehead's tacit approval.

That year, a revenue agent attempted to search his premises. "Somebody had reported to the law that I was sellin' whiskey, and was makin' homebrew beer," James noted. "... It was a little ol' young law, and I guess he wanted to build up his reputation or somethin'," he recalled. "But he did wrong to try to build it up offa *me*."

Knowing that state revenue agents did not have legal authority to search a tenant's premises without the consent of the owner— the planter who leased to the lowly sharecropper—James gave full play to the ever-present arrogance he ordinarily kept in check in dealing with whites. It was with great relish that he recounted their confrontation, which occurred on James' front porch.

" 'Hey, Skip!'

" 'Yap!'

" 'Skip, they tell me you're makin' whiskey and homebrew beer around here.'

"I say: '*They* tell you? Who "they" is?' I say: 'Who the hell is *they*?'

" 'Er-ruh, I got . . . a warrant for you; search your house . . .'

" 'You got a warrant for *me*? How you get a warrant for me? Where is it at? Lemme see it!'

" 'Oh well, I don't have to have one—'

" 'Damn you don't!—you *better* have one if you want to come in *here*.'

"He's standin' right out there on the bottom step of my house, and wanted to come up on the porch. I say: 'Wait a minute! Show me your warrant or your writ or whatever you got.'

" 'Well, I got the authorities to come—'

" 'No, you ain't got no authorities to come in *here*, unless'n
you show it to me. With all honor and due respects to you,
man, don't you come in here until you show me that warrant.'

" 'I guess I'll have to go back and come again . . . '

"I say: 'I don't care how many times you come back. If you
show me that you can come in here I don't object it. Now
here's my bossman sittin' right over there on the porch over
yonder. Check with him. If he tell you to use your authorities
to come in here and search this house you can do it. You
bring him with you, then. Other than that, don't you come
in here. You get the hell away from here, you understand
that?'

"I think I gave him to know that I had just what *he* had—
I had a good gun then. He never did make an attempt to draw,
though, after I talked to him like I did. I thought perhaps he
would . . . He knew I meant what I said 'cause I was lookin'
right at him just like I'm lookin' at you. And he know that if
a Negro talked with you *that* straight—with the way things and
times was down there then—you better not fool with him 'cause
you'll have to kill him or get killed.

"But I guess he didn't wanna do that . . . He . . . just figured
he would bluff me and make him some quick money off me.
And he'd-a got a quick head cut off there instead, that's right!
Or maybe *me* one. Anyway, that law turned right around and
walked on to his car and got in it."

Having called the agent's bluff, James could not resist taunting
him in his own fashion. "I say: 'There's my bossman sittin' on
by the porch—don't you see him? You be sure to go on by and
speak to him when you leave.' "

Needless to say, James knew that the lawman wanted no part
of the planter. "When the bossman did come out, took him
a notion to go to town," James recalled, "I stopped him and
told him about it. He say: 'Who was that over there, Nehemiah?'
He called me by my *real* name.

" 'That was a little old cop, little old law you-all got up there,
and he couldn't show me authorities to search my house. I told
him: "Now you go over and see Mister Whitehead—" '

"He looked at me and smiled. 'What did he say?'"

"I say: 'He ain't said nothin'—just left. He didn't come out to see you, did he?'

"He say: 'No. But *I'll* handle him if he comes back.'"

This episode fairly delineates James' ideal relationship with the white planter: as colleagues in illegal collusion, with James enjoying the refracted power of the white aristocrat. Although it was this relationship, and the primacy of the planter in the Mississippi scheme of things, that enabled James to lord it over a lowly white, he credited himself with displaying a fortitude lacked by other Negroes. ". . . If I had been one of them there tremblified and scared Negroes, like some of them, he'd of just walked right on in by me, and did anything he wanna," he said of the revenue agent.

But despite his secure position as Whitehead's personal pet, James could not maintain his comeback as an exalted form of local lowlife. He was likely defeated by both a bad conscience and bad commerce; in the late 1930s, he would have been hard-pressed to make much of a living from music, given the condition of the national economy, which was still devastated by the Depression. In any event, around 1937, or some two years after his departure from Texas, James would move to Selma, Alabama, where his father worked as the principal of a seminary. Once again, he attended weekly minsterial councils chaired by his father, and assiduously read the Bible.

At this time, the born-again James was more akin to "Jonah in the wilderness" than to someone who had found inner content. After some four years of immersion in the Bible, he had yet to even become a minister.

The premium his father placed on education was partly responsible for this state of affairs: James could not respond to the traditional Baptist "call to preach" and begin bellowing the Bible upon "getting religion." In order for his salvation to pass muster with his father, he had to study continuously.

But studying the Bible under his father's tutelage set off a conflict in James that probably contributed to his periodic backsliding, and ultimately to his inability to find a comfortable sanctuary in either the church or the barrelhouse. It in-

volved him in an emotional tug of war between two opposing
forces: his parents.

His father was a firm Missionary Baptist; his mother, an African Methodist. The two parents never spoke to each other.
Both of them were sheltering, protective figures; his father
from a materialistic standpoint, his mother providing a ready,
rubber-stamp endorsement of himself, never holding him ac-
countable for his conduct. Once a local consort of James' had
brought an infant to her doorstep, declaring he had fathered
the baby. Phyllis James had indignantly turned the woman
away; if her son said he wasn't its father, there was nothing
more to say about the matter. To James, his father was a figure
who had deserted his martyred mother to become a "big shot"
preacher.

James' conflict of faith and family was so acute that a year
after he was finally ordained as a Baptist in Meridian, Mississippi
around 1942, he became ordained as a Methodist minister in
Hattiesburg. Moreover, it had taken him a full ten years to formally enter either camp.

Although he was to later refer to his "ministerial career," it
is apparent that James had no such career to speak of. He never
pastored a church or had any affiliation with a religious forum
that was not run by his father. He largely remained in his father's
shadow, a kept man.

The levee camp tough who had remorselessly gunned down
opponents was terrified of his tyrannical father. ". . . He was hot-
tempered. In fact, he would whup me now if he was livin', and
if I disobeyed his orders," James said in the mid-1960s. "Now
I never would sass him or cause him to get offended; if he
got angry I'd just get out of his way, that's all." He did not
see his father's lack of interest in him as a flaw in his father;
most likely, he felt that he did not merit the attention. The
only open criticism he would have for Reverend E.D. James
lay in his marriage to an elementary school teacher from Tuscaloosa: a former classmate of Joe Louis', she was some thirty
years younger than himself.

Afterwards, James was to recall it as one of the most dramatic
moments in his life. It was not the story of his emptying a bar-

relhouse with shotgun blasts, but of asking his father for change so he could buy a package of cigarettes.

The father, guessing the purpose of his request, pointedly asked him what he needed the money for.

Summoning up his nerve, James replied quietly: "I think that's my business."

He saw the look of shock on his father's face. Then, wordlessly, the father handed him some coins.

Such was James' great moment of liberation. Never having a childhood with his father, he had relived his adolesence as a middle-aged man.

Eventually the strain was too much for him. "I couldn't lead his life and mine, too," he declared, explaining his eventual drift from him.

One suspects that James never really walked in his father's footsteps, and may have been known primarily as the errant son of a highly-respected pastor, indulged on the basis of nepotism for his periodic pratfalls. While the Bible had a firm hold on his intellect, the church enjoyed no similar grip on his conduct. His divided tendencies ran so deep that in the 1960s, as a blues rediscovery, he occasionally toyed with the idea of starting up a "homebrew" business in his Philadelphia apartment. At the same time, he would ruminate about joining the church. He appeared to be in a kind of limbo, neither Christian fish nor conniving fowl, and one suspects that this ineffectuality entered his life as soon as his father had re-entered it.

22. *Resumption*

James' independence from his father was, in his rosy rhetorical view, another of his life's triumphs. "Now I coulda been styled among those great philosophers and all that stuff, if I hadda continued studyin' in Texas and in Selma," he was to recall. "But I just didn't wanna reach that stage because it was a course I didn't wanna pursue. I just wanted enough education to take care of myself. I decided in other words that I'd be a plain, common, ordinary old Skip," he would say. Such was the face James put on his failure to scale the heights like his father, who had, he noted, preached all over the country, even speaking from a pulpit in New York. He felt that the simple Skip he became was an undistinguished fellow compared to his father, "one of them big D.D. [Doctor of Divinity] preachers."

For all of its ambivalence, James' attachment to his father had managed to stalemate his musical ambitions to such an extent that he did not hazard a resumption of his blues career in Alabama. Instead, he toyed with the idea of founding a music publishing company in Birmingham, in emulation of the ill-fated enterprise Clarence Williams had begun in New York with Porter Grainger and Shelton Brooks twenty years before. A lack of capital prevented him from carrying out this plan, which would not have been a successful venture in any event. He did not even know enough about publishing to seek to dun Decca Records for its 1939 versions of *Devil* and *Cherry Ball* purveyed by Johnnie Temple, who made a blanket representation of originality. ". . . All-a my recordin', I writes my own lyrics," he was to tell Gayle Wardlow.

James's forgotten records would soon come to the attention of white jazz enthusiasts. In 1943 a 35-year-old jazz collector named John Steiner formed a record label with a friend named Hugh Davis "largely because in that period we learned that we could get an allotment of then scarce shellac. . . . " The two then set about to locate "the best jazz, blues and especially reproducible copies [of 78s] we could locate." In Richmond, Indiana, where it was reposing as the property of Decca Records, Steiner acquired a test-pressing one of James' Paramounts, *Little Cow And Calf Is Gonna Die Blues*. Its 1944 reissue on the Steiner-Davis label has been called "the first country blues to be reissued for the white collectors' market." The label, however, bore the legend: "Fine Jazz Documents," and the term "country blues" (a misnomer) had yet to be coined. The market for the self-accompanied Southern blues that would be indiscriminately labeled "country blues" was more than two decades to come, and James' title sold about 300 copies. It was so esoteric within the piano blues field that James' name was never mentioned during the then-current vogue for boogie-woogie piano that had produced the blues-derived pop hit *Cow Cow Blues* for Tommy Dorsey.

To his associates of the early 1940s he was known as "James," the surname supplanting his given name and nickname, as it had previously in Arkansas. In this period, he remained in Birmingham, working as a "surface" man, loading timber and steel to be conveyed within iron ore mines. Shortly afterwards he married the camp cook, a woman named Mabel. She had sometimes sung tunes like *The Blues Ain't Nothin' But A Good Woman Feelin' Bad* to his accompaniments; James would still not venture to sing blues himself.

What most impressed Mabel James about her husband-to-be was the gentlemanly air that was out of keeping with his coworkers, and with her previous experience of seeing blues singers, who had a habit of throwing whiskey bottles at women. James even made a formal marriage proposal to her mother.

The gentlemanly singer had grown so civilized that he was no longer disposed to kill or maim people. The P-38 he carried after the Second World War was intended largely for display purposes, and when two men began following him down a railroad track one night after he left work, James dispersed them by turning around, drawing his gun, and deliberately firing over their heads.

The onset of the United Mine Workers' strike in Birmingham in March of 1948 caused him to return to Bentonia. Although the strike was settled a month later, James never returned to the mines. Instead, he resumed his dormant musical career in his hometown.

James' belated return to blues was surprisingly ill-timed, given the small prospects of success a solo blues career now held. The population of Mississippi plantations, and with it, the potential audience for local performers, had diminished drastically during his years away from the blues scene. Between 1940 and 1950, the state would lose a quarter of its black population, including Muddy Waters and Son House. Since the Depression, the Mississippi audience for blues had been steadily shrinking, thanks originally to the Agricultural Adjustment Act of 1934, which rewarded planters for letting their fields lie fallow and thus decreasing the oversupply of cotton. The need for manual laborers had further diminished due to the mechanical cottonpicker, developed by John Rust. This mid-1930s innovation had been designed with a view towards improving the lot of the plantation worker; after being employed on Cooperative Farms, a Delta plantation whose trustees included Reinhold Niebuhr, it was approvingly noted in a Delta newspaper that the picker would result in "shortening of working hours and the elimination of children from the cotton field . . . " What actually happened was something far different: human labor was all but displaced. A two-row picking machine driven by a single laborer could scoop 3200 pounds of cotton a day: a black field hand could pick 200 pounds a day, and was prone to fatten his load with debris.

Musical mechanization, in turn, eroded the live blues market. Since the mid-1930s, the once-pervasive jukehouse culture of Mississippi had begun to give way to the jukebox, which all but replaced live performers. By 1942, the blues singer of James' ilk had seemed so passé that his discoverer H.C. Speir had quit the music business, "believing it was gone forever."

It was in this inhospital climate that James once again became a blues singer. He was probably tempted to do so by the recent success of Muddy Waters, a Delta emigré gone to Chicago who had gained a modest hit with *Country Blues*, recorded a month after the United Mine Workers' strike began. James no doubt heard Waters' records; he also seems to have met Waters early on in his comeback. When Waters was to arrive at the 1964 Newport Folk Festival in a car, James immediately recognized him, strode over to him and introduced himself. In return, Waters gave him a pop-eyed look of unpleasant surprise, and hastily drove off. What had formerly transpired between them in Mississippi is anyone's guess.

Another impetus to James' comeback was the continuation of a blues market in Bentonia, a likely consequence of its still flourishing bootlegging industry. A cousin of Henry Stuckey, Burd Slader, was performing locally à la Muddy Waters with an amplified guitar, and James periodically performed with Slader, as well as another neophyte named "Son" Banks. He considered Slader a better musician than Henry Stuckey, who had returned from a sojourn in Nebraska and once again became his basic duet partner. For a time the two veterans played for Saturday night parties thrown by Slader, who had originally learned guitar from them.

James also played for Bentonia frolics sponsored by a local sharecropper and bootlegger, Jack Owens. "First time I saw him he was with Adam Slader playin'," Owens was to recall. "That was Burd Slader's brother." Along with Owens and two other forgotten Bentonians, they were to perform blues as a means of raising money to rebuild the Old Liberty Church, a still-standing Baptist institution. James' erratic religious pretenses struck Owens as essentially humorous: "He try to be a preacher once," he laughingly told Edd Hurt. "Take the guitar this week an' preach the next week." He claimed that James even played secular music in church: "He didn't care what he doin' . . . He'd just soon go in church an' play a reel [secular song] . . ."

Owens himself would become the unwitting bearer of another set of false pretenses—the idea that he, James, and other undocumented local blues musicians represented a "Bentonia school" of blues playing. When James knew him, he was little more than a putterer with rudimentary picking ability that would be enshrined almost twenty years later in his debut recordings of 1966. Inspired by James' northern celebrity, he continued honing his skills, displaying more verve than James was able to muster in his post-1964 concert career. Instead of being appreciated in his own right, Owens would subsequently enjoy a curious (and still continuing) celebrity as the bearer of an illusory Bentonia blues "tradition."

But Owens had never worked as a professional blues musician; he was a sharecropper who spent most of his life in and around Bentonia, whose retinue of local musicians, he maintained, generally played in standard tuning, or what he called "straight natural on the guitar." The "tradition" he bore primarily consisted of musical scraps from James' table in the form of such pieces as *Devil*, which he conventionalized and converted into a heavy-textured plantation blues. The most interesting resemblence between them was not musical (Owens could not follow his voice fluently with melodic guitar figures), but lay in their odd blue eyes, which (if Owens is correct) denoted no familial relationship.

It was from the example of derivative amateurs like Owens —often, the surviving dregs of a defunct musical culture—that blues scribes were to develop the pet notion that blues-playing of the 1920s had a provincial cast. As one commentator put it: "Originally the lack of communications and isolation of rural communities in the South had fostered various musical styles, each peculiar to a particular region or locality."* But the turn-of-the-century South was far less provincial and isolated than would appear to latter-day researchers, who would only visit its various towns after the railway networks that formerly linked virtually every Southern hamlet had been destroyed.

To white Southerners of the railroad era, the idea that black music reflected local styles would have seemed absurd; of blacks in general, the Mississippi planter Alfred Holt Stone wrote in 1902: "They have been wanderers since emancipation ... the plantation Negro changes his residence far too often for his

*Mike Rowe, *Chicago Breakdown* (Eddison Press Ltd., London, 1977), p. 11.

children to form local attachments or to develop anything akin to such a sentiment."* To *arrivistes* of the post-blues era, Bentonia would take on an isolated cast it had only begun to assume in 1933, when the Yazoo and Mississippi Valley Railroad ended its fifty-year run of passenger service. The early repertoire of James and other bluesmen of his generation attested to the wholesale saturation of the South with the same collection of songs, borne by itinerant musicians who had obviously exploited the enormous empire of the railroad, and in the process made traveling the single most commonplace subject of the blues couplet.

Except for its lyrics, the teenage James effort that was *Sliding Delta* bore no significant difference from its later recordings (under various names) by a host of musicians, including New Orleans' Papa Charlie Jackson, Memphis' Frank Stokes, and South Carolina's Simmie Dooley. Similarly, "rag" songs like *Make Me A Pallet On The Floor* were known throughout the South, never associated with any particular region or even state. *Coonjine*, James' original piano piece, had likewise been Little Brother Montgomery's earliest effort, forged in Louisiana: "Most kids learning how to play piano at that time learned that song because it only takes two or three fingers to play it," Montgomery was to recall. "I was playing *Coon Giant Baby* in 1910 when I was four years old." In Jackson, both Ishmon Bracey and Tommy Johnson rendered the same song on guitar.

Rather than reflect the original conditions of the blues environment, intimations of individuality and local imitations of particular stylized musicians were a belated blues development. It was likely only with the development of blues fingerpicking that the guitar songs of Southern blacks became specialized, and their techniques distinguishable.

At the same time, the repertoires of blues singers began to show the same individuality, or semi-individuality. Instead of learning songs from wayfarers in the fashion of the previous generation that had given universal coin to the likes of *Sliding Delta*, the performers of the 1920s appeared to latch on to free-

*Stone, *Studies In The American Race Problem* (Doubleday, New York, 1908), p. 142.

floating lyrics. Though James never owned a phonograph, one would find couplets on his Paramounts that had been sung on contemporary records by performers from South Carolina, Texas, and Georgia he could not possibly have met:

> I lay down last night an' tried to take my rest
> But my mind started ramblin' like a wild geese in the
>   West.
>
> (Ramblin' Thomas: *Ramblin' Blues,* 1928)

> Well I took this brownskin woman, from my best friend
> And that rascal got lucky an' stole her back again.
>
> (Pink Anderson and Simmie Dooley:
> *Every Day In The Week Blues,* 1928)

The lack of anything resembling regionality in James' blues lyrics indicates the likelihood that his accompaniments were not products of some local musical commune. Had Jack Owens been a professional musician in James' heyday, which was the heyday of the railroad, his music would have been too diverse to pidgeonhole in terms of a local style. As it was, the James he remembered was not the professional of his former days, but the sedentary semi-professional he had become in the 1940s. "He made a crop, ploughin' and hoein'," he said of James.

Impatient with the small pickings available in the Bentonia area, which were netting Owens sums of five and six dollars on Saturday nights, Henry Stuckey advised James to move to Omaha and work in a band with him. "Man, I ain't doin' nothin' but fishin' and sportin' and golfin'," he told James, in an attempt to tout his recent locale, where he had relatives.

Instead James' market remained delineated by local parties given by the likes of Owens, Burd Slader, and his own cousin Buddy Polk, who ran a jukehouse. Sometimes he traveled to Yazoo City with Stuckey. In a Moorhead jukehouse they visited in 1950 the pair encountered another aging blues singer, Kid Bailey, who had recorded two obscure sides in 1929 and was probably the Delta's only remaining pre-Depression blues holdover. Traveling with Stuckey gave him the luxury of dispensing with his wife's company, for she shrank from Stuckey's presence:

"He had a deep, beautiful voice," she recalled, "but he was so ugly I didn't like him."

After James' mother died in February of 1950 he briefly returned to Birmingham, where he saw his father for the last time. Soon he was back in Bentonia. It is apparent that the death of his mother deprived him of his former status with R.K. Whitehead, for James was no longer attached to the latter's plantation. For a while he cut timber; for eight or ten months, he worked as a tractor driver on Sonny Hart's plantation in Satartia, as his wife toiled as a cook. His next job was a joint farming stint with his cousin Buddy Polk, on Leon Hancock's plantation.

James once claimed that a dispute with Hancock terminated his stay in Yazoo County. Polk, who had borrowed $500 from a Yazoo City bank in order to establish James as a renter who would furnish his own farm equipment and supplies, would offer another story. Later, James would term Polk's claim that he had been fleeced of his cotton crop by the blues singer a "damned lie." His eagerness to put distance between himself and Bentonia spoke for itself; once he left the town, around 1953, he never returned. It is doubtful that he was referring to local racism when he proclaimed, in the 1960s: "I wouldn't play in Bentonia for a hundred dollars a minute."

23. *Recognition*

It was during the period when James was evidently determined to vanish that he became an object of curiosity and, in time, a cult figure to record collectors. The wonder is that it took two decades for his legend to take hold.

Although there is nothing intrinsically esoteric about a blues singer accompanying himself with a guitar, the self-accompanied blues genre was only belatedly discovered in the North, thanks to the tunnel vision of the earliest patrons of black music. These were devotees of jazz music, already so numerous in 1933 that the vice president and general manager of Decca Records, E.R. Lewis, would state in a trade publication: "Another market [for race records] exists among the group of record collectors . . . You will find among these collectors those who are very much taken with negro band music which they describe as 'primitive' and which are equivalent to what appeals to the college group under the less elegant expresion, 'hot music.' " That very year, Leadbelly had begun a career as a New York concert entertainer, following his prison discovery by John Lomax. Leadbelly was a plantation product whose music unfailingly bore a heavy dance beat. Although his style of musicianship was basically conventional for a blues artist, he was presented as a unique, singular specimen of black "folk" music, occupying his solitary niche as America's black guitarist-in-residence for the next seventeen years.

The purchase of the American Record Company by Columbia Records in 1938 brought the work of Robert Johnson to the attention of its resident jazz enthusiast, John Hammond. When his attempts to locate Johnson for a 1938 Carnegie Hall concert proved fruitless (the artist having been recently murdered), he

played two of Johnson's records for his audience. Hammond
acquired what amounted to a fetish for Johnson; he never bothered to promote other blues singers on Columbia.* Guitar blues
remained such an obscure genre that when Elvis Presley suddenly emerged in 1956 as America's most popular entertainer,
none of the commentators who wrote about his music appeared
to know that he had based his debut record on a 1946 Arthur
Crudup recording, the fact that Crudup had continued to record
for the RCA Victor label through 1951 notwithstanding.

The obscurity of individual blues performers was largely attributable to the prevailing perception of blues as being simply
an expression of racial feeling. This idea relegated all thoughts
concerning the characteristics and quality of individual blues
performances to a non-sequitur, and made all singers of blues
seem interchangeable. The jazz writers and folklorists who
turned their attention to blues invariably fostered this notion
of blues as a kind of non-entertainment; as the earliest American
jazz study put it in 1940: "In song, the Negro expressed his
true feelings, his hopes, aspirations and ideals . . ."** As late as
1960, a folklorist, Alan Lomax, would sound this patronizing
note in a preposterous explanation of the evolution of blues:

> Around the turn of the century, when the Negro
> began to be absorbed into American society . . . he
> began to wail the blues . . . what the Negro felt when,
> in the first years of the twentieth century he was
> pushed off the land, set adrift as a casual wage-hand,
> losing his family and village roots and learning to
> live as a lonely, predatory male, all Americans began
> to understand during the depression and feel even
> more deeply today in this day of social breakdown.***

*It was probably Johnson's truncated guitar boogie that appealed to Hammond,
who presented boogie-woogie pianists like Pete Johnson and Meade Lux Lewis
at the same concert. Likewise, Leadbelly began trafficking in "walking bass"
figures, to the extent that they became almost obligatory in his accompaniments.

**_Jazzmen_, edited by Frederick Ramsey, Junior (Harcourt Brace, New York),
p. 104.

***Notes to _Roots Of The Blues_, Atlantic 1348. It was at the turn of the century
that the "absorbed" Negro became subject to Jim Crow laws.

So long as blues were perceived in this fashion, they were at best a dreary social or racial document, and not a medium of art or entertainment. The idea that blues represented the "feeling" of "the Negro" went hand in hand with the idea that blues music expressed ingrained racial characteristics. So it was that Lomax, in 1960, would write speciously of the "African rhythms in the blues."

With blues viewed as a generic racial product, there was no point in evaluating the merit of any given blues performance. One blues was as African as the next.

It was the 78 RPM record collectors who first applied artistic standards of any sort to blues music, and impressed the notion of blues as an art form. The reason for this attitude lay in their relationship to the records: the latter were merchandise to be bought, or items to be owned. Since the records were hard to come by, collectors would only invest energy (and money) in those that were thought to justify the effort.

Yet as their enthusiasm for the music spread, the aesthetic values of collectors did not. As blues gained a more substantial following in the 1960s, it would be rhetorically lionized as art, but appreciated as entertainment. In this respect, blues acquired the same type of audience as rock music and contemporary "folk" music, whereby earnestness was equated with ability. Paradoxically, the authors of critical tomes on blues music would rarely have a bad word to say about a blues performance, a blues song, or blues singer. To hear a blues singer disparaged for a lack of talent it would be necessary to listen to another blues singer.

The first person to concern himself with the actual merits of Southern guitar and piano blues and to approach the singers as individuals was an eccentric, solitary jazz collector living in a Brooklyn YMCA, James McKune. McKune seems to have begun fancying blues and gospel records around 1944. The records he was able to acquire were primarily cast-offs from jazz collections, regarded as worthless by everyone but himself and three or four fellow enthusiasts. In 1951, he was able to sell a copy of *22-20* to one of his confreres for twenty cents.

McKune's pretenses set the tone for early blues record collectors. With nothing to guide him but crude gut reaction, he affected the role of connoisseur, instinctively able to discern blues classics from dross. A great record was a record that McKune liked. A mediocre record was a record he didn't like.

In essence, McKune and his fellow record collectors were like wine sniffers. It was not only the vintage of the product that arrested them, but its rarity. Although blues record collectors universally claimed to approach the form on sheer aesthetic grounds, none of them venerated records that were easy to come by, and thus lacking in value as items to trade or sell. The surpassing vocals of Blind Lemon Jefferson, who was avidly (but not artfully) copied by the same bluesmen they collected, held no charm for them: his works had been best-sellers. Aside from the tangible rarity of a record, its appeal to early collectors was a matter of ineffable taste. McKune happened to like James' brand of blues-playing almost as much as Charlie Patton's, and his tastes were assimilated by other collectors. It was his early disciple Pete Whelan (a collector since 1954) who would promote the gospel of what became known as country blues via the Origin Jazz Library, the first reissue label to feature a running series of obscure Southern guitar blues. Instead of becoming an influential figure as his idiosyncratic tastes congealed into a form of classicism, however, McKune rapidly became a forlorn, irrelevant figure. By 1965, he was a semi-derelict who could be seen wandering about the lower East Side, sockless and seemingly brain-damaged from alcohol. When he was murdered in 1971 by a man he had apparently picked up on the street for a homosexual encounter, his name was completely unknown to contemporary fans of Skip James and Charlie Patton.

Although the ranks of blues collectors expanded steadily in the 1950s, the records they collected were still all but unknown beyond their own circle, which amounted to something like twenty persons. When Sam Charters wrote *The Country Blues* in 1959, he made no mention of Skip James, or of most of the "country blues" greats who would become celebrated in the next decade. The first written mention of the singer, in fact, would occur in 1960, when Charters compiled an album, *The*

Rural Blues, designed to augment his book. It featured a fragment of *Little Cow and Calf,* along with the comment: "Skip James seems to have been the only musician to develop a piano style that is clearly within the rural blues idiom. . . . He was one of the most exciting and one of the least known singers of the Twenties."

One of the reasons that James (who did not have a piano style as such) remained "one of the least known singers of the Twenties" was that pigeonholing blues specialists were unable to perceive any links between him and recognized singers. Little Brother Montgomery, then living in Chicago, could have told anyone who asked him that James hailed from Bentonia, Mississippi. But since Montgomery and James were taken to inhabit separate "rural" and "city" worlds, no one thought to ask Montgomery about James. Johnnie Temple, another easily accessible Chicago blues singer, would eventually point researchers in James' direction.

Ironically, it was the label "country blues" that enabled artists like James to acquire a distinctive identity, and with it, an eventual following. The term would take root among record collectors and chroniclers to such an extent that it was commonly accepted, by 1961, as a valid musical idiom. That year the *Atlantic Monthly* would refer to "that subsidiary branch of jazz-folk music known as Country Blues," and proclaim: "Country Blues have 'arrived.' " No one bothered to ask the question, "arrived from where?" or wonder why such a supposedly early form (the column spoke of the "almost archeological purity" embodied by one country blues album) had been such a late arrival.

The term had actually arrived courtesy of Folkways Records, via a 1957 album titled "Big Bill Broonzy Sings Country Blues." The blues that Broonzy sang on that occasion were not evocative of anything remotely rural: they included his renditions of hits by Indianapolis' Leroy Carr, Chicago's Tampa Red, and *Louise, Louise,* the Johnnie Temple hit of 1936 (said to have been plagiarized from Tommy Johnson). The album came with detailed notes by a jazz writer and children's book illustrator, Charles Edward Smith. Smith always appeared to write off the top of his head, presenting flimsy fancies as historical or aesthetic truths, and his coinage of the phrase "country blues" was in keeping with this tendency. He simply assumed the existence of the genre: "The country blues draw upon the warp and woof of folk music . . . " He made no attempt to explain what country blues were, or bothered to specify the contribution he claimed blues had made to jazz: "In the blues—and that means first of all the country blues—one finds the most important single source for the root music of jazz."

Smith had been a colloborator of Frederick Ramsey, Jr. in the latter's 1940 *Jazzmen*, the first American-authored book-length study of jazz, and the notions he advanced were prevalent among armchair jazz collectors, untested by research. The primitiveness that blues were thought to embody pointed inexorably in a rural direction. As Ramsey had written in 1950, for the first LP compilation of blues music (presented as an adjunct to jazz):

> A lone worker in a wide, parched field, a mother with a child, a slave with a complaint, a lover without love, a moaning, eerie unison of voices rising and falling across hot plains, the sharp, rollicking click of guitar strings at a sukey jump, a sad song in a shack along some lonesome railroad line, all gave blues their sadness, their joy, *their country start and their country ways.* [emphasis added]*

There was nothing to support the notion of blues as a music of any particular origin, rural or urban. Its history was simply invented by writers. In jazz-collecting circles, the term "country blues" essentially implied a contrast with what collectors—with equal absurdity—labelled "classic blues." These were the theatre blues of performers like Bessie Smith and Ma Rainey, singers who were lionized in jazz circles, thanks to the jazz bands that often accompanied them. It was thought that their songs embodied a professionalism and urbanity that self-accompanied blues lacked; the jazz writers who conveyed this impression, like Ramsey and Smith, never bothered to analyze their music. Had

---

*Notes to *Jazz Vol. 2: The Blues*, Folkways FJ 2802.

they done so, they might have inverted their notion of what represented "primitive" blues singing. Characteristically, the voices of these legendary singers occupied an amateurishly constricted range within a single octave, typically never traveling beyond a fifth within a given song.

Any musician who accompanied himself was construed as a country blues singer. So it was that Sam Charters' *Country Blues* (1959) devoted most of its pages to artists like Broonzy (a fixture of Chicago blues), Lonnie Johnson (a St. Louis bluesman), and Leroy Carr (an Indianapolis musician). Although it was the focal point of his work, Charters made no attempt to explain the characteristics of "country blues": he merely brandished the term as a superlative. He concocted a dualism (country/city blues) in much the same way that folklorists would create diametrical opposites of "folk" and "pop" music, the one profound, the other shallow. The "country blues" are described as "intense," "intensely personal," "moving," and "sensitive," as compared with "dull, obscene party blues," or "thin, suggestive or tasteless blues." The country blues singer has "emotional depth" and "earnest, deep sincerity." He is something like a noble musical savage.

Despite Charters' use of the term "country blues" as a counter word rather than a descriptive term containing any intelligible meaning, blues collectors seized upon it as a catch-all for self-accompanied guitar and piano works by Southern bluesmen, while invariably claiming that Charters' study was inauthentic because it had featured few authentic country blues singers. The first full-scale LP reissue of a James tune, *Devil Got My Woman*, appeared in 1961 on an Origin album titled *Really! The Country Blues*. It purported to give listeners a taste of the unadulterated country blues that Charters had overlooked.

Perhaps because it facilitated recognition of blues and was thus gratifying to the enthusiasts who authored blues commentary, the term was to be questioned only by a single writer. In 1965, Paul Oliver would note:

> "Country blues" and "city blues" are terms that
> have relatively little meaning in the blues today for
> the distinctions have been blurred by the influences

of mass media. It is likely however, that undue emphasis has been placed upon them even when reference is made to earlier periods in the history of the blues: some of the best examples of "country blues" have been recorded by city-dwellers in, for example, Memphis, Birmingham and Atlanta. With the fixed associations of such terms—ones unused by Negroes—are the beliefs that such lateral divisions may also be made by instrumentation. Thus the guitar is "country", the piano "city". That no such simple distinction exists is clearly evident from the testimony of blues singers from rural areas.[*]

Regardless of its application, the label "country blues" was inauthentic, for the terms "city" and "country" were faulty antonyms. In ordinary usage, it was the town that formed a contrast with the city, and the country that formed a contrast with the town. Thus a Mississippi planter would write, in 1901, ". . . there is not much difference between the Negroes of the town and those of the country."[**] Blues singers had used the term in the identical sense:

> He's a country man, but that fool done moved to town
> He really done sold his cotton, and now he's walkin' 'round.
> (Bo Carter: *Country Fool,* 1940)

None of this literary typecasting was done, moreover, with any actual knowledge of the backgrounds of the artists who were perceived as country blues singers. One would have been hard put to cast Skip James as a simon-pure country blues singer; he had developed his piano style in towns and cities, and was to credit his frequent association with Jackson musicians with honing his guitar skills.

Although the term became pervasive and remains so to this day, neither the collectors nor commentators who seized on the gimmicky label "country blues" have ever been able to elucidate

---

[*]Oliver, *Conversation With The Blues* (Horizon Press, 1965), p. 11.

[**]Alfred Holt Stone, *Studies in the American Race Problem* (Doubleday Page & Company, New York, 1908), p. 111.

any meaningful musical distinctions between "country" and "city" blues artists. The only generality one could rightly make between rural and urban artists lay in their typical degree of vocal volume and raucousness, which does not begin to justify the use of a catch-all term. More often than not, "city" singers had a sedate vocal delivery. The reason for this difference in tenor had less to do with geography than a lack of social license. On a plantation, where cabins might stand an acre apart, musicians were free to become as noisy and boisterous as they cared to, without fear of disturbing neighbors. Thus the young Henry Stuckey recalled by Skip James would "holler and stomp till you'd think there was two-three people there." This situation did not obtain in Chicago "kitchenette" apartments of the 1920s, which were occupied by as many as ten people at a time. But while the sedate urban delivery was almost obligatory, the typical raucous country delivery was not, and rustic artists like Bo Carter and Mississippi John Hurt were as placid as the countryside about them.

The real stylistic distinctions between bluesmen were not those of "country" and "city," or those involving the supposed regional styles that are often discussed (but never intelligibly) in blues literature. The work of most singer-guitarists of the 1920s was classifiable in terms of the dance music that was the province of the plantation "house frolic," and the street music that was the province of the town and city. A performer who plied the streets of Jackson resembled one who played on the streets of Atlanta or Dallas more than he did a dance-oriented performer of his own vicinity. The typical dance accompaniment, established by a recurring vocal and instrumental accenting pattern, generally offered a repetitive, full-sounding accompaniment containing little or no variation, and a stable bar structure that typically amounted to a 12-bar stanza.

The typical street accompaniment had a nebulous bar structure, owing to the fact that the artist followed the obligatory nine or ten-beat blues vocal phrase with any riffs he felt like playing. At the same time, the typical street accompaniment had a skeletal instrumental work behind its vocal. But even this distinction begins to break down in the work of upstarts like Memphis Minnie, James, and Robert Johnson, who typically follow conventional phrasing patterns and concoct full-dress guitar accompaniments, while generally omitting a dance beat. It is as if these artists stood halfway between the two worlds, or had begun as plantation rustics, defecting from their original musical environment. Their music suggests uncharted travels.

However, it is rarely possible to determine the origin or orbit of any blues singer on the basis of his guitar playing. The frequent claim that there is a characteristic Mississippi blues style, for example, is unsupported by anything tangible in the music of Mississippi musicians. Nor can one distinguish between Delta blues and blues of other Mississippi areas.

It was the lack of any firm regional identification that made musicians like Skip James so mysterious and alluring to their earliest white listeners. As Temple's and McCoy's Jamesian renditions were more obscure than the original, there were no telltale linkages between James' recordings and those of any known musicians of the 1920s and 1930s. At most one could plausibly assign a rural background to him on the basis of a blues allusion:

> I walked the levee, honey from end to end
> I'se just tryin' to find, my calf . . . again.
> (*Little Cow and Calf Is Gonna Die Blues*)

Virtually the only nuance that hinted of his Mississippi origin was his substandard diction, which reflected the virtual nonexistence of the state's educational facilities for blacks, at least in his formative years, a situation the missing blues singer was still seeking to repair.

24. *The Delta*

James was asked on two separate occasions by the author if he had left Bentonia in the 1950s for any particular reason. Once he claimed that a dispute with an employer, Leon Hancock, was responsible for his departure. By another account, he had been working for a planter named Sonny Hart: "I had a special reason for leavin' Mr. Sonny because I had promised to go to Memphis for my relatives." When asked what he had done in Memphis, James replied: "I didn't do anything but play [music] there." On no other occasion did James mention having any Memphis relatives, or even acquaintances.

The real reason for his abrupt disappearance is suggested by his recounted musical activities in Memphis. Having been unable to garnish a real livelihood as a blues player in Bentonia, the plough hand of yore was suddenly in great demand in Memphis, where he was a stranger: "I played there at clubs and places; I'd pick up maybe fifteen or twenty a night; I'd play two, three, four nights: I'd make at least eighty dollars a week." For anyone else in the country, blues would be strictly a weekend activity, one that could only be pursued on electric guitar, an instrument James never played.

If one substitutes "cafe operator" for "musician," James' otherwise inexplicable departure from Bentonia becomes suddenly illuminated. His cousin had been dismayed and bewildered to find his abandoned pick-up truck in center of Bentonia, its cotton surreptitiously sold, its driver vanished.

James had likely met someone who offered to sell or sell an interest in a Memphis or West Memphis honky tonk (or bootlegging) operation. Unable to scrape up the required front money (perhaps $500) and unable to endure the possibility of losing out on a lucrative enterprise, James then turned to his only financial resource. One can readily imagine James and his wife waiting for his partner's car in his cousin Polk's pick-up truck after cashing in their cotton, and then climbing into the escape vehicle.

However he left Bentonia, it is certain that James did not become the full-time musician he claimed to be in Memphis. At most he made a half-hearted attempted to keep pace with blues by performing a rendition of *Black Rat Swing*, a still-popular 1941 hit associated with Memphis Minnie:

> You're one black rat; someday I'm gonna find your trail
> And I'm gonna hide my shoe, somewhere in your
>   shirt-tail.

This tune was probably sufficient to enable him to make some pick-up money in the early 1950s; it was not enough to sustain a career.

His days as a commercial blues commodity of any kind were far behind him. The basic cause—and effect—of his obsolescence was his failure to play an electric guitar, the instrument that had been the rage of blues ten years earlier, and was now a staple of blues performance. When a French jazz specialist named Jacques Demetre was to visit Chicago in 1959, he would find the careers of singers like Johnnie Temple floundering.

> Among the old-timers whose careers are over (or almost over unless a "blues revival" starts in this country) I met Tampa Red, Curtis Jones, Red Nelson and Kokomo Arnold . . .
> Even if they are not starving, the lives of these old-time blues men are really pathetic from a psychological point of view. They, who were making many records and entertaining wide Negro audiences, have stopped their musical careers and now go gradually to the sad shadow of the forgotten people whose art does not have the recognition it deserves . . . Negroes in the Northern cities—and I guess in the Southern towns as well—no longer want the old style blues . . .

they no longer enjoy the natural "old-fashioned" guitar of the first blues specialists and they are looking
for the electric guitar. They need a solid after-beat
in the music they hear and they do not find it in
the old records of Big Bill Broonzy, Johnny Temple
or Tampa Red . . . the Negro masses forget very
quickly the old artists and other things of the past.[*]

In this respect, the Negro masses were no different from the
white masses, which had even less use for their own pop hold-
overs of the 1920s and 1930s. An "old-fashioned" blues musician
like James was actually more employable than his white coun-
terparts.

The most remarkable thing about blues was how hidebound
and resistant to modernization the idiom remained. There was
no blues counterpart of Hank Williams, who had begun his recording career with an idiomatic blues piece (*Move It On Over*,
a version of *Tight Like That*) in 1947 and had both modernized
and nationalized hillbilly music by applying the Tin Pan Alley
conceits of romantic love to a genre that had previously been
impervious to them. Blues songs of the 1940s and 1950s were
still typically sung from the point of view of a hardhearted, un-
feeling narrator, a stance that had been designed, W.C. Handy
pointed out, for "small town rounders and their running-mates."
Incredibly, the callous blues conceits of the 1920s were perpetuated for decades, in such boorish works as a 1953 Big Joe Turner
blues hit, *Honey, Hush*:

> Get in the house stop all that yakety-yak
> Oh fix my supper don't want no talkin' back . . . .
>
> Come on in, stop that yakety-yak
> Don't make me nervous 'cause I'm holdin' a baseball
>   bat.

The failure of blues song to concoct anything other than a
coarse, unsympathetic narrator mandated its obsolescence
in the 1950s, when romantic rhythm and blues ballads
came into vogue.

*Notes to *Memphis Slim and the Real Boogie-Woogie*, Folkways FA 3524.

Even when James had originally resumed his career in apparent response to Muddy Waters, the blues form had lost most of its earlier popularity. Although blues writers like to invoke the names of Waters and Howlin' Wolf as evidence of a revival of "down-home" blues in the early 1950s, the fact is that no such revival actually occurred. Their success (on Chess Records) did not prompt any record label of consequence to begin recording blues singers, and the likely reason for this non-response was that their hits (as was generally true in contemporary rhythm and blues) were purchased via disk jockey payola. Had companies of the period perceived any real public demand for blues, they would have promoted them, just as they had done in previous decades. As it was, one of the two record companies of the period that could pass muster as a blues label—Sun Records of Memphis—had no success whatsoever with the various blues singers it recorded. Nor did any of the isolated singer-guitarists who briefly graced larger labels in the late 1940s and early 1950s sell enough records to justify follow-up sessions. With the exception of Muddy Waters, blues singers who performed on electric guitar were not notably successful, either.

Whether played on acoustic or electric guitar, blues was no longer a medium that beckoned inventive or gifted performers. Whether he had an urban or rural background, the blues singer unfailingly gave off an immediate impression of illiteracy, and this fact, as much as his indifference to love, made him a peripheral figure in the rhythm and blues market of the early 1950s. With rare exceptions, the blues singer had been unable to outgrow the unsavory dive that had been his original habitat, and it was inevitable that in a postwar age that marked the first stirrings of racial progress since Jim Crow, the sleazy blues singer would largely loom as a racial embarrassment. Even the limited literary attention he attracted was too much for racial progressives of the period, one of whom complained: ". . . The self-respecting Negro artisan is crowded out of the pages of books by the more picturesque but atypical migratory singer of 'blues.' "[*]

[*]H.C. Brearly, "Are Southerners Really Lazy?," *The American Scholar*, Winter 1948-1949.

In all probability, James was not actually situated in Memphis, but in West Memphis, Arkansas, where Johnnie Temple had seen him and where the Tunica gambler "Hard-Face" had known a piano and guitar-playing nightclub operator named Curly in 1961. That "Curly" was the current alias of Skip James is indicated by James' later acknowledgment that he, as he pointedly put it, "knew *of*" a Tunica gambler named Hard-Face in the early 1960s.

Hard-Face recalled that "Curly" (which may have been a misnomer for James' middle name, "Curtis") also had a band. The likelihood is that James did some playing in West Memphis as a pianist in a rhythm and blues band of some sort, most likely one modelled after Muddy Waters. This would account for his familiarity with Waters' pianist, Otis Spann, who was not a featured performer in the latter's band. At the time of his rediscovery, James regarded himself as a rival of Spann's; one of the three albums he would eventually own would be an Otis Spann offering. Although his revived career in the North would not display any intimations of postwar blues, James had a keen appreciation of what his newfound audience wanted of him. As he was to put it in November of 1964: "Lots of people plays mostly jazz, an' this comical and hillbilly stuff, and classical, and so forth. Well, it takes to some extent and in some places. But we're getting to the place where it don't take so well, don't fit in, to the fancy of the youngsters comin' on. And they haves an intensity mostly for blues now. And they likes the blues played in the old original style, like what I first heard, when I was first comin' on."

Working as a sideman in a band would account for otherwise inconceivable claims he made about this period: that B.B. King approached him in Memphis with an offer to join a "rock and roll band," and that a company named "Buckley" in Nashville made him a recording offer in the late 1950s ("I was scared to take a chance on it," he said). Conceivably, King offered James a one-night slot as a pianist; Bullet Records (a small Nashville concern that had recorded King, as well as Walter Davis) might have expressed an interest in him, in which event James—who was likely a quasi-fugitive—would have shrunk from the prospect of publicity.

If James finally fled West Memphis to escape legal difficulties, he might have gone to Tunica at the suggestion of Hard-Face, who lived in that town. Such a deliberate disappearance on James' part would also explain the fact that his musical career seemed to putter out for no specific reason. By his own account, he was to perform only once or twice after leaving Memphis for Tunica, forty miles south.

It was there, apparently in the early 1960s, that James was to hazard what was to be the first and last new composition of his revived career, a song in "cross note" called *My Last Boogie*. He had created it in delayed response to a request some "churchy" ladies in Birmingham had once given him for a boogie, after playing a boogie record for him. At that time, James had resisted the urge to play blues.

In Tunica, he took a succession of non-musical jobs. His most profitable sideline was raising fighting cocks. For a time he was engaged as a truck driver, delivering fish and vegetables to New Orleans once a week.

James also sold fishing worms from a bait-box on the Tunica cut-off, which attracted numerous patrons who fished for catfish. For three dollars a day, he worked as a boat-hopper. "One day a lot of people were out fishing on the far side of the cut-off . . . that day there came a storm. The waves, I imagine, were ten or twelve feet high . . . Some people got drownded.

". . . The man I was workin' for, Charley Wells, asked me to load up with him and his motorboat to go out and try to rescue those people.

"I told him: 'No—I couldn't do that.'

"An' he insist once or twice for me to go with him. I told him: 'You wants to go ahead, man, then go, 'cause I'm not; you can pay me off now if you want to, though.'

"He said, 'Oh, well, it's not necessary to do that. You're just afraid to go.'"

His next job was as a tractor driver, in which he earned between $36 and $50 per week. "That was big money, then, it'd take a real good tractor driver to make that," he said. Kidney trouble, he said, caused him to give up this position. He then became an ordinary plantation hand. One morning, six or seven months after he had taken the job, an overseer reported him missing from the cotton fields, and a town constable was dispatched to his shack to fetch him. He was discovered nursing a drink of whiskey. His explanation that he felt ill that day did not take with the sheriff, and James landed a thirty-day sentence on the county farm for drunk and disorderly conduct.

James was gratified when a month of unrelenting rain fell in Tunica, preventing him from performing the road repair work he had been sentenced to perform. After his release, the planter he had worked for tried to rehire him, only to receive a tongue-lashing.

"N.C. James," as he was now called, decided it was time to move on. He had never cared for Tunica, he would later insist, but had only stayed there because his wife liked it. In 1962 he was to drift to Dubbs, some eight miles below Tunica, and languish there as a tenant of S.A. Arnold's plantation. Prior to that time, he had spent a short period on another plantation in the vicinity, leaving, he said, because the owner worked him too ardously. Exactly how he passed the time on Arnold's is anyone's guess; his wife later said that he had worked as a babysitter. When he would be rediscovered, the owner would remark that he had never done a day's work there.

The Delta was dying, just as blues music had died as a profession. It was said that Tunica County was one of the poorest counties in Mississippi, and in the early 1960s, the median income for Mississippi blacks was $900 a year. The state was losing 30,000 in population each year, chiefly because blacks were deserting it. Although the decline of the cotton plantation was largely responsible for this loss, it was felt that blacks were running from the brutality of the state.

Not long after James' probable arrival in the Delta, an event occurred there that fixed the image of the Delta—and Mississippi —in the national consciousness for years to come. This was the murder of Emmett (Bobo) Till in August, 1955 by two white Mississippians after Till, a teenage visitor from Chicago, had been impudent with the white proprietress of a grocery store in the town of Money. Although the Delta had historically been an area of relatively genteel planter paternalism, storied among black Mississippians for its opportunities to make money, it now became almost a national metaphor for racial terrorism, its identification with blues a thing of the future.

To northern journalists who took the measure of Delta culture, the black inhabitants of the Delta appeared to be anachronisms of another age. Nicholas Von Hoffman would write in 1964: "... I doubt if the poorest field hands in the Delta, whom the whites lovingly call 'the blue gum niggers,' would choose freedom and strife over peace and subjugation."*

Most Delta blacks were dependent on the white handout. With their dependence came a mannered subservience. Skip James was no exception. What was peculiar about his position was that he had always been affronted by Jim Crow, but had never taken any step to distance himself from it. In the 1940s it would have been an easy matter for him to move to Chicago. But James was not an earnest protester of the Southern status quo: his idea of success was not working in a Chicago packing plant, or bettering himself through non-plantation labor. He was someone who devoted himself to "using the system," and it was the familiar sharecropping system that he set about using, in the 1950s and 1960s. He had a definite role to play in the declining Delta, which was shored up by agricultural subsidies. His role was that of the solitary plantation tenant, a figurehead who could be entered onto a list of tenant families, and thus fatten the Federal dole that was available to the planter who provided his lodgings. Because he was in effect earning income for planters merely by his presence, he would feel little pressure to work, which was the situation he wanted. His suitability as a tenant arose from the provisions of the Agricultural Adjustment Act, by which the Federal government had subsidized cotton growers in terms of their number of tenants but made no distinction between families and single tenants. Whereas the large family was the most desirable tenant of the pre-Depression Delta plan-

Mississippi Notebook (David White Company, New York, 1964), p. 16.

tation, the loner like James became the ideal tenant of the post-Depression plantation.

James was far more outspoken than the ordinary Mississippi black of his time. When race riots erupted in 1967, he would say: "If it hadda been just a few Negroes like my daddy[*] and myself and a uncle or two I got, this riot wouldn't been existin' now: everything woulda been settled fifty years ago. All along my early life, I'd tell boys: 'Man, you let somebody stand up and beat you like that and you won't hit 'em back? Oh, shoot!' I feel like beatin' that guy myself, then; I don't give a darn how white he was." Yet the only skirmishes he ever reported having with whites were verbal ones. James would appear to have picked his white targets very carefully, either sizing them up as cowards or exploiting his favored position on the *Woodbine* plantation to flex his muscles. His survival attested to his discretion.

Although James had the temperament of a racial firebrand, and irate memories of various indignities wrought by Jim Crow, he was too comfortable within the system to reject it. Moreover, he had no intellectual frame of reference that would enable him to arrive at the kind of catchphrases of equality that would be characteristic of a civil rights leader. He had never been exposed to the Declaration of Independence, the Constitution, or any of the documents that lay at the base of racially progressive rhetoric. He had only his intuitive senses and his own experiences to sort out racial matters, and his experiences were not ones that had suggested the equality of the races. The only whites with whom he ever had prolonged contact were planters, exalted by wealth.

In his eyes, blacks suffered sorely by direct comparison with whites. The races were composed of the same substance, but their intangible spirits differed. "Now then, if I stick a pin in you, your blood runs red," he was to say in the 1960s. "If you stick a pin in me, my blood runs red . . . But I couldn't compare my blood with yours." His own blood, he thought, was not as

---

[*]This was James' stepfather, Harrison Banks, whom he approvingly described as a "mean bastard." Although James never mentioned it, Banks partly established these credentials by abusing James' mother. "He was a jealous old man," Jack Owens told Edd Hurt. "He'd whup her all the time."

good as that of white people. Although James did not often make generalizations about race, he believed that white people were basically more upright than blacks. "White people don't like you to lie or steal," he said, as though this constituted a curious Caucasian peculiarity. Blacks, he believed, were primarily interested in what he called "the lower things in life," particularly "sociality" (sex), and it was partly in the interests of elevating himself above them that he pronounced the very word with contempt.

At the same time, James' basic intractability immunized him from ever becoming a true Uncle Tom. No one, white or black, was able to intimidate him, and he would have open contempt for most of the elderly Southern blues singers he was to meet on the 1960s concert circuit. ". . . Guys like John Hurt, and Son [House], you know, they're just shaky," he would say. "A white could tell 'em, 'Go ahead and put your head in that hole, nigger.'" Of Mississippi whites, he said: "Those guys believed in gettin' two and three and four and five, gettin' you in a store, gettin' you across barrels, and get ax handles and beat the shit out ya . . . And I'll bet you they never did put *Skip* down there. Uh uh."

His subservience was always a contrived formality, but yet convincing enough to cast him as a "desirable darkey." "I always was malleable and I stayed in my place," he said, "and I had a good reputation as that." His thoughts were another matter altogether: he came to believe that there was a curse on the white race, and that a catastrophe would eventually befall it because of its treatment of blacks.

Owing partly to his belief in the superiority of supernatural forces, James had no interest in the mundane advancements of blacks that marked the civil rights movement, such as the voter registration that was the basis of most early civil rights activity. "Right now they are demanding for people to . . . vote," he was to remark in 1966. "But I don't care how qualified you are. If you don't wanna vote, there's no compulsion. These politics and politicians, I just tell 'em: 'Disconsider me. Proceed on, in whatever course you're pursuin'. And I'm sorry, but count me out of it. I'm not even interested . . .'

"I'll tell you something: sometimes it's a good idea to play ignorant. I say: 'I never voted and don't know how; what is votin',
anyhow? What's it mean, mean? What, what? I'm just so ignorant,
I'm an illiterate; I can't read, can't write. I can make an X and
that's all, and don't want to do that unless you do it for me.'"
This was the kind of dumb darkey act that played well in
Mississippi, where fewer than five percent of native blacks had
been registered to vote in 1963. But James had other reasons
for his aversion to voting: all politicians, he thought, were corrupt. "They try to get the majority to go their way, these guys
. . . The people will vote and put him in office, though they
know he's a rascal to start with. And after he gets in there,
he's a double rascal, 'cause he's got the authority . . . After he's
in office, he don't need your assistance any more . . . When he's
in power, he's one of the best enemies you have." Only one
candidate appealed to him: "I'll vote for Skip," he declared.

In a progressive (some would say revolutionary) period, James
had become a social anachronism. Outsiders were horrified by
the feudal control the Delta planter enjoyed over his tenants:
James found it reassuring, provided that he had an "in" with
the boss that others lacked. Nothing raised S.A. Arnold in his
estimation so much as the sight of the planter pummeling a
local sheriff on the steps of the Tunica County Courthouse in
the early 1960s for having the temerity to arrest one of "his
niggers" for bootlegging without his permission.

James' backwardness was so acute that he did not recognize
the backwardness of Mississippi, which had little changed from
the antebellum days when a native had told Olmsted: "This isn't
the country for schools." In 1940, the median education for state
residents amounted to 7.2 years of schooling. When a coffeehouse
comedian named Biff Rose took a swipe at the state during James'
comeback, he bristled: "He styled Mississippi as the most ignorant
and low-degraded state in the South." To James, this view was
a slander: while allowing, "there are some illiterates in Mississippi,"
this was less important than the fact that "some of the most studious, efficiency-prepared professionals—star-gazers, scientists,
doctors, prognosticators, teachers, lawyers, astromers—all professional men of deep profundity—were from Mississippi."

But in attempting to refute Rose, James only provided a pathetic example of his own backwardness. The self-styled "walking encyclopedia" who claimed to be able to write assorted words in Latin and Greek stated: "I think there are some talents out of Mississippi that can entertain these thirty-eight or thirty-six, whatever you might style it, but I think it's about forty-two states."

James rightly regarded himself as being highly erudite for a black Mississippian. "My vocabulary," he was to remark proudly, "has congealed as much as it can hold, and I cannot stand any more." Although their weakness for gaudy but faulty erudition made blacks a stock figure of racist humor and prompted observers to note "[t]he racial relish for impressive words and resounding sentences,"* James did not speak gibberish. He used non-technical words with almost total accuracy.

His thirst for learning led him to delve into a book of his father's, *The Science Of Sound*, in search of musical knowledge. He came away with a mangled understanding of musical fundamentals that he would later brandish in an attempt to escape the onus of illiteracy: ". . . What is 4/4 time? What is your time is? What do time consist of? Well, time is . . . as a count. You start to count, say: 'Well, I'm gonna take me two steps.' One, two; one, two. Well that's two. Well, you might say: '4/4'—well, that's a little faster.

"You know quite naturally a whole is different from a quarter. And a quarter is different from a half . . . If you put it in 6/8ths, you're still takin' the value from that. If you put it in 16ths, your time done got speeded. But you *still* can cut it. And everytime you cut it, that makes your time faster.

"Then you can put it in triplets or 32nds . . . Then you can put it it 64ths . . . That's just about your limit in speed, and that's your limit in music. You can't get any further. When you reached that, you done reached your height in time, beatses, accents, and whatever you want to call it."**

*Clifton Johnson, *Highways and Byways of the South* (Macmillan, New York, 1904), p. 334.

**Although James' mangled musical argot made him seem comically pretentious to blues afficionados who were exposed to such discourses, most of the latter had no greater formal knowledge of music. Similarly, blues literature abounds with erudite-sounding descriptions of blues songs and styles that would make legitimate musicologists cringe.

236   I'D RATHER BE THE DEVIL

Unfortunately, James did not similarly concern himself with
the science of medicine. When he fell ill in January of 1964,
his reflexive reaction was to blame his condition on a female.
"... A woman was the cause of it all," he was to say that November, when his condition was still uncured. James was convinced that she had "got some whiskey in me some way or
another. Got some doped whiskey."

On the calculation that his wife knew nothing of his extra-
marital affairs, which had been common knowledge in Bentonia
(causing Owens to report: "He had a heap of girlfriends ... he'd
court anybody, you know, let him ..."), he decided that the malefactor must have been a local girlfriend who had fallen in love
with him. "She wanted me in this way—to just give up Mabel
altogether ... She decided if I didn't, why she'd just fix me so
that I wouldn't be of no service to myself, Mabel, or nobody
else. Unless'n it was her." This explanation neatly dovetailed with
his ailment, which involved a tumorous growth on his penis. As
James put it, the malefactor was trying to "kill my coozie. She
fixed me so I couldn't do myself any good [sexually] and my
wife either ... She'd just ruther see me suffer and die."

His understanding of illness was a sad throwback to the West
African mores a missionary had remarked upon fifty years earlier: "not a death occurs among them that is not attributed to
witchcraft," he had written. The death of a male prompted a
literal witchunt: "A man's wives are the first to be charged with
his death, even without evidence, because they are supposed
to have a latent desire for it."[*]

In the Delta, blacks outnumbered whites by two to one. To
blues researchers, the Delta of the period appeared to be both
a cultural and musical wasteland. After making a field trip there
for Arhoolie Records, Chris Strachwitz wrote in December of
1961: "In a way the Delta is deserted. Those who could afford
it have moved north to Chicago or out to the West Coast ..."
It was not thought that the area still housed any musicians.

[*]R.H. Mulligan, *Fetish Folk of West Africa* (Revell Co., London, 1912), pp. 38,
238.

PART FIVE

25. *The Prospectors*

Since the February day he had spent three hours in Tunica in search of Skip James in 1964, Gayle Wardlow had not turned up any new leads on the whereabouts of the missing blues singer. Four months passed; time that was frittered away partly because he had little leisure and money to act on his urge to find James, and partly because the Delta in which James had disappeared a decade before was on the verge of exploding.

Although Wardlow resented the rhetoric of northerners who routinely condemned the South, he felt the same drift of oppressive air that had led Sam Charters to write, the year before:

> Northwest Mississippi is one of the most vicious areas of human intolerance and brutality on the face of the earth. . . . A stranger in a town like Avalon or Port Gibson is followed as he goes down a street. If a car is left outside of a store a sheriff is leaning against it waiting to ask questions when the driver comes back outside. Someone with a camera will be forced out of a shack area, someone asking questions will be forced to leave the county.[*]

The gathering civil rights movement intensified this white paranoia, and Wardlow was not exempt from its effects. In the spring of 1964 he had turned up a 70-year old blues singer named Henry Butcher in the Delta town of Moorhead. As Butcher began playing on a sidewalk for him, fretting his guitar

[*]Notes to J.D. *Short and Son House/The Blues of the Mississippi Delta,* Folkways Album FA 2647.

with a piece of bone and singing in the deepest voice Wardlow had ever heard, a crowd of black youths had assembled to hear the performance. A police car had abruptly shown up, and Wardlow had been ordered to leave town.

The Mississippi Summer Project was scheduled to begin that June, and the entire state was being converted into a pitched camp. One thousand Northern "freedom riders," most of them college students, would be arriving to register black voters. Before the month ended two of them would be murdered, along with a black Mississippian.

Wardlow would have braved the Delta sooner had he simply known where to go in pursuit of Skip James. He never considered the possibility that James' relatives in Bentonia might be withholding information from him, thinking him a law enforcement officer. He had phoned James' cousin in Yazoo City, and was told that the singer lived in Tunica—a place he had already searched, fruitlessly. He tried phoning a black speakeasy in Tunica and asking about James; the person he spoke to had never heard of him.

The gambler named Hard-Face who had spoken of his friend "Curly" cutting out on a bootlegging warrant had also mentioned that he had departed for Alabama one night. Since Wardlow had learned from James' cousin that the singer's father had died in Birmingham and left an inheiritance for him, he attempted to learn something about the father. But none of the black churches he called could give him information about a pastor named James.

He was left with snatches of information about the missing singer, gleaned from Bentonia; they added up to an ambiguous portrait. He had been known in the 1920s as a "wicked" Georgia Skin gambler and a "big drinker." After returning to Bentonia from Alabama in the 1940s, in the company of a "mean woman," it was said, he no longer drank. But the reformed blues singer had nevertheless cheated his cousin and was, Wardlow believed, now a fugitive from the law.

To relieve the frustration and loneliness of his quest for vanished blues singers, Wardlow had a habit of dropping in on Ishmon Bracey, the one-time Jackson blues singer he had found the previous year. On one of his visits, hoping to jog a memory, he told Bracey about his trip to Bentonia, and his discovery that Skip James had been reared there. Bracey merely grunted; it seemed as if the ex-blues singer knew nothing about James.

The success of Mississippi John Hurt and word of Wardlow's peregrinations had stimulated other blues enthusiasts to such an extent that they were willing to brave deadly Mississippi in search of other singers. These figures were prospectors; they had no interest in conducting blues research as such, but hoped to emerge with a marketable blues rediscovery. The most coveted missing bluesmen were James and Son House.

One posse of prospectors was organized by Nick Perls, a wealthy art dealer's son who had become absorbed with blues while attending school in Washington, D.C. With two other companions, Perls drove from New York to Robinsonville, Mississippi in search of Son House, who had been recorded by the Library of Congress there in 1941. They found a lone local blues player in the form of Sol Henderson, a sharecropper who rendered amateurish versions of House's *Jinks Blues*. Henderson was all that was left of the town's once-sizeable retinue of blues singers, which had included Robert Johnson.

"The last time me an' him played together," he said of Johnson, "it was a time out here on Friar's Point. That's the time he got killed . . ." A woman had stabbed Johnson, he said, when the singer had slapped her. "Wasn't no surprise to me," Henderson said, "I figured a woman was gonna kill him 'cause he never meddled nothin' but a woman when he get to drinkin' . . . Never bothered no man; he never bothered 'em. . . ."

Perls and his cohorts believed they had received the inside story about the singer's legendary death. What they had received was another bogus blues tale.

So notoriously unreliable were black informants in the Jim Crow era that previous generations of folklorists had scarcely bothered to document their musical statements, which were held to routinely contain "extraordinary exaggerations and misstatements."[*] The first generation of blues researchers, on the other

*R.W. Gordon, "Folk Songs of America: Negro 'Shouts,' " *The New York Times Magazine*, April 24, 1927, p. 4.

hand, gingerly swallowed most of the stories they received from their sources. When a localite responded to Perls' question about Skip James with a startling statement that he had followed a woman up to Poplar Bluff, Missouri several years before, the trio decamped for that town. They left upon learning that no one in Poplar Bluff had apparently heard of James.

Acting on a local tip about Son House, which came complete with a street address, the group continued up to Rochester, New York. They discovered that the old blues singer was now languishing on welfare, with an alcoholic tremor that made his guitar work torturous.

At about the same time as Perls and his cronies set out for Mississippi, a second Mississippi-bound caravan left from California. It consisted of a trio of budding guitar players, John Fahey, Bill Barth, and Henry Vestine. Fahey, a native of Takoma Park, Maryland who had since moved to Berkeley, had originally been a bluegrass enthusiast. He experienced a swift conversion in the late 1950s when a record collector he met at a Unitarian meeting, Richard Spottswood, played Blind Willie Johnson's *Praise God I'm Satisfied* for him. Fahey became so affected that he broke into tears. In 1958 he visited Clarksdale, Mississippi in search of his favorite blues singer, Charlie Patton. His failure to find much information might have ended his days as a field researcher had he not (in 1963) idly sent a post card to "Bukka White—Old Blues Singer" to Aberdeen, Mississippi after hearing about the discovery of John Hurt in Avalon. Just as Hurt had recorded an *Avalon Blues,* so had White recorded *Aberdeen, Mississippi Blues.*

The postcard was eventually forwarded to Memphis, where White had been living since the late 1930s. He was working in a tank factory and had drifted away from music. Although Booker was a non-stop talker, he was a poor source of information on other blues singers. He hardly knew any recorded musicians of the past.

Booker's rediscovery would illustrate the large gulf between blues singers as they existed in the imagination of scribes and record collectors, and as they were in life. His *Fixin' To Die,* recently recorded by Bob Dylan, had impressed white listeners as a heartfelt lament. But White had merely tossed it off as a studio composition, ventured after discovering that his original retinue of songs (mostly standards) did not find favor with his recording director. None of his tunes appeared to be of any particular value to him.

Booker not only lacked the musical integrity that collectors ascribed to country blues, but any other form of integrity as well. When he learned that Fahey was a devotee of Charlie Patton, he recorded a breezy reminiscence of Patton, whom he had never met.

Unlike John Hurt, White had worked as a professional blues musician. His criterion for music-making had been monetary, and when it no longer paid to perform blues, he let his abilities lapse. Even at that, he was exceptional for being only damaged goods. Most of the professional musicians from the 1920s were dead.

From K.C. Douglas, a Jackson transplant living in Oakland whom Fahey interviewed in April, 1964, he heard that the storied Tommy Johnson could not possibly still be living: the singer had been a Skid Row type, subsisting on wood alcohol. When Douglas had met him in 1940 the singer's waist had already grown so skinny that one could encircle it with two hands. Douglas believed that Ishmon Bracey, the second most popular blues singer in Jackson, might be alive, and it was Bracey who the prospectors turned to in search of Mississippi leads.

When the trio arrived at Bracey's home, the singer immediately offered to record twelve songs for them in exchange for $400. After they indicated that they could not afford this fee, Bracey countered with another offer: in exchange for $30, he would sell his capsule reminiscences to them.

Using motel stationery, Fahey drafted an officious-sounding agreement with Bracey.

> I John Fahey agree to pay Rev. Ishmon Bracey $30.00 in return for information recorded on tape recorder—appx. 2 hours—to be used only for educational purposes, & not for commercial purposes, not for publication, one copy only of tape to be made

for UCLA Center for Study of Camp Folklore, the
above restrictions binding said copy also

Bracey proceeded to educate his guests in the fine points of
blues con artistry. Rather than declare that he did not know
some obscure singer they mentioned, he would make an inconsequential comment about the performer, as when he spoke
of the mysterious Isaiah Nettles: "He played pretty good but
he could sing better than he could play." He remarked that
he had run across Nettles in Vicksburg, a city where any Mississippi singer was likely to play at some point.

When a question about Skip James came up, however,
Bracey was more specific. Parroting information he had recently heard from Gayle Wardlow, he told them that James
had come from Bentonia. Fahey quickly took out a pen and
wrote the name of the unknown town on the box containing
the spool of tape he had used to record Bracey. Having succeeded at their real educational objective, the trio quickly left
Jackson and drove to Bentonia, which now officially numbered
511 residents.

On arriving there, Barth went to the county clerk, who had
never heard of James. He drew a similar blank at the local post
office, where he was advised to ask for James at the town drug
store. There Barth encountered the same results.

The trio then took to cruising back and forth through town,
their eyes scanning the yards of black houses for elderly-looking
blacks. At the north end of town they saw two such persons
talking in a yard, and drew up alongside of them to broach
the subject of Skip James.

"Skip James left town thirty years ago with a woman and went
up North," one of the men declared.

At the west end of Bentonia they spotted another resident
who appeared to have been old enough to know James. Mention
of his name brought the gruff response: "He's *gone*," causing
Fahey to wonder if something had happened between the man
and the missing singer.

The group then began canvassing shacks on foot. The first
person they encountered thought James had left town twenty

years earlier. The second, who thought James had left ten years before, was able to direct them to the house of James' maternal aunt, Martha Polk.

Thirty years before, the aunt had received her brother as an overnight guest, and set into motion the conversion of her blues-playing nephew. Now ailing and bed-ridden, she asked her guests to await for her husband's arrival from work. When James' uncle appeared, he told them that he had seen the missing singer the year before, at the funeral of the latter's father in Birmingham. He said that James was living somewhere further north in Mississippi in a town called "Dunbar," situated south of Tunica.

The few people who had previously recognized James' name had proclaimed him the best musician in Bentonia. To this appraisal, Polk added that his nephew "can play anything"—including kazoo and trombone. Nothing was mentioned about the strife between James and their son, who had told Wardlow of his unsuccessful search for the vanished cousin who had bilked him out of $500.

The trio decided to leave Bentonia, even though no town named "Dunbar" appeared on their map. They suspected that the name of the town was actually Dundee or Dubbs, two Delta communities located about fifty miles below Memphis, set eight miles apart from each other, off Highway 61.

In their excitement, the searchers had overlooked an anomaly in the information they had just received. In order for James to have attended his father's funeral, some relative of his must have been able to contact him in the Delta. Yet the Polks never indicated that they or any other relation knew how to get a message to James. As James' closest relatives, the Polks should have been able to give the trio a better idea of his whereabouts than to mention a town that apparently did not exist. It would seem that they were willing to point James' pursuers in the right direction, but not to lead them directly to him. This willingness to approximate rather than pinpoint James' location, were it in fact such, would make sense only if his discovery stood to enmesh him in some form of trouble.

After combing the black district of Dundee, it appeared obvious that Skip James had never lived there. En route to Dubbs, which lay northeast of Dundee, they stopped at a gas station. Noticing a youthful black lounging near one of the pumps, they asked if he had ever heard of a place called "Dunbar." Without hesitation, he replied gruffly: "Yeah. It's around." Then Barth asked the man if he had ever heard of an old musician named Skip James.

He recalled a night he had spent at Benny Simmons' barber shop in Dundee. A drunken old man had sat around bragging that he had been a great musician who played piano and guitar. The man had claimed to have made records. Nobody in the shop believed him, including the man who was relating the incident. "We thought he was bullshitting," the man said.

At Simmons' barbership, Barth and Fahey were immediately directed to the nearest shack, some four hundred yards away. There, on the front porch, sat an old woman in a rocking chair. At first she denied knowing Skip James.

"Now just what do you want with him?" demanded Mabel James, who would later claim that she had taken Fahey and Barth for revenue agents.

When their interest in James had been explained to her satisfaction, she agreed to take them to Tunica County Hospital, where James had lain since January.

The rediscovery of the bedridden ex-blues singer was unceremonious: James appeared to have no reaction to the event, or his improbable visitors' interest in him. When they showed him a discography listing his known records, he commented unenthusiastically: "Now isn't that nice?" However, their arrival interested him enough to quietly begin working on rhymes for a new blues composition, *Sick Bed Blues*, which he would eventually set to the melody of Blind Lemon Jefferson's *One Dime*, and which quickly became his wife's favorite piece.

His discoverers arranged for a news photographer to take a bedside photo of him, greatly agitating her in the process. "Man come in and takin' my pictures so fast!" James recalled. "Well, then, that kinda got baby a little bit upset; she didn't know what was his object, you know." Evidently Mabel was still under the impression that her husband might be in legal difficulty. When she learned that James had been obtaining whiskey in the hospital, she secured his release the following day.

Shortly after returning home to Dundee, James sat down before a tape recorder. He had not touched a guitar for some seven years, nor recorded for some thirty.

Rusty strains of a truncated *Devil Got My Woman* demonstrated that James' voice had not coarsened with age. As he began retuning his guitar, he muttered: "Whew! Hot like a dog." Then he began playing *All Night Long*, his unrecorded guitar version of *If You Haven't Any Hay*. He stopped after a few verses, retuned his guitar, and began *Hard Times*.

At Mabel's cry of alarm: "Here comes the bossman!" the tape machine was hastily cut off. The nervous Northerners discovered that S.A. Arnold was nothing like the ogre they had expected in the form of a Delta planter. He began laughing when he looked at the discography they displayed as evidence of their interest in music (rather than civil rights) and noticed the listing of a tune called *Drunken Spree*. He provided them with an escort to mollify townspeople who might mistake them for civil rights workers. Shortly afterwards, he brought his daughter out to visit James. When Skip played a bottleneck version of *John Henry* for his boss, who had no inkling he had ever been a musician, the planter rewarded him with a ten dollar tip.

Nevertheless, to the astonishment of his rediscoverers, James indicated his contempt for Arnold by routinely cursing him behind his back.

As the days passed, James showed no interest in practicing or in laying the groundwork for a musical comeback. Instead, he would have Barth and Fahey serenade him on his front porch.

"Aren't they a cute couple?" his wife would ask rhetorically. Privately, James would tell her: "They're slick, but they can stand another greasing."

Periodically, James would direct them to the back of his shack to look at his hogs. In their absence he would guzzle moonshine. When Fahey interrupted him one day to convey his tolerance of alcohol, James immediately offered him a drink of liquor. One gulp almost made Fahey vomit.

The next day, a bootlegger arrived on the scene and offered to sell Fahey a pint of moonshine for $1.50. Skip then consumed the bottle himself.

By this time, James' discoverers had begun to feel like interlopers. The standoffish singer mistrusted them to the extent of showing the Takoma contract they brandished to his boss. After glancing at the contract, Arnold promptly drove James and his discoverers to the office of his own lawyer, a Mississippi state senator. "... The contract that they had, he [Arnold] didn't like," James recalled a few months later. "... There's some certain clauses in there they thought they'd put over on me, and they didn't give me a chance to go through it all the way ... the clause he didn't like ... he had it took out and a new contract made," James recalled. Even at that, the planter privately advised James: "Don't sign nothin'."

He had no eagerness, he said later, to become a blues singer again. "Bill and John, they just outtalked me," he said five months later. "... [T]hey talked so fast I could hardly hear a word sideways ... and then I wasn't feelin' too good noway. I just decided, right after I talked with baby, that's my wife, she said: 'Well, James, you oughta try it,'—she got angry a little bit ... she said: 'I don't know why in the world your mother gonna send you to school, for, and give you that learnin', an' you don't use it. She coulda eat that money up in ice cream.'"

S.A. Arnold finally told James: "You'd be a fool to hang around here when you have a chance to start a career."

James would look back on Arnold's reassurances as a basic reason he decided to cast his lot with his discoverers. He quoted Arnold as telling him: "Anywhere you go, if you need any help, if anybody mess with you, I'll see the sonofabitches pay you what you deserve." He added: "And I know he meant it. His word is superior to any other word I have had yet."

James had no inkling that the three-man audience he hosted at his shack actually represented a significant chunk of his potential comeback constituency. In the entire country there were no more than twenty hard-core blues enthusiasts. Nearly every one of them was a record collector who had a pronounced distaste for any blues not enshrined on a 78 recording, or an aspiring performer who was primarily interested in copying blues songs. James had a storied reputation, but it was a reputation that extended to a handful of people, far fewer in number than the population of Bentonia.

As a commodity, James existed in the form of three 1931 recordings featured on two Origin Jazz Library anthologies. The first, issued in 1961, had taken a year or two to exhaust its initial pressing run of 500 copies. The second album (*Mississippi Blues*) had appeared the year before James' rediscovery: like its predecessor (*Really! The Country Blues*) it generated a pressing of 500 albums. European sales accounted for something like half of Origin's audience; in America, its clientele chiefly consisted of New Yorkers and Californians. The company's guiding light, Pete Whelan, ran it as a hobby.

The almost simultaneous rediscoveries of James and Son House in June of 1964 were to mark the beginning of the blues "revival" as a paper phenonomen. A feature article in *Newsweek* bore photos of both singers, along with an effusive tribute to them: ". . . these two were the only great country blues singers still lost," it claimed. "No wonder the excitement last week when it was learned that both Son House and Skip James were found."

Henceforth, blues would take on an exalted rhetorical media life in which the music would appear to be important and beloved. One who followed references to blues in popular and specialist publications would gain a completely different picture of the music than one who followed the sales figures of blues records, which to this day do not amount to one percent of the music market. In the 1920s, when blues had been virtually ignored by white society, the music had actually been far more commercially significant, thanks to its enthusiastic patronage by blacks. The blues "revival" of the 1960s actually represented the placement of blues upon a white respirator.

From the viewpoint of his recent discoverers, James' discovery was a form of deliverance for him. Instead of being a déclassé plantation darkey, he would now be recognized as an artist.

But to James himself, the alternative to his dismal present was not an irresistible proposition.

"I done got too old to be worried with so much music," he was to say that November, five months after he had resumed his career. "It's too hard on your brains, on your fingers, and on your energy . . ." Besides demanding an onerous effort, leaving Tunica also meant postponing the prospect of punishing the woman whose perfidy, he was certain, had placed him in the hospital. Resuming his blues career when his own health was precarious was to tempt fate. If he were to die during his resurrection as a blues singer, the celestial credits his years of preaching had obtained would be washed away by fire and brimstone. For while God would at least look the other way as Skip fired upon a female in the street, He would not forgive an act as odious as blues-playing. So it was that James would, within five months of his rediscovery, begin to hint at his retirement from secular music. He planned to play "two or three years more . . . if the Lord'll let me live that long."

In the meantime, making the records that his discoverers promised to arrange for him did not bode any sure financial return. He was not even sure that they would pay him. Out of fear that their pledges might prove empty, James concocted a melodramatic account of his previous experience with Paramount Records. "I was so badly deceived . . . after which, I gave up music altogether . . . All I got was forty dollars . . . If you had been as badly deceived as I was, you wouldn't be playin' now," James would say.

This story not only served as a caution, but as a salve for himself. It was like his tale of his broken marriage. His own decisions had nothing to do with his failure to record after 1931; he was the unhappy victim of other people's machinations.

James' instinctive mistrust of his discoverers was not without a basis. Although blues devotees of the 1960s prided themselves for having a genuine aesthetic appreciation of blues music that was not characteristic of the "race" recording moguls of the 1920s, they had an even keener appreciation of commerce. It was thought that the blues field was on the verge of becoming lucrative.

Although the blues field in 1964 tended to attract people who could charitably be described as connivers, the petty nature of the burgeoning blues business obscured the fact that the real purpose of James' discoverers and sponsors was to make money off him. It had been the profitable example of John Hurt (then earning $200 a week on the "folk" circuit) that had drawn Northern blues prospectors to Mississippi, as well as the soaring prices of old blues records, which were now so coveted as to command $100 in the form of a rare Skip James record. Soon James would become enmeshed in business transactions that were quite shameful, thanks to the shamelessness of his assorted sponsors.

The machinations of these mentors would be disguised by an aura of pious altruism, assumed by virtually everyone in the blues business. Indeed, to judge from contemporary writings on blues, there was no such thing as a blues business, and no one was in such a business—everyone affiliated with it would be identified as a "blues enthusiast" or "blues specialist" or "blues researcher." (Fahey, the owner of the Takoma label, had represented himself as an "ethnomusicologist" on the notes of his first blues issue.) These pretenses were made possible by the peculiar confluence of the blues "revival" and the folk movement.

26. *The "Folk" Movement*

The precarious livelihood Skip James would eventually eke out after leaving Mississippi was garnished primarily through his misrepresentation as a folk singer. His concert debut would take place at a folk festival, three weeks after his discovery; his major recordings would appear on a label dedicated to folk music. He would be frequently be categorized as a folk musician, or something called a "folk" bluesman.

James never represented himself as anything other than a blues singer. He had no idea what a folk musician was, no idea what a folk song was, and no idea what "folk blues" were. He paid no attention to the kind of billing he received, and only scant attention to anything written about him, even the text that accompanied his albums. If he even noticed the word "folk" in any context applied to himself, he probably saw it as simply a meaningless expression of white-speak. For his part, he was simply an entertainer whose services were available to any bidder.

The label "folk" music was generally affixed to the songs of déclassé ethnic or sociological groups whose individual members were thought to possess no individuality. The members of the group were thought to be so transparent that their songs were " . . . the crude but forceful expression of the impression, emotions, and experiences of that singular race, through the only medium of self-utterance which they know . . ." This description of gypsy folk song, written in 1908,[*] could have been written by any folklorist of the pre-1950s who assessed black music. The author's notion of gypsy song as a "racial art product, coming

---

[*]Edward Baxter Perry, "What Is Gypsy Music?" *The Etude*, September, 1908.

straight from the heart of the people . . ." was intrinsic to the perception of folk music, applied to blacks.

To folklorists, racial purity and musical purity went hand in hand. The earliest study of black folk music (Henry Krehbiels' *Afro American Folksongs*, authored in 1914), was actually subtitled *A Study In Racial And National Music*. Krehbiels wrote: "The creator of a folksong as an individual is a passing phenomenon . . . His potentiality is racial or national, not personal, and for that reason it is enduring, not ephemeral." This was a pompous, euphemistic way of stating that when one listened to a work song, one was hearing "nigger music," the product of someone who was not an individual, but a representative "nigger."

Many folklorists had little use for either blues, or, it seemed, blacks. The folklorist who was to author liner notes for Skip James' first major comeback album had recently claimed, a few months earlier, that whites did not understand blacks. "Perhaps nowhere is this myopia more apparent than among many fans of Negro blues," he stated. "We often find among them a curious negrophilia such that every Negro utterance, however trite, or every Negro musical activity, however incompetent, is more valuable than any statement by anyone anywhere, ever. It is, I suppose, one of the more offensive forms of patronage fostered by our times."[*]

Folklorists had their own preferred forms of patronage. By and large, the devotees of black folk culture were people who liked Negroes — in their proper place. Their proper place was to remain on the level of the downtrodden plantation darkey and to perpetuate the "folkways" of the Jim Crow era. So it was that Newman White would lament in 1928:

> The Negroes are becoming less and less a folk-group . . . The Negro is told to be himself, even to be proud of himself; but he is also told to be ambitious, to "rise." Implicit in most of the exhortations of Negro leaders is the inevitable "Imitate the white man" . . . The mass of Negroes are still nearer to the

[*]Bruce J. Jackson, introduction to Newman White's *American Negro Folk Songs* (Folklore Associates, Inc. reprint of the 1928 edition, Hatboro, Pa., 1965), p. vi.

> folk stage than they are to their leaders, but one can
> foresee even now the end of the old Negro folk-song.*

Had folk ideologues had their way, there would never have
been a forum for the Mills Brothers, the Ink Spots, Nat "King"
Cole, Lena Horne, Billy Eckstine, or any black artist who did
not perform plantation music.

No country could be more inhospitable to the values of folk
music scholars than the commercially-oriented society of America, in which what was obsolete was valueless. The typical American outlook towards the idea of "tradition" that was exalted
by folk scholars was precisely that of Skip James: "I'm not interested in the past. I done experienced that . . ." Blues music
itself was a reflection of a racial regard for music of the moment:
it had arisen around the turn of the century, displacing banjo
and fiddle music. By the 1950s, it had been basically rejected
by black audiences.

Even within the nonsensical terms of the folk music field, blues
had no legitimacy. Not a single folk song collector who actually
lived during the blues era accepted the notion that blues was
a form of folk music. The original folk music mongerers of
America knew as much, because they had first-hand contact with
what was termed the "folk Negro"—essentially, a plantation
darkey. They saw at a glance that blues did not have the universal
circulation of spirituals, which were (in the 1920s) regarded as
the authentic folk songs of blacks. Moreover, they recognized
that blues were the product of a deviant segment of black society. Writing in 1925, Odum and Johnson described their compilation of secular songs (including blues) as "representative only
of what may be called the Negro lower class."** In 1928, Newman White dismissed the blues as "mainly of an underworld
origin." Whereas folk music was supposed to be representative
of a "folk," blues were regarded as degenerate and disreputable
within their own community. A Mississippi woman who had an
avid taste for blues music would say of its exponents: "When

---

*White, pp. 4-5.

**See Odum and Johnson, *The Negro And His Songs* (1964 reprint of the 1925
edition, Folklore Associates, Inc., Hatboro), p. 159.

I came along, you know, they called 'em 'jukehouse people,' or otherwise they just didn't like 'em. Them there Saturday night folks: good people don't be out with 'em; that's a bad class of people, bad type of people . . . bad character."*

Not surprisingly, the first blues singer to be represented as a folk singer was a convicted murderer, Leadbelly. Yet to his promoter John Lomax, America's most famous folk song collector, blues were a decadent Tin Pan Alley product, a corruption of an imaginary genre he called "field hollers." There was no logic to Lomax's representation of Leadbelly as a folk singer, but, in the field of folk music, there was no such thing as logic. It was simply a tower of babble, to such an extent that Lomax could blithely maintain that folk songs were songs that were handed down via "tradition," while brandishing as his prime exhibit of folk music a performer whose forte was songwriting.

After being transplanted from a Louisiana prison to New York in 1933, Leadbelly became the first simon-pure professional "folk" singer. The real contribution that Leadbelly made to the cause of folk music lay in the fact that he personalized the imaginary idiom. Whereas previously folk music had seemed to exist in terms of a collection of songs, it now became a genre that resembled pop music, attached to personalities and performers. Their material was secondary.

By 1950, when Leadbelly died, it was clear what a folk singer actually was, as opposed to what was written about him. He was someone who was unemployable as a singer in any other context; a performer whose work was so far removed from "the people" that only a handful of persons had the slightest interest in it. So it was that the lionized products of Leadbelly characteristically sold in the neighborhood of 100 copies apiece.

Within ten years of Leadbelly's death, "folk" music had erupted as a popular alternative to rock and roll. To its growing constituency of the late 1950s and early 1960s, folk music was non-commercial music, redolent of a handcrafted rather than mass-produced product, the work of humans instead of a machine. This was exactly what those who retailed folk music

---

*Calt and Wardlow, *King Of The Delta Blues* (Rock Chapel Press, 1988), p. 109.

wanted its audience to suppose, so that they would pay for the privilege of enjoying such an exalted product.

There was nothing remotely non-commercial about folk music and its assorted products, because none of them came without a pricetag. The consumer often paid a higher price for a "folk" album that he paid for an ordinary commercial item ($11.95, in the instance of a 1950 Folkways anthology, "American Folk Music"). The folk movement was simply a tiny industry that sold pretensions along with a product, its foremost pretension being that it was something other than a business, and that its humble products were somehow better and purer than crass articles of commerce.

In essence, the folk music that was retailed in this guise was a contradiction, actually a crude form of commercial double-talk, its supposed non-commercial nature its foremost *selling point*. This form of double-think enabled record labels to produce and sell "folk" products at prevailing prices without having them judged in terms of dollar or aesthetic value. When translated into the realm of commerce it actually represented once its flimsy rhetoric was peeled away, the premises of the folk movement meant simply that a record producer could dispense with the patina (and cost) of professionalism, but at the same time produce a profit. All that was really required of the folk singer was that he evince an attitude of sincerity; whether he was a capable or talented musician was thought to be besides the point.

Above all else, folk music of the early 1960s was characterized by a pretentious loftiness, consisting largely of an affectation of purity. As the sleeve jacket notes for Peter Paul and Mary's first album in 1962 announced: "There is just something *Good* about [the album] . . . Good in the sense of Virtue. . . . Honesty is back." The writer did not mention that this conglomerate of human Virtue included both a musical director and a manager who decreed that its feminine member should create a mystique by never talking on stage, and that one of the Holy Three (Peter Yarrow) had claimed composer credits for a black spiritual (*This Train*) featured on the album.

The reason that such a false confection as "folk music" could succeed was because it was congenial to a pre-existing consumer, namely the stylized teenage "beatnik" who emerged in the wake of *On The Road* (1957), and his modified successor of the early 1960s, who would sometimes be called a "peacenik" or "folknik." Although the life-span of the "beatnik" as a recognizable social entity lasted no more than five years (1959-1963), this figure was the real cause of the folk movement and with it, the ancilliary blues revival of the early and mid-1960s.

As the high school Beat considered himself essentially a noncomformist, and neither liked nor applied the label "beatnik," the recognizable literary and musical emblems of the "Beats" did not appeal to him. Unless he considered himself an artist, literature and poetry occupied a peripheral place in his life, running a distant second to music.

The coffeehouse that was to become the basic forum for "folk music" of the 1960s had originally loomed as a citadel of Beat culture, a place where one would presumably meet fascinating intellectuals and play chess. In the hopes of having such encounters or seeing authentic adult Beatniks, numerous high school Beats made weekend pilgrimages to Greenwich Village coffeehouses, where they sat sipping espresso and wondering where the Beat action had fled.

Whereas the adult "Beat" such as Jack Kerouac brandished an enthusiasm for cool or progressive jazz, his youthful counterpart had almost no taste for instrumental music. He or she readily gravitated to folk music, both in the form of retailed albums, and as played in urban and suburban coffeehouses by amateurs and professionals alike. The "Beat" often played acoustic guitar, learning a few rudimentary folk songs. By 1958, outright "folk" music in the form of the Kingston Trio had resulted in a No. 1 best-seller, a revival of the 1866 ballad *Tom Dula*. By the early 1960s, much was heard of a "folk revival," as if the sudden popularity of folk music had any precedent in American culture.

Were it not for the peculiar sensibilities of the Beat listener, there would have been no "folk revival," and no forum for any of its artists. There were four distinct components of the Beat outlook that fostered an appreciation of folk music, and with it, blues. The first was the essential quietism that was the basic hallmark of the Beat. "Folk" music reflected this quietism in the same way the coffee house did: it had the forcefulness, generally, of a lullaby or ballad, being played on an acoustic instrument, and by a single person or small group that did not even begin to approximate the volume or mayhem of rock and roll. This subdued ambience was also basic to blues music, as it was manifest to the early 1960s' listener: the most deafening singers of the 1920s, such as Charlie Patton, were smothered by static and poor recording quality. Even at that, most blues were too clamorous for Beats.

The second characteristic that pre-disposed the Beat to folk music was his avowed nonconformity, which was seen as positive on principle. The typical teenager of the late 1950s and early 1960s had a horror of taking up any amusement that was not certified by the crowd: something as marginal and as far removed from mainstream music as what passed for folk music would have brought an expression of acute distaste to his features. To the Beat, the unpopularity of folk music was its primary selling point: had it been the rage of high school students instead of rock and roll, he would have looked elsewhere for musical diversion. The fact that high school students, in the main, had never heard of folk music or the names of performers like Leadbelly gave the entity a snob appeal and its Beat listener a pretense of sophistication that was critical to its favorable reception by him.

The third factor was his attitude towards conventional learning, wisdom, common sense, and culture, which was that these things, being conventional, were superficial or of negligible import. Because of this overweening attitude, the Beat would suspend all value judgments as he listened to music. His child-like receptivity towards folk music prevented him from exercising the jaded ears of the average listener, who would likely see it as something crude, simple, passé, uncultured. This willing suspension of common sense facilitated an inherent regard for blues singers, whose message was seen as no less valid than that of a more accomplished musician or a more intelligent lyricist. By contrast, the ordinary blues singer would make a completely negative impression on a conventional white middle-class

listener of the period: he would immediately be seen as an illiterate, as a scruffy alcoholic or derelict, or as someone who
lagged far behind the level of civilization represented by a Nat
"King" Cole or Dizzy Gillespie, a figure who could not read
or write and who knew nothing about music.

The fourth aspect of Beatdom that certified folk music was
the Beat indifference to, and in many cases rejection of, the
ideal of romantic love, which gripped conventional teenagers
of the period and saturated pop music, rock and roll, and
rhythm and blues alike. The prevalent teenage custom of "going
steady" had no appeal for him, and he scrupulously avoided
this phrase even if he had a steady girlfriend. The universal
teenage female preoccupation with marriage (culminating ro-
mance) held no significance for female Beats.

It so happened that virtually none of the songs that were labelled as folk music had any romantic component. The "folk
ballad," as certified by scholars like Francis Child, was a song
that "told a story." It was not a song of sentiment.

Only in the field of folk music would it have been possible
to stage a three-day music festival involving 70,000 spectators,
without employing a single security person. There was no danger
that the lamb-like devotees of folk music who flocked to the
1964 Newport Folk Festival were apt to behave like normal
youths of the period or denizens of the riot-ridden 1960 Newport Jazz Festival, drinking beer and getting into fights. They
were reverential gawkers.

27. *The Fan*

The eighteen-year-old blues enthusiast stood gawking at an enclosure where performers of various sort were registering in
a trailer. His face pressed against the metal fence, he peered
about for anyone who looked like a blues singer.

It was July 24, the second day of the four-day festival. I had
just completed my freshman year in college, where I had spent
more time listening to Charlie Patton records than studying.
Almost no one of my acquaintance cared for blues, and the
ones who did were usually strange misfits: the high school John
Lee Hooker fan who had since committed suicide, the college
coffee house performer who claimed to have hoboed his way
through the South, playing blues, but who had actually spent
the time in a mental institution. For the most part, my infatuation with blues was a solitary, thoughtless preoccupation. It
was only much later, when I began to reflect upon the peculiarity
of passing the prime of adolescence absorbed in scratchy-sound-
ing records, that I recalled how the music had first insinuated
itself within me. I had developed a taste for blues when I was
too young to know that it was a special type of music, a music
of blacks, a music outside of the mainstream.

The first strains of a blues song I had heard came from my
best friend, near an integrated housing development. As an
adult I could still hear its echoes and see two tykes trudging
down the street, one seven, the other nine, the older black
child singing: "I'm a Mississippi bulldog, sittin' on a Harlem
dump."

"What's Harlem?" I asked, when the one-line song had concluded.

"It's a dump," the friend replied.

The same year, 1953, I had passed an exciting evening listening to the Leadbelly records my father was blasting on a phonograph, the tunes forever etched in his memory. And the following year, as a fourth grader, I watched with stark facination as two classroom ballerinas tap-danced their way through Joe Turner's *Shake, Rattle and Roll*.

Soon I was a pint-sized rock and roll addict, avidly and unknowingly absorbing a variety of blues songs that were retailed as rock and roll, sung by the likes of Turner, Carl Perkins, Elvis Presley, the Cadillacs, and even Pat Boone. It was a music for young punks and would-be criminals, and I aspired to become as tough as the faces I admired on Post Office wanted posters. As I outgrew these anti-social affectations, and settled into a pretentious Beat style, I began sampling my father's jazz albums, finding in boogie-woogie piano the same excitement I once had found in rock and roll. It was not until 1962 that I even recognized blues as a distinct genre of music, and began resolutely searching out blues albums, cutting through the slick surface of the form presented by the likes of Josh White, tunneling my way, so to speak, to its raw bottom strata.

It was an exasperating but exciting venture to stumble about in search of quintessential blues sounds, never knowing what lay hidden behind the cover of an unfamiliar album found in places like *Sam Goody's* and *The Record Hunter*, always adorned with liner notes that promised great music. More than once I excitedly brought home a record, only to be greeted by a hollow, enfeebled product. The hit-or-miss search ended when I came upon albums issued by The Origin Jazz Library, available in a single New York retail shop. Its scratchy reissues featured unpublicized nonentities like Charlie Patton and Skip James, who nevertheless stood at the core of blues.

There was something penetrating about their sounds, and something addictive (to me) in the way their voices and guitars played off each other, and the way their guitar notes were inflected. They played completely differently from the way folksingers, professional or amateur, played, sporting a real guitar *sound*. For all the attention he paid to sonority, the folk guitarist might as well have been playing a banjo. Although their guitar-playing was completely mannered, with an almost classical emphasis on tone, their voices were completely unvarnished. Patton sounded like the personification of the gutter.

After learning that Skip James and Son House (Patton's alleged disciple) would be at the Newport Folk Fesitival, I rigged up a cardboard sign reading NEWPORT and began hitchiking on a Friday afternoon. Newport was four hours north of my home, and the festival was to begin that evening.

The driver was going straight to Newport, his hometown. When I scurried into the back seat of his car, I saw a mound of empty beer cans. The man informed me he had been driving non-stop from Fort Bragg.

As he drove, he drank and made small talk about his stint in the Special Forces in Vietnam. He drunkenly displayed his scarred leg, stippled with scars from machine gun bullets. The war, he thought, was unwinnable. "The people don't give a shit," he complained. "When we're there, they're our friends. When the Communists are there, they're their friends."

I asked the serviceman what he thought of the idea of dropping atomic bombs there, which had recently been propounded by Barry Goldwater. "It wouldn't make any difference," the soldier said derisively. "There's nothing to bomb. But what the fuck. Sure. Drop 'em."

I was standing outside an enclosed fence, where a group of performers were gathered. Someone I had spoken to had mentioned that Robert Wilkins was also playing at the festival. When I asked one of the white performers if he knew where Wilkins was, the man replied: "Wilkins? Is he colored?" He made a sour Southern face.

There was a lone black man standing within the enclosure, doing nothing in particular. He looked to be about forty years old, his dark face unfurrowed by wrinkles. He was dressed so poorly as to stand out, the formality of his attire accentuating its shabbiness. None of the clothes looked his own: his dun-colored hat, twenty years out of date; his frayed white shirt, buttoned to its rumpled, oversize collar; his dark blue double-

The author, blues fanatic, and his sister Maggie visiting
Gary Davis a few months before meeting James.

breasted suit, the jacket bulky as an overcoat, the pants so broad as to conceal the contour of his legs; his shoes, dingy and dilapated beyond recognition. Even his expression looked shopworn. He was otherwise unremarkable; a standing signpost of poverty, plainly a pauper who was trying to put a respectable face on his poverty. I took him for a groundskeeper.

"Excuse me!" I called through the fence. When the man turned towards me, I asked: "Can you tell me where to find Robert Wilkins?"

The man walked over to the fence and began talking. He was apparently trying to be helpful.

"Robert Wilkins?"

"He's a blues singer."

Then I noticed the plastic square affixed to his lapel.

"Skip James! Are you *Skip James*? I heard your records!"

For the next twenty minutes we stood talking outside the enclave, the fan feverish and galvanized, the blues great subdued and nonchalant, but relishing the excitement and interest he had aroused.

I had only imaginary pictures of actual blues singers, and the Skip James of my imagination had been a nebulous, composite creature. I thought the singer of *Little Cow and Calf* was actually a white man, thanks to his name, his placid singing, and his clear diction. This impression was corrected by *Devil Got My Woman* and *Hard Times Killin' Floor*, where the singer sounded so ethereal that the sadness he projected seemed almost radiant. His *If You Haven't Any Hay*, the only other James tune I knew, seemed like the work of another person. I had never heard a vocal piano accompaniment played so rhythmically, each note sounded with the sharp precision of a vocal exclamation. The subdued sound of his voice and the couplets he sang gave an unalterable image of someone sitting alone, living a life on the run:

> I'm goin' I'm goin', comin' back no more
> If I go to Louisiana mama lord they'll
> They'll hang me sure.

The picture he projected was that of a man wanted for some unimaginable crime, unflustered by fate.

But all of these fancies dissolved with the discovery that Skip James was an actual person, and a lively conversationalist.

"You liked my records?" he asked with mock incredulity. In respose to my raving, he replied: "I thought I sang like a girl." Then he asked if I had seen the advertisements for his records, which he described in detail, or had heard various titles he had recorded in 1931.

The singer wanted to know if I had heard Johnnie Temple's version of *Devil Got My Woman,* which he proceeded to disparage, and if I had met his wife. "You haven't met my wife?" he asked increduously. "The prettiest woman in the South." Later I learned that she was still in Mississippi.

When I found out that his hometown lay near Jackson, I asked James if he had met Tommy Johnson. "Tommy Johnson, he was Lonnie Johnson's brother," James stated (incorrectly, it turned out). "Did you hear his *Coal-Black Mare?*" Gleefully, he recited its lyrics.

"What's *If You Haven't Any Hay* about?" I asked.

"Out in the country we used to go hack-ridin'; hay-ridin'. Sometimes there'd be someone who didn't have any *hay.* So, he'd best get on down the road." He chuckled, and began citing a low-down lyric: "You heard *Make Me A Pallet On The Floor?* Well, I styled it this way: 'Give me the keys to your back door. So I won't be bothered 'round the front no more.'"

All of his songs seemed to consist of such little jokes, immensely pleasing to their author, whose grinning recitation bared a set of rotten teeth. The singer told his new fan that he was only now getting back into the music world.

When a managerial figure led James to the two-story "blues cottage" that housed singers, I decided to follow him. I was intoxicated with exposure to a musician whose voice had echoed endlessly in my mind during the past two years. It was like meeting a dead person come to life. Had I known how our lives would intersect over the next four years, I would not have initiated that first conversation.

Skip James at Newport

28. *Newport*

"Since the Second World War a number of older blues singers
have been performing as concert artists for an intellectual white
audience that has usually confused the style with American folk
music," Sam Charters wrote in 1960.* By 1964, however, the
promotion of blues singers as folk artists was in full swing,
thanks to the inveterate opportunism of the folklorist and the
growing vogue for blues among white youths.

The original festival of 1959 had featured a single blues singer,
Memphis Slim, an urbane 44-year old Chicagoan whose tastes
in music ran to pieces like *September Song* and *Summertime*, and
whose folk pedigree rested purely on his association with Folkways Records, which was then hawking him as a "traditional"
blues singer. The 1964 version was a quasi-blues festival, with
over a dozen such performers, representing almost a third of
a musical menagerie that was equally divided between contemporary, "traditional" white Southern, and blues acts. Never before had so many blues singers been assembled in a single setting. The "blues cottage," a remote two-story house on the festival grounds where most of them were quartered, was a
continuous hubbub of activity.

Fifty-year-old Robert Pete Williams, a recent parolee from a
prison farm, had never been north of Louisiana, or appeared
in a concert. Dressed in a snap-brim fedora hat and a brown
suit, he looked like a caricature of a pimp. He had quick, nervous
gestures and a Cheshire smile that surfaced and retracted with
the suddenness of a switchblade, for no apparent reason. As

*Notes to *The Rural Blues*, RBF Records RF 202 (1960).

he stared at the young white girls milling about the "blues cottage," he could not comprehend that he was appearing in a music festival.

"What's this, a whorehouse?" he asked me.

The girls were blues fans, I laughingly explained. But Williams looked unconvinced. "This place looks like a whorehouse," he said.

Now he began cajoling his new roommate. "I don't care nothin' about playin' up here," he sneered. "We can have ourselves a party. I got plenty of money; I got enough for chicken, wine, girls . . ."

It was girls that most interested Williams. He announced that he was going to set a chair against the door of his room and keep everyone out until I returned with girls for both of us. He demonstrated what he called his "secret knock" that was to be used to signal my arrival.

"I don't care if she's white or colored," Williams said. "Long as she ain't no shabby."

A seemingly embittered Jesse (Lone Cat) Fuller stayed in his own room, living his nickname. "All I wanna do is get paid for it," he said of his appearance.

Sleepy John Estes, who had called himself "Poor John" in the 1920s, shared a room with his former recording mates, Yank Rachel and the bufoonish Hammie Nixon. While Rachel sat smoking a pipe or playing the six-month-old rock and roll hit he had worked up for the festival—*Hi-Heel Sneakers*—Estes and Nixon recalled their earlier days as sleazy blues singers.

Estes' pet trick had been to get money from the suckers on Beale Street by posing as a blind singer. Now he was actually blind.

Fred McDowell and his wife Annie sang a succession of spiritual duets, McDowell's bleating nasal voice barely carrying over his electric guitar. His wife had a pop-eyed, deranged look, and McDowell's musical piety did not blend well with his purple shirt.

The former Robert Wilkins (now Reverend Wilkins) attempted to distinguish himself from the blues riff-raff about him by boorishly bragging about his wardrobe.

"These shoes cost me sixty-five dollars," he told the ragged Skip James.

"Is that so? I'll have to get me a pair like that," James said sarcastically.

Someone asked James what his song expression "cherry ball" meant.

"Everyone has a cherry ball except the Reverend," he said, lookin at Wilkins. "You don't like 'cherry ball,' do you?" When Wilkins turned away uncomfortably, James said: "See that? He speaks against it."

One look at Al Wilson was sufficient to stamp him as a high school nerd, now become blues nerd. The 21-year-old budding blues guitarist wore a severe crewcut and formless khaki trousers. Nerds like Wilson seemed to gravitate towards blues singers, I thought: it was the equivalent of courting the homeliest girl in school, the only one who would not rebuff a request for a date.

But James was having none of Wilson's courtship. He eyed him with unconcealed disdain as the chubby, slovenly guitarist eagerly stuck to his side, hanging on his every word. "Why don't you take a bath?" he asked his fan, who looked stunned and speechless. A few moments later, Wilson began picking out a blues tune on the National guitar he had brought to Newport. Now he awaited James' appreciative remarks.

"You know," James said, "you ought to lose some weight. You can't play blues unless you stay in shape." To escape further heckling Wilson began keeping his distance from James.

In search of an idol who would not reject his social advances, he made a pilgrimage to Son House's apartment in Rochester several months later, only to discover that the great blues singer was the laughing stock of his neighbors.

"Hi, Son!" they taunted him as Wilson escorted him to the corner liquor store, their patronizing, simple-minded tone suggesting House's dim-wittedness.

As House grew sodden on the wine Wilson bought for him, the blues fan suffered another letdown. The simple-minded blues singer became a surly drunk, bitterly cursing his wife as though she had ruined his existence.

The 47-year-old Muddy Waters had not had a hit record for ten years, and his appearance at Newport (which paid a small honorarium) was symptomatic of his commercial decline. He was in the position of a musician whose works had grown obsolete, but had not acquired the vintage antique status of museum pieces like Skip James. Although placed on the white respirator, he had yet to carve out a niche among white audiences. In 1960, he had appeared at Newport's Jazz Festival. At its 1964 Folk Festival, he would be roundly ignored, thanks to his electric guitar and his band, which certified his folk inauthenticity.

To Skip James, however, Waters was the reigning sultan of blues, and the only musician he recognized at the Festival. Their brief encounter within the blues cottage was terse and tense, as though James were waiting for an opportunity to one-up Waters in some way, their sparring preceded by what James called Waters' "glad handshake." Later, he recalled: ". . . He say, 'I think you got it.'

"I said, 'I wouldn't say that.'

"He say, 'Oh, yeah.'

"I say, 'Why is that?'

"He say, 'Little Brother's in Chicago, still playin.'"

"I say, 'Well, *I* haven't been playin'.'"

"He say, 'When you start back playin'?'

"I told him 'bout three weeks, four weeks . . .

". . . He say, 'You ain't been playin' no longer than that?'

"I say, 'How you like that?'

"He say, 'Oh, I like it.' "

It never occurred to James that Waters was simply being polite in registering surprise that he had only been playing for a few weeks.

Although James had not been engaged as a featured Newport performer, and was not scheduled to appear in its regular evening concerts, it was he who was the reigning sultan of the "blues cottage." Over two days he was continually followed by fans and flunkies who found him an extraordinary figure—a blues legend come to life.

By now, he had worked up versions of *Crow Jane* and *Catfish Blues*, the latter salacious:

I want you to take me baby, and lay me down 'cross
   your bed
I'm gonna suck your titties till your
Nipples turn cherry-red ...

Under the prodding and coaxing of his followers, he began re-
creating *Illinois, Special Rider,* and *I'm So Glad,* with the claim
that he had not played them in thirty years. All the while, he
was quiet and subdued, and did not seem to share the enthusiasm of the listeners who flocked around him. "You never
smile," one of them said.

Another fan asked how he felt. "I feel pretty fair," he
said.

"Only 'pretty fair?'" the fan replied.

"I think 'pretty fair' is pretty good, don't you?" James shot
back, fixing the fan with a stare.

Later, he would remark that he was suffering such physical
pain that he had begun to think seriously of suicide.

When someone popped a beer can open behind him, James
gave a violent start. He had mistaken the sound for gunfire.
It was the first, indirect inkling of the squalid environment he
had stepped out of.

James' nine-minute outdoor performance in an afternoon
blues "workshop" (actually a mini-concert) on July 25 was, to
many blues devotees, the most dramatic moment of the festival.
His four songs produced an electrifying effect on his audience,
and there was a general air of euphoria within his immediate
circle of backers, who had wondered in the light of his actual
concert debut three weeks before if he would shape up as a
viable blues act. On that occasion, as they were ferrying James
northwards, his discoverers had decided to put him on in Memphis' only coffeehouse, *The Bitter Lemon* (a local drug haunt).
James had gotten drunk and seemed barely able to play. They
were further alarmed because he had voided his bladder in the
car as they drove to Washington, D.C. with their quarry.

The drama of James' Newport resurrection, and the large as-
sembly of blues singers there, had created a pre-Woodstock illusion of a blues rebirth. Years later, as I listened to the Vanguard recordings of the James concert, I recognized the sen-

timental, juvenile nature of my joyous excitement when I witnessed James' seeming resurrection. The drama had been the
result of the uncertainty that James could perform, which had
given his performance a triumphant quality. But it was the soap
opera triumph of an impaired performer. James could barely
play guitar, and he limped his way through skeletal accompaniments to *Devil, Sick Bed Blues, Cypress Grove* and *Cherry Ball.*
His struggle had been stirring, not the results themselves.

After listening to James at Newport, one of Son House's
discoverers walked over to Bill Barth, a member of James' two-
man entourage. "We found the wrong guy," he said enviously.
James appeared to be on the brink of becoming the dominant
figure of a blues renaissance: all he needed was enough practice
to clear the cobwebs from his fingers.

On the basis of his Newport performance, James could have
obtained a recording contract with the prestigious Vanguard
label, whose officials had taped its concerts and workshops. But
the blues prospectors who were nuturing his comeback were
solely concerned with their own profit. They never so much
as entertained the idea of signing James to a well-distributed,
well-regarded label that would earn him the maximum profit
and publicity. James was treated as a trophy of the tiny Takoma
label, which had only one record on the market (by Booker
White) and had been created with a view towards providing
a forum for its founder John Fahey. It is doubtful that anyone
in James' retinue was even aware of the fact that the singer
was even capable of self-interest, or entitled to exercise it. Looking back at the various persons who avariciously attached themselves to blues singers of the period, a record collector comments: "It was really a plantation mentality. Everyone wanted
to own a nigger."

22 days after his Newport appearance, James was whisked to
a private studio in Silver Spring, Maryland and recorded for
Takoma. Another session followed four days later, on August
20th. The songs that ensued would remain unissued for the
next 29 years. By the time they finally surfaced, on a 1993 Genes
Company CD titled *She Lyin'* (a misnomer for *See The Line*),
they had a familiar quality, thanks to the fact that James had

since recorded most of the same tunes for other labels.* Yet the difference between the newly-rediscovered Skip James and the anemic, apathetic James of later recordings is astonishing. Although James had not gotten his real bearings on guitar, his singing had the dramatic intensity of his Newport appearance; *Devil Got My Woman* was probably the most stirring vocal effort of his entire comeback.

Shortly afterwards, James was hospitalized in Washington. "He went downhill after that," the engineer of the Takoma session, Gene Rosenthal, noted.

Racked by illness, James was out of commission for the summer and fall. Fahey decamped for California, leaving him in the hands of intermediaries.

By the end of the year, James had failed to sign a Takoma contract, although he gave the impression that he would be willing to record for the label once his health improved. ". . . I guess after my time expires in this company, if they do as they promised, I may re-enlist and proceed on playin' another year or so . . . When I quit this one, I ain't joinin' any other one . . . When that abscess come to a head, I'm not gonna go bustin' no other one."

---

*Genes' owner, who had originally engineered the session, acquired the tapes from Takoma in 1970. His treasure trove, he states, will eventually run to four CDs.

29. *Washington*

In the meantime, he scarcely had any musical jobs. His basic outlet was a local coffeehouse, *The Ontario Place*, which had been founded largely as a forum for John Hurt, its reigning local attraction.

As James became more practiced, he became a disappointment to the hard-core blues addicts who had believed that his dramatic appearance at Newport foreshadowed a stirring comeback. Almost immediately, his singing lost its Dundee/Newport intensity, which had been designed to compensate for his inability to play. The new pieces he began to trot out, like *Worried Blues* and *I Looked Down The Road*, were unexceptional, run-of-the mill blues. Only in playing relatively simple, straightforward tunes like *Cypress Grove, Cherry Ball*, and *Hard Times* did he appear to be his 1931 instrumental equal. The inexplicable alterations he had made to *Devil* deprived it of its most interesting brushstrokes. *I'm So Glad* now took on the nature of a banal ditty, played without speed or forcefulness. His piano playing had suffered even more erosion, and pieces like *If You Haven't Any Hay* and *How Long* came across as slow, stodgy ballads, their melodies paramount. Unexpectedly, a blues great had metamorphisized into a mediocrity, using his blues idiom as a crutch to convey him rather than a canvas to paint upon.

For his current white audience, in the main, it was sufficient for him to merely "play the blues," which was the selling-point of his revived career. In his heyday, to play the blues meant practically nothing, since every black Southern performer played them. To stand out among the crowd it was necessary to rise above the herd or somehow make a forceful impression. So it was that James and his most talented peers had become blues greats.

The intervening years, the prolonged periods of penance, and the passing of the blues life had all chipped away at the blunt edges of his music. Once James had touted the ability of blues song to "deaden the mind" of its female listeners. At its best, the blues guitar was almost a cutting instrument, its tones and inflections containing a piercing quality. Once James had attained this quality by isolating the most acrid tones in conventional chords. Now he had changed the way he sounded a B7th; instead of implying it and omitting the fifth, he created a cretinuous-sounding full chord, and created another tonic chord of the same construction by sliding up the neck of his guitar. He became so enamored of this figure that it became a musical calling card. To the devotee of his old records it was funeral music, signifying the death of James' once-potent musical magic.

No one could account for its unexpected loss. To some extent, concert presentation robbed James of initiative. He was paid a flat performance fee, garnishing only audience applause for whatever impression he made with what he called "Skip's music, his fingers, and his art." Such was the way of the legitimate music world—a foreign world to James, who had always (whether on the street or at a house "frolic") had an economic incentive in the form of potential tips to give his performances their greatest possible allure.

The staring eyes and impassive faces of sedentary white listeners made him acutely uncomfortable on stage. "Sometimes they just look at me like I was ... I don't know what—a bear or somethin'," he was to remark. Even when he finally understood that the zombified manner of the white concertgoer was meant to convey respect, it continued to rattle him. He tried to play with as much inattentiveness to this unsettling audience as he could muster, frequently closing his eyes and looking heavenward as he sang, as if in the throes of emotion. There was no emotion: only uneasiness.

Only once did the author find James thoroughly relaxed and in top musical form at a concert engagement. The audience consisted of almost entirely of black teenagers affiliated with a Head Start program in Nyack, New York, none of whom had

any previous acquaintance with blues. They took readily to
James' jaded lyrics, many of which struck them as the wise-ass
quips they could imagine someone actually saying. Every violent
allusion he made provoked open mirth:

> I'm gonna find her, I'm gonna find her, with my
> smokin' .44
> And when I find that black woman, her nappy head
> won't be hard no more.

Buoyed by such uncharacteristic listener responsiveness, James
gave an uncharacteristically confident, forceful performance.

But the blues "revival" was completely white in character, and
James served his tepid audiences a musical equivalent of themselves. Most blues rediscoveries of the 1960s did not alter the
tenor of their original attack. But this was largely due to the
fact that they knew no other attack: an impassioned blues
shouter like Son House had never played for whites before being
yoked to the blues "revival." James, on the other hand, had
frequently entertained Southern white gatherings, largely on the
basis of his ability to play placid pop pieces like *Carolina Moon*.
He seemed to assume that diluting his blues with a comparable
aura of gentility would make them more suitable to white audiences.

In truth, he had little to gain by purifying his newly-adulterated
blues of the past; the handful of hardcore blues addicts who
looked askance at his adulterations could not have filled a coffeehouse.

That became clear when James made his New York debut
at the Gaslite, a popular MacDougal Street "folk" coffeehouse
forum, in January of 1965. The attendance was so dismal for
his three-night engagement that when I attached myself to
James' two-man entourage, the desperate owner tried to shame
me into paying admission. "It's pretty sad when a man's friends
don't support him," he said. Blues were still off the beaten path,
a musical form that the majority of whites had either never
heard of or had only a vague sense of, thanks to the paucity
of interracial publicity it had received. The increasingly conventional blues conformist Skip James was bent on becoming was

still too esoteric to make him anything but a commercial liability on even the coffeehouse concert circuit.

So it was that James spent most of his first six months as a blues rediscovery stationed at the local *Ontario Place*, where a new set of sycophants descended upon him. Instead of blues addicts like Al Wilson, they consisted of neophytes like Ed Morris, who pestered James for guitar lessons. After James showed Morris a few tunes, he discovered that the fledging guitarist had set himself up as a guitar instructor, giving paying lessons to other novices. James was indignant to the point of never giving lessons to "groupies" again.

Another budding guitarist who learned from James was a 34-year-old carpenter, John Cephas, whose earliest music had been imitative of Blind Boy Fuller. James was the first "name" blues singer he had ever met. "I was so enchanted and fascinated with his sound that I practiced and listened to him for hours on end, just trying to figure out what he was doing," he would later recall.* He mustered up versions of James' *Cherry Ball* and *Hard Time Killin' Floor*. As a black musician in a field where guitarists beneath the age of 50 were invariably white, Cephas was an anomoly, as well as a pedestrian player whose career only bloomed once the 1960s' generation of blues singers died off.

In 1983 Cephas recorded his *Tribute To Skip James*. It was the kind of gesture of fellowship that James himself would have been incapable of making. When a German blues enthusiast would write him a letter asking for his reminiscences of Little Brother Montgomery, James would fling it aside, remarking: "Shit on Little Brother. I'm not interested in him; I'm interested in Skip." He took little notice of other musicians, except to disparage them. "He's a poor songster," he said of Son House. "Some folks don't know any better, they think that's music," he said of Big Joe Williams.

Although James had no career to speak of, he had both a manager and a road manager. The manager, "Banana Ed" Denson, worked as the business manager of Takoma Records, which meant that he handled all of the business of the two-man com-

Blues Guitar, edited by Jas Obrecht (GPI Books, San Francisco, 1990), p. 50.

pany. Denson knew nothing about blues music and gave off the appearance of being a hanger-on when he attended the Newport Folk Festival in 1964. In James' company he had a disagreeable habit of pulling out a harmonica and blowing amateurishly on it, as though the pair were on a musical par, or engaged in some folk "hootenanny." He was enamored of psychedelic drugs, and would rhapsodize, "Skip's got a mind like LSD," as though that made him a figure of infinite depth.

Denson had signed a one-year personal managerial contract with James, apparently because the artist was leery of attaching himself to an unknown record company. Thanks to his part-ownership of Takoma, his role represented a blatant conflict of interest. He appeared to function primarily as a stalking-horse for the company, preventing James from wandering off to another label.

James' road manager Bill Barth was one of the most agreeable and least avaricious persons who surrounded blues singers of the period. He was also one of the few white blues guitarists who did not have a passion for self-promotion. By 1964, he could play at least as well as James, but always kept in the background. It was Barth's job to see that James' guitar was in tune, that he appeared at his jobs, and was paid for his work.

The amateurishness of James' handlers is indicated by the fact that they had no promotional materials to offer prospective clients. For the most part, they bided their time, thinking that James would be in a position to acquire coffeehouse jobs once he had completed an album.

It was not only because of his innate standoffishness that James did not mix well with the "blues fraternity." Most of the assorted blues enthusiasts who mingled with him behaved as though they were his benefactors, whose very presence was somehow ennobling the life of a downtrodden blues singer. Such was the attitude of the self-aggrandizing white blues guitarist who was to author numerous instruction books in the field of "country blues," and give off the impression that he had been one of James' associates. The mention of his name would make James bristle, and recall their acrimonious 1965 encounter at a New York coffeehouse. "I had just got off-stage . . . He say: 'Skippy, you got a new guitar?'

"I say: 'Yes.'

" 'Oh boy, that's great! Lemme see it!' I passed it over to him: 'Oh man, this is a *white* man's guitar!'

"Now I had already give him information in music; sit up two, three hours one night tryin' to give him music, and that's the kind of consideration and appreciation I get . . . I said: 'Why do you think a white man should have that guitar?'

"He say: 'Oh, Skippy, I don't want you to blow your top, now. I know—'

"I say: 'No, you don't.' I said: 'Now here's what: it could be a white man's guitar, but a black man got it, and I think I got a white man's integrity.'"

In James' view, the obnoxious blues guitarist had been putting on a display for his girlfriend. "He wanted to show off 'fore that old tackhead [brainless female]. I coulda did the same thing, 'fore my wife or some colored girls there; some of my fans. I coulda showed my hindparts, too, *if I wanted to*."

After James' death the young "tackhead" became a popular concert blues entertainer, performing note-for-note versions of songs like *Devil Got My Woman*. This literal approach to his songs would have struck James as a faulty way to render blues music. In James' view, imitativeness was the mark of an untalented student: "If you're musically inclined, you can just go on, hear somethin', and that sound will stay within, until you get some- place where you can try it, say: 'Yeah, I'm gonna change this thing, play it this a-way.' You got a send-off, right in that other fellow's version which you heard . . . you can still add on to it, re-arrange it, and change it, fix it any way you want it. . . ." Such had been his own approach to blues-playing.

The members of the blues illuminati were unprepared for James' independence and outspokenness. Their ideal compan- ion had been Mississippi John Hurt, a perpetually pleasant, pas- sive individual who announced: "I don't care if someone calls me 'boy.'" James acquired a reputation for being thin-skinned, primarily because his openly patronizing fans did not know how to approach him with anything resembling decorum or respect. One of his temporary road managers finally asked him: ". . . 'With your temper that you have, why is it you ain't done got killed down in Mississippi?'

"I say: 'Why you think that? What is your object?'

"He say, 'Oh, well . . . I didn't have no reason. . . .' He say, 'You ain't scared of nobody, is you?'

". . . I say: 'Scared of nobody? *What?*'

"He say: 'I just notice how you talk . . . .'

"I said: 'I talk *straight* and I don't do nothin' to nobody. . . . What I say I mean, and if I don't say nothin' I don't mean nothin' . . . I speak facts, and I want you to tell *me* facts. And if you do somethin' I don't like, I'll tell you about it.' "

Such outspokeness did not endear James to blues fans of the period. What they really sought in James was a social companion: someone who would share their relish for old blues records, who would reminisce about his old buddies in the blues field, teach his songs to his new-found friends in the manner of a Pete Seeger, and share joints with them. On every count, James was a disappointment. He listened to collectors' records with strained politeness. He had no enthusiasm for Mississippi bluesmen of the past. He was the opposite of the blues name-dropper; when asked about the fabled Mississippi bluesmen Rube Lacy and Kid Bailey (both of whom he had met), he would say: "I know *of* Rube Lacy," or "I know *of* Kid Bailey," and fail to elaborate. When he would show a song to someone, it was invariably an undistinguished piece like *I Looked Down The Road* that played a peripheral part in his repertoire. When James had been offered marijuana by one of his discoverers, he had smoked without comment and promptly fallen asleep. He was not interested in any drug. In short, James behaved as if he were bent on pursuing the musical career that Fahey and Barth had dangled before him in Dundee. He had not learned that their talk had been basically a fantasy.

30. *The Sick Man*

James had no inkling that he was largely surrounded by inept, ambitious schemers whose petty machinations had stalemated his recording career. By the end of 1964, the two-man, two-bit Takoma label had merged with the two-man, two-bit Piedmont label, which had been founded to record Mississippi John Hurt and now boasted of two artists, Hurt and Robert Wilkins. The addition of Takoma's retinue (consisting of James and Booker White) would, it was felt, result in a superlabel that would corner the blues market. When one of Piedmont's partners was abruptly voted out of the new company, which may have been the true purpose of the merger, he began tying the fledging label (Bullfrog Records) up in court. The intended James recordings were put on indefinite hold.

To their eternal discredit, James' self-styled benefactors took little interest in the state of his health. They saw to it that he was equipped with a set of false teeth, but never concerned themselves with the cause of the ailment that had made him a hospital case at the time of his rediscovery. It was said on the blues circuit that James' condition was due to syphillis.

Between sets at the *Ontario Place*, he would fearfully scrutinize his penis, which was disfigured by a tumor, in the men's room. By late 1964, James had a gaunt, sickly appearance and was in constant pain, thanks to the untreated cancer that had drawn him to the Tunica County Hospital. "Heap of time I'll be playin'," he said at the time, "I'll be sittin' on the stage in misery. Pain."

Curing his condition became an abiding preoccupation with him. The little money James picked up as a blues player was siphoned off into the hands of a black con artist in Washington whom James considered a "specialist" and a "medical man." When he visited New York in January of 1965 to appear at the *Gaslite*, he spoke at length on this subject.

"At this period of time, as I have duties to perform in music, and try to carry my work on, seems to me that my health is failin' me so *fast*. I can't find a medical doctor or a surgeon to do me any good because they can't diagnose my case: it's beyond their comprehension. I been to a couple of hospitals and they operated on me. They cut on me and they experimented on me, till perhaps they have gone too far and destroyed the main part of my strength and health." By this, James was referring to his penis.

"I know I've been X-rayed and X-rayed . . . they've cut on me and then they've sent off some of my flesh, and had it inspected and all that," he continued. "But it's not no contagious disease as they had to confess and give up to that end." At the time, James was smarting because his discoverers had attributed his condition to syphillis.

"Heap of times I goes to medical doctors, my case gets worse. Every time they experiment on me, that makes me worse." Having established that the cure was the disease, James discussed the treatment he was then taking in Washington from an "herb doctor."

" . . . He told me—he *guaranteed* me that he would cure me. An' he already have told me things which have happened to me, and how it *did* happen . . . He's an international man and he has lots of patients, so I have been informed. And he asked me, say: 'What would you give me to take up this case?'

"I said, 'Well, I'll tell you: I don't like to set a price or estimate on another man's work. I'm not a doctor; I can't set no price.'

" 'Just give me an idea. What do you think it would be worth to you?'

" 'I dunno; to get my health and to get this misery offa me, it'd be worth a thousand dollars to me in a way, almost. It may be worth a million.' I said, 'But still, I can't set no price on it: *you're* takin' up the case.'

"He say: 'Aw, just make a guess.'

"I said, 'All right, twenty-five or thirty dollars.'

"He said, 'Aw man, I wouldn't even *start* the case for that.'

"I said, 'Well, just set your price then. You guarantee you would cure me; you guarantee your work?'

"He said, 'Yes.' He already had examined me. He said, 'Now I'll tell you something.' He said, 'There's something inside you that should come out.' Say, 'Don't you feel sick in your stomach?'

"I say, 'Yes.'

"He say, 'That misery that's in your privates, where they'se been operatin' and experimentin' on you: they keep a-cuttin' and they're liable to cut yourself to death.'

"He say, 'Now you was *fixed* . . . by a woman. A brownskin woman that was tryin' to destroy you and your wife; depart you and your wife.'

"I say, 'Yes, that's right . . .'

". . . He told me it happened by intercoursin' with a woman, understand? And, she's messed me up that way, tryin' to cross out my nature . . . And since I never did go her way, quite naturally she has it fixed so that things keep gettin' worse and worse. Just so that if I never did 'socialize' with *her* any more, then I never would be able to associate with nobody else."

James paid the con artist $35 in advance: "That was just to get the herbs he uses and so forth." His treatment would cost a mere $265.

It was pathetically easy for James to accept this explanation, because it lodged the blame where he was already convinced it belonged: on a female culprit. His view of women was so jaundiced that he did not have to analyze the woman in question to arrive at the conclusion that she was bent upon destroying him. Any female he encountered was likely to plot his ruination, or the ruination of any other man. "I'll tell you," he stated, as he complained about his "jinks of death," "a lot of people have experienced those things about women. They've did all they could for 'em . . . I know men have set women down, didn't 'low 'em to work, didn't 'low 'em to do nothin' . . . Then that woman had that man killed. 'Cause of one guy that she *thought* that she was gonna get to marry." It was his jaundiced view of women, he said, that was the basis of his blues songs: "See, those kinda ideas I catch and I just convert 'em into music, songs, where they'll fit, and heap of people . . . hear those songs and know exactly—it'll hit somebody."

But James' songs never generalized about women, or articulated his view of man as the weaker, more ingenuous vessel: ". . . A woman is wise from the beginning, and she's continually and constantly seekin' and graspin' at the weakest spot of a man. She gonna get it, too; she has got it." This sexual power, he believed, made them arrogant and dangerous. "You may tell a girl that you don't have time to consume with her; say for instance you tell her: 'I'm gonna run downtown, and I'll be back in a few minutes. We can wait till I come back, or perhaps at some other time before I contend [have sex] with you.' Well, she may then begrudge you and envy you and sic her associates on you."

Old Testament portrayals of women as underminers fed into this delusion. "There's no tellin' what people are requestin' of you as an innocent person . . . You could be beheaded like John the Baptist for no reason at all . . . Now John was slaughtered for just one dancin' girl, Salome."

James' view of the dark machinations of the opposite sex may not have been simply born completely of Biblical abstractions and proverbial prejudices. A cousin was to characterize him as a "horse," a term used by old-fashioned blacks to mean a conjurer, and James himself made an engimatic, inexplicable reference to his association with conjurers: "I learned to sit under the feets of people who are styled as gazers." He recalled unspecified visits to "prognosticators," and these persons were likely to have been conjurers. "Yes, I have talked with some," he said. "They have told me things which have happened to pass and come true; they have warned me, too; they have told me things what would happen and they has happened."

"I used to go to New Orleans, place they call Algiers, across the river . . . That's where those 'wise' people supposed to have been," he said. When James was to describe the powers of conjurers to the author, he used himself as an example: "I can be talkin' with you, in a word or two; I can just get out of sight. You turn around: 'Where is Skip goin'?' And I could be sittin' right here . . . And, I could disguise myself and get in a bottle . . . I could be get out of that bottle and be sittin' right 'side you."

Had James actually dabbled in conjuring at some point (which would support his claim, "there are mighty few places I haven't been or things I haven't been into"), he would not have learned to miniaturize himself, but he would have learned that innocu-ous-looking people were capable of hatching sinister plots that required the assistance of a conjurer.

If James had not actually practiced conjuring, he had certainly absorbed some of its cliches. "In conversations, I can sit down and I can tell from a few words if a person is worthwhile for me to consume the time to converse with 'em," he said. "I can see a person come in that door there, and before they get to me I can just read 'im. I can look at a woman and tell just about what type of girl she is . . . what she'll stand, and what she want, an' whether she'll 'Judas' or not. What her object in life. I can just look at her eyes; on her mouth; nostrils; how high her temple; ear . . . You can tell whether to approach her or not, as a friend . . . Look at her fingernails and mostly tell about the sexual part of life."

Just as his infallible antennae had failed to warn him of the underminer in Tunica, so did the $265 James paid to lift his "jinks of death" fail to alleviate his condition. In early 1965, he became a patient at D.C. General Hospital. To James' horror, he was castrated after doctors discovered his tumor was can-cerous.

31. *Air Puddings*

After being discharged from the hospital in early April of 1965, James gained weight and took on a healthy appearance. Although the operation left him with a permanent loss of appetite, he remained paunchy. In place of the physical pain he had formerly endured, he now felt psychological anguish. The amputation had been a trauma akin to the loss of Captain Ahab's leg. Like Captain Ahab, he plotted vengeance against the party responsible.

But first, he had other matters to attend to. Once he recuperated from his operation, he began ridding himself of what he considered to be excess career baggage: Denson and Barth. Once removed from James' sphere, Denson would return to Berkeley, California, where he found a congenial cultural climate in the burgeoning hippie movement. By the late 1960s he had become the manager of Country Joe and The Fish, who attained a hit record with their anti-war *Fixin' To Die Rag*.

Barth, who had a genuine love of blues music and a genuine attachment to Skip James, was quietly devastated to find himself dropped by his own rediscovery. To him, James became a figure of ingratitude, all the more so because James had lost his own $400 guitar (or so he had said) after getting drunk at a concert in Philadelphia, and had never offered to replace it. The following year, the deposed road manager wrote an intoxicated letter to a friend: "have you seen James. I fortunately have not, though if you see him you may tell him i been to a black witch, an his time aint long. remember, a BLACK witch, this is important, you'll see an interestin re-eaction i betcha."

James never kept in touch with his former handlers. His pet phrase of the period—"I put that baby to bed"—reflected his breezy attitude towards fellowships, as did another favorite saying: "Squat that rabbit and jump another one."

Once Fahey's retinue disappeared from James' life, James was cultivated by Dick Spottswood, the ousted partner of Piedmont Records. A librarian who had begun collecting blues records in the early 1950s, he owned one of the two existing copies of *Special Rider/I'm So Glad*. His wife Louisa, an heiress to the DuPont family, was said to have bankrolled his venture in the record business. At Newport, Spottswood constantly hovered over James and appeared to regard him almost as his personal property.

It was Spottswood's intention to feature James on his own just-created label, Melodeon, as soon as James was physically well enough to record. It had almost no distribution, and did not offer an advance comparable to Prestige's contemporary $350 allotment to the average blues singer.

In January of 1965, Spottswood's partner Pete Kuykendal induced James to sign a publishing contract, assigning the rights to his songs to Spottswood's music company. The cynicism of this transaction is difficult to express, or exceed. Whereas publishing contracts are normally an adjunct of recording contracts, there was, in this instance, no recording contract. James was too sick to record a full-length album. He therefore stood to gain no benefit from a publishing contract. The beneficiaries were the publishers, provided that the ailing James died and his songs were posthumously recycled in the fashion of "folk" staples. They had gone to the trouble of sniffing out all of James' known 1931 song titles, even lost works like *Yola My Blues Away*, which the artist no longer remembered, even as a title; to him it was *Yolee Blues* (his corruption of "yodel"). They copyrighted standards that James performed but could not possibly have composed, like *Crow Jane* and *Catfish Blues*.

Had a "race" record label operated in such a fashion, it would have acquired a notorious reputation among present-day blues chroniclers. Their descendents of the 1960s are just well-meaning blues enthusiasts, out to preserve a neglected art. Eventually,

AGREEMENT MADE THIS 27th DAY OF **January** 19 65 BETWEEN
WYNWOOD MUSIC COMPANY , HEREINAFTER AS PUBLISHER AND

NEHEMIAH "SKIP" JAMES

JOINTLY AND/OR SEVERALLY DESIGNATED HEREINAFTER AS WRITER.

WITNESSETH

(1) THE WRITER HEREBY ASSIGNS, TRANSFERS, SELLS, AND DELIVERS TO THE PUBLISHER, ITS SUCCESSORS AND ASSIGNS, ALL OF HIS RIGHTS, TITLE AND INTEREST IN AND TO A CERTAIN HERETOFORE UNPUBLISHED ORIGINAL WORK, WRITTEN AND/OR COMPOSED BY THE WRITER, NOW ENTITLED,

"I'M SO GLAD"

INCLUDING SAID TITLE, MUSIC AND/OR WORDS THEREOF, AS WELL AS THE ENTIRE EXCLUSIVE RIGHT TO PERFORM PUBLICLY AND TELEVISE, AND ALSO INCLUDE THE RIGHT TO SECURE COPYRIGHTS, AND RENEWALS THEREIN THROUGHOUT THE WORLD, AS THE PROPRIETOR IN ITS OWN NAME, OR OTHERWISE, AND TO HAVE AND TO HOLD THE ABOVE STATED WORK, COPYRIGHTS AND RENEWALS THEREOF AND ALL RIGHTS WHATSOEVER NATURE THEREUNDER EXISTING.

(2) THE WRITER HEREBY WARRANTS THAT THE SAID WORK IS HIS SOLE, ORIGINAL AND EXCLUSIVE WORK, THAT THE WRITER HAS FULL RIGHT AND POWER TO MAKE THE WITHIN STATED AGREEMENT, AND FURTHER THAT THERE EXISTS NO CLAIM ADVERSE TO AND/OR IN THE SAID WORK, WHICH IS FREE FROM ALL ENCUMBRANCES, LIENS AND AFORE MENTIONED CLAIMS WHATSOEVER.

(3) IN CONSIDERATION OF THIS AGREEMENT THE PUBLISHER AGREES TO PAY THE WRITER, JOINTLY THE FOLLOWING ROYALTIES:

(A) 50% OF THE NET AMOUNT RECEIVED BY THE PUBLISHER IN RESPECT TO ANY LICENSES ISSUED AUTHORIZING THE MANUFACTURE OF PHONOGRAPH RECORDS OR OTHER INSTRUMENTS WHICH SERVE TO MECHANICALLY REPRODUCE SAID WORKS IN THE UNITED STATES AND CANADA.

(B) 50% OF THE NET AMOUNT RECEIVED BY THE PUBLISHER, FROM SALES OF PHONOGRAPH RECORDS AND/OR SHEET MUSIC OUTSIDE THE UNITED STATES AND CANADA.

(C) 3 CENTS PER COPY, IN RESPECT OF REGULAR PIANO COPIES AND/OR ORCHESTRATIONS, SOLD IN THE UNITED STATES AND CANADA FOR WHICH THE PUBLISHER RECEIVED PAYMENT.

(4) THE PUBLISHER HERE IN AGREES TO RENDER TO THE WRITER ON OR ABOUT FEBRUARY 15TH AND AUGUST 15TH OF EACH YEAR, SO LONG AS IT SHALL CONTINUE PUBLISHING AND/OR LICENSING SAID WORK, COVERING THE SIX MONTHS ENDING DECEMBER 31ST AND JUNE 30TH OF EACH YEAR RESPECTIVELY, ROYALTY STATEMENTS ACCOMPANIED BY REMITTANCE OF THE AMOUNT DUE.

(5) IN RESPECT TO THE AFOREMENTIONED ROYALTIES THE WRITER IS HEREBY GRANTED THE POWER TO OBTAIN AN ACCOUNTING OF SAME ROYALTIES UPON HIS WRITTEN REQUEST WITHIN TWO WEEKS AFTER RECEIPT OF SAID REQUEST, BUT NO MORE THAN THREE TIMES PER CALENDAR YEAR, INCLUDING THE TWO AFOREMENTIONED ACCOUNTING DATES.

(6) THE PUBLISHER IS FURTHER GRANTED THE RIGHT TO CHANGE, ALTER, TRANSLATE, OR EDIT THE WORK THEREOF, IN ANY WAY IT MAY BE NECESSARY FOR THE PUBLISHER TO CAUSE LYRICS TO BE WRITTEN IN OTHER LANGUAGES FOR, AND AS PART OF THE WORK, THE PUBLISHER SHALL IN SUCH EVENT HAVE THE RIGHT TO DEDUCT FROM THE HERETOFORE AGREED ROYALTIES PAYABLE TO THE WRITER, THE COST OF THESE OBLIGATIONS THEREOF, BUT THIS AMOUNT WILL BE EQUAL TO NO MORE THAN 50% OF THESE INCURRED OBLIGATIONS.

Publishing contract for *I'm So Glad*

(2)

(7) The Writer hereby grants, and conveys an irrevocable power of attorney empowering and authorizing the Publisher, its nominees, successors or assigns, to administer any and all fees relating therefrom; also to file application and renew the copyrights in the names of the Writer, and upon such renewals, to execute proper and formal assignments thereof so as to secure the Publisher, its successors and assigns, the renewal terms relating to said copyrights and/or works.

(8) The Writer agrees to indemnify and save harmless the Publisher against any loss, expense and/or damage by reason of any adverse claims made by others with respect to the work, and agrees that all expenses incurred in defense of any of these claims made by others with respect to the work, including counsel fees, as well as all sums paid by the Publisher, pursuant to a judgement, arbitration or any adjustment or settlement which may be made at the discretion of the Publisher, or otherwise shall at all times be borne by the Writer, and may subsequently deducted by the Publisher from any money accuring to the Writer under this agreement or otherwise.

(9) The Writer agrees that he will not assign this Agreement nor any sums that may be due hereunder, without the written consent of the Publisher first endorsed hereon.

(10) Except as otherwise herein provided, this Agreement is binding upon the parties hereto and their respective successors in interest.

(11) Your signature below shall make this contract valid and in effect signifying your agreement to the terms indicated herein.

(12) This agreement covers __One (1)__ compositions.

Nehemiah Skip James
NEHEMIAH "SKIP" JAMES   WRITER

_____
ADDRESS

_____
WRITER

_____
ADDRESS

WYNWOOD MUSIC COMPANY

BY _Peter Hugley___

_____
WRITER

_____
ADDRESS

their calculations would pay off handsomely: they would collect royalties for a hit rock song James never recorded for Spottswood and did not even write, *I'm So Glad*.

Not long after leaving the hospital, James resumed his recording sessions for Spottswood. "They had to tie a pillow to his foot because he was stomping so hard," Hank O'Neal, a blues enthusiast who attended the session, recalls. When the sessions (held at Spottswood's home) were formally completed, on July 28, 1965, Spottswood paid him $200.

James, who had balked at signing any recording contracts, received a Melodeon contract in the mail almost a year later, in August of 1966. The contract was only dated "1965"; it assigned the rights and master recordings for seventeen titles—virtually his entire repertoire as it was then known—to Spottswood Music Company. This figure meant that James was being paid less than $12 per side—a lower recording rate than than he had earned from Paramount at the height of the Depression. Moreover, it represented enough material for two albums, rather than the eight titles Spottswood had already placed on the market. By signing the contract, James would have been either committed to a second album (which no one had spoken to him about making), or would have in effect given Melodeon an option on his services, preventing any other company from recording him. The contract was ambiguously worded: it assigned Spottswood's label the rights to the titles he had recorded, rather than rights to specific performances of those titles.

The contract had been represented to James as a mere formality, reflecting his year-old recording session. Nothing was done to call attention to the fact that it perpetuated a relationship with Spottswood that James wanted no part of, or appeared to supersede any other contract James might have since signed with another company. It was other people who pointed these implications to James, and notified Spottswood that the contract would remain unsigned until it was rewritten.

Because James had already signed a contract with Vanguard Records, signing the undated Melodeon contract would have enabled the owners of the latter company to sue James' new

MASTER AGREEMENT

Between: Nehemiah "Skip" James and the Spottswood Music Co., Inc.

Nehemiah "Skip" James hereby sells, assigns and transfers to the
Spottswood Music Co., Inc. all rights, titles and interests in and to
the following master recordings owned by him, entitled:

1. Hard Time Killin' Floor Blues
2. Washington D. C. Hospital Center Blues
3. Devil Got My Woman
4. Special Rider Blues
5. Motherless and Fatherless
6. Let Jesus Lead You
7. Drunken Spree
8. Cypress Grove Blues
9. Sick Bed Blues
10. Illinois Blues
11. Cherry Ball Blues
12. All Night Long
13. Worried Blues
14. Crow Jane
15. Catfish
16. I'm So Glad
17. I Don't Want a Woman to Stay Out All Night Long

Nehemiah "Skip" James grants to the Spottswood Music Co., Inc. the
sole and exclusive right to manufacture, sell, lease, license, advertise,
or otherwise use all types of records containing the performances
embodied in the said master recordings upon such terms and conditions
as may be desired by the Spottswood Music Co., Inc. Nehemiah "Skip"
James grants the Spottswood Music Co., Inc. the right to use and allow
others to use his name, likeness and biography in connection with the
publicizing, advertising, or sale of records manufactured using these
master recordings. Nehemiah "Skip" James grants to the Spottswood Music
Co., Inc. the sole and exclusive right to use and control the use of the
said master recordings, matrices, mothers, stampers or other copies or
derivatives and records produced from the master recordings and the
performances embodied therein, in Canada, the United States and throughout the world. Nehemiah "Skip" James warrants that he possesses full
right, power and authority to enter into and to perform this agreement,
and there are no outstanding claims of any kind due upon them.

Spottswood Music Co., Inc. agrees to pay Nehemiah "Skip" James $.20
(twenty cents) per LP record sold when that record contains only music
by James and proportionate royalties from LP album sales containing
music by James and others. Royalties for 45 rpm record sales shall be
$.02 (two cents) per selection per record sold. Royalty statements
with check shall be made quarterly. In the event these master recordings are leased to another firm, royalties shall be half the amount
received by the Spottswood Music Co., Inc. under the lease arrangement.

Nehemiah "Skip" James acknowledges receipt of $200.00 (two hundred
dollars) as advance payment on royalties.

This agreement is binding upon the parties hereto and their respective
successors in interest.

In witness whereof we have hereunto set our hands and seals this _____
day of _____, 1965.

                                    _____
                                    Nehemiah "Skip" James

                                    R.___ K. _____ ___
                                    Richard K. Spottswood, Pres.
                                    SPOTTSWOOD MUSIC CO., INC.

                    Contract proferred by Melodeon

An emaciated James recording for Melodeon in 1965
(Courtesy Hank O'Neal)

company for infringement. In all probability, such was the aim of the blues "patron" who had drawn up the contract.

What was particularly reprehensible about this ploy was that the contract was accompanied by an offer of $125 in already collected fees from his record, were James to sign it. The person who dangled this offer to James had simply counted on him to snatch at the bait, without bothering to scrutinize its contents.

As it was, the Melodeon effort was an embarrassment to James, who was not easily embarrassed by his own efforts. The record, which was released in November, 1965, was titled *Skip James: Greatest Of the Delta Blues Singers*. "Skip James is the greatest artist that ever came from the Mississippi Delta . . . ," gushed the author of the liner notes, Ed Morris, a man with whom James was not even on speaking terms. A Melodeon flysheet likewise billed it as:

> Eight superb blues from the greatest of the veteran Mississippi Delta blues singers . . . Skip James' guitar accompaniments set the standard that all others must follow.

James was not even from the Mississippi Delta, but this was of little concern to blues revivalists, who apprehended the words "Mississippi Delta" as a blues selling point.

Despite its mediocrity, the album received favorable reviews from a press that was predisposed to tout blues artists and susceptible to the glib hyperbole of blues salesmen. *Downbeat* awarded it five stars. ". . . James is almost the elusive poet of the blues," *Times* critic Robert Shelton gushed in his June, 1966 *Cavalier* review of the record. "His melancholic sweet voice seems to drift and sway in a sort of introspective series of laments. Of all the native blues men, James stops this listener firmest in his tracks."

Such pap enabled Louisa Spottswood to later say of the album: "We released it for artistic rather than commercial reasons primarily . . ." After ten months on the market, the record had sold 736 copies.

By then, James was giving off the impression that his recordings were the product of a sickly hospital patient who had been cajoled into making them. When the Spottswoods were criticized for having recorded an ailing artist, they claimed that Melodeon had only begun to record Skip James after his release from the hospital. Almost thirty years later, in 1991, unreleased Skip James Melodeon material would be resold and retailed by Biograph Records. The session date provided by Spottswood—November, 1964—indicated that he had recorded James during his period of acute physical "misery," and during the time he was formally under contract to Ed Denson.

The final recipient of James' pink slip was his frowsy wife, Mabel, who had made a suitable consort when he had been a miner, plantation hand, and presumably, honky tonk operator. Now that he had become a concert performer, he saw her as beneath his station. This was particularly evident to James when he traveled to Philadelphia with John Hurt and lodged with the latter's stepniece, an Avon lady whose business cards read "Mrs. L.L. Meeks."

Lorenzo Meeks had been reared in Greenwood, Mississippi, leaving the area in the 1940s to cook for a Southern family that relocated to Philadelphia. By the 1960s she was working as a part-time Avon saleslady. She was a soft-spoken, unassuming widower whose life revolved around the sanctified church and her daughter Rae Roots. For diversion she watched daytime television and read innumerable mystery stories. She subscribed to women's magazines, *McCall's*, and *Ebony*. Unlike Mabel James, she did not dress in dungarees and wrap a handkerchief around her head. She was not the sort of woman to plunge an icepick into a Delta sharecropper, leave the dead body sprawled in a plantation ditch, and give a detailed anecdotal description of the appearance of an icepick wound, as Mabel James had done.

Later, Lorenzo would complain of James: "He's like two people." With women, James was an old hand at dissembling: "My love was like ice water—I could turn it off and on," he once said, quoting a pat blues phrase. Now he set about turning off the tap that had once flowed in Mabel's direction. Because James was normally distant he could not make the impression of coldness he wished to convey by becoming remote and silent. So he began addressing her with the formality of someone who had just met her, and at the same time venturing only critical remarks.

When she uttered a casual curse, he would look affronted and say, through bared teeth: "I wish you would not use that vulgarity language in my presence." Startled, she would fall silent in terrified incomprehension. Overnight, her husband had turned into an unfriendly stranger.

In the summer of 1965 the author called at James' small apartment at 1609 19th Street in Northwest Washington. Instead of finding James, he found Mabel alone sitting in a darkened room. "I'm sick," she blubbered.

Her jaw quivering, she said that James had disappeared. No one would tell her where he was. "Skip's always thinkin'," she added ominously. "Skip's got mean things on his mind." In a peculiar past tense construction, she remarked: "Skip never listened to anybody." She could not speak without stammering. As she gulped from the bottle of Scotch she persuaded her guest to buy her, she casually propositioned him, attempting to sweeten the overture by displaying her husband's wallet and promising to present him with $300 James kept in a bank account.

James never returned to Washington. Later he explained his defection from Mabel on the grounds that she drank too much and feigned sickness in order not to look after their apartment. But he had not bothered to convey these complaints to Mabel, or make any separation announcement. He simply left her to her own devices; once she realized that her husband was gone for good, she moved in with a local niece. An intermediary, Louisa Spottswood, eventually sent him his father's books and the suit that constituted virtually his entire personal property aside from the piano he would have abandoned on the street had a fan (Hank O'Neal) not rescued it. Afterwards, he claimed to have sent money to Mabel, but it is doubtful that he did so: even when they lived together he had begrudged buying her anything. When she had spoken of her desire for a cooking set, he snapped: "I don't have time to bother with those things."

James had jumped headlong into a housekeeping arrangement on the basis of what was actually a scant, brief acquaintance

with his "bride." In all probability, his alacrity was borne not
only of a desire to drop Mabel, but to remove himself from
the sphere of parasitic "blues enthusiasts" he was forced to do
business with in Washington. He first took up residence at 5634
Pearl Street, where Lorenzo resided with her daughter and son-
in-law, both quiet, unassuming Catholics, and her sister, a re-
clusive woman known as "Tee" who rarely spoke and was
strangely spinsterish for someone of her age and appearance.

In April of 1966, the couple moved into their own dwellings,
in a detached building at 5274 Jefferson Street. Occupying the
ground floor of a two story apartment, they paid $65 per month.
It was set in a quiet neighborhood in West Philadelphia, which
was some forty percent black. Its most famous black resident
of recent note had been Sonny Liston, who had settled in West
Phiadelphia in 1962, but soon departed, claiming that the local
police were harrassing him. The overall ambience of the city
had not changed appreciably since Jack Johnson, who had lived
there in the early 1900s, had termed it "The Sleepy City." Blues
singers who had previously taken up quarters in Philadelphia
included Bessie Smith and Lonnie Johnson, who had been working as a janitor at the Ben Franklin Hotel when he was rediscovered in 1960.

James believed that it was only through sex that a man could
control a female. Now he had only his honeyed pimp's tongue
to employ as a weapon. "What is love?" James asked upon meeting my girlfriend. "Love," he explained grandiloquently, "is the
willingness to make sacrifices for your companion." Before in-
stalling himself with Lorenzo, he patiently explained that living
with him would entail a sexual sacrifice. Perhaps grateful for
a respite from widowhood, she had dimissed his sexual debili-
taton as a nonsequitor.

James told her that he had no objection if she wanted to
keep another man who could perform sexually but that he
"didn't want to hear about it." Formerly, he had told Mabel
with a laugh: "I grant you complete freedom to do anything
you wanna do—so long as I'm right there."

Lorenzo Meeks appeared to bring out James' latent gentility.
She was neither deferential nor domineering, but firmly dis-

approved of his drinking. Under her prodding, he became a moderate drinker, foregoing whiskey entirely for the sake of beer.

She also aggravated James' incipient piousness, which had lain largely dormant when he had been attached to Mabel. Although she was not a churchgoer, she was quietly devout and completely "churchified" in manner and deed. To the black sheep Baptist who was Skip James, this was equivalent to throwing down a gauntlet. More aggressively and vociferously than he had during his days with Mabel, he brandished his rhetorical Christianity, as though Lorenzo's presence constituted either a challenge or a living rebuke.

To make matters worse, she adhered to the sanctified church, which James considered a church of frauds. Although she was always unassuming, James imagined that she thought herself better than he, particularly when she brushed off his male chauvinism as "old fashioned." Her perceptibly lighter complexion fed into his feeling that he occupied a lower order in his household: he believed that sancts were more color-conscious than Christian, and even had a story (apochryphal, in all probability) about a "blue veined" sanctified church in Texas to illustrate this view.

"Now it was a friend of mine was goin' with a yellow girl," he claimed, "and she was in the choir of that very same church. He was darker than I was: slick-black. When she brought him to turn one day, she didn't tell 'em all that she was gonna bring him . . . After a while, he could see everybody lookin' at him and whisperin' about him. And when the time commenced for their spirituals, they looked right at him and sang:

> Only the yal-*ler*, hunh!
> Only the *yal*-ler, hunh!
> Only the *yaller*, hunh!
> Shall see God.

"When he heard that he got up and started walkin' up the aisle . . .

> Alla you *yel*-ler, hunh!
> Sons of *bitch*es, hunh!
> Kiss my *ass*, hunh!
> Go to hell.

And he walked right outta that church and never went back."

Lorenzo's perspective, whatever it was, remained too nebulous and low-key for James to confront in the fashion of the hero of his tale. She was a creature of pleasant small talk who took no interest in James' large utterances. Her relatively urbane diction had a noticeable pruning effect on James' elocution. Instead of the paragraph-sized plantation-style sentences that formerly marked his utterances, he now spoke concisely, without periphrasis, and with more consistent conjugations.

Yet James was noticeably more relaxed around his relatively uncouth former wife, an outright social inferior. In the genteel company of Lorenzo he became sterile as a person: his low-class tendencies stalemated, his former earthiness replaced by stuffiness. Although he took readily to an atmosphere that reeked of propriety, his punctiliousness was performed with utter unenthusiasm. As Lorenzo's "husband" he reminded one of nothing so much as a student suffering in a classroom; as Mabel's husband he had characteristically behaved as though school were out for the day.

Lorenzo found him incomprehensible, and often disconcerting. "He's like a Jekyll and Hyde," she would say, when she discovered that his mild manner was a mask. She appeared not to notice the essential coldness that marked her husband's personality, regardless of whether Dr. Jekyll or Mr. Hyde was on display.

With James' upscale marriage came relatively upscale management and a relatively upscale record company. This change occurred in the summer of 1965, shortly after he moved to Philadelphia. At the fourth annual Philadelphia Folk Festival held in Spring Mount, Pennsylvania, he was approached by Dick Waterman, who had just opened up a blues booking agency at 34 Parker Street in Cambridge, Massachusetts. In order to impress clients with a reminder of its main attraction, Mississippi John Hurt, Waterman had named his one-man firm "avalon productions."

Securing Hurt's services had been the reason for the booking agency, for Hurt was the only blues singer for whom there was anything resembling a commercial demand. Waterman talked James into his fold by telling him that he could arrange to have him record for Vanguard Records, whose proprietors had been interested in him on the basis of his 1964 Newport appearance. James would earn a $1000 advance, well above anything he could earn from the vanity blues labels of the period. The two-album contract Waterman negotiated was actually modest by Vanguard's standards, which usually called for a three-year contract involving three albums.

Waterman was later to complain that James' acceptance of $200 from Spottswood had made it difficult for him to sell the singer to Vanguard. Had James been more sophisticated, he might have complained that Waterman's method of retailing him to the public made it difficult for him to get work. He did not sound like an appealing performer on the basis of Waterman's flysheet description of him, which read:

> Withdrawn and introverted as a young man, Skip James developed his musical style into an emotional personal expression. Equally brilliant as an instrumentalist and singer, he has been called the "bluesman's bluesman" because others are awed by his introspective manner and complete involvement into [sic] his stark blues.

Waterman wrote as though James were virtually a mental case, which was how blues addicts tended to view Waterman. He had first become involved with blues by accompanying Nick Perls and Phil Spiro to Mississippi in search of Son House. He was not a member of the hard core blues fraternity, which (aside from Al Wilson) held him in contempt. Perls let it be known that Waterman had only worked as part of the Son House caravan because he had a driver's license and was able to spell himself as a driver. When he began as a booker, Perls would denigrate him as a "loser" who was clutching at a career straw, having been a failed photographer. Although Waterman and Perls had become embroiled in a bitter feud during their brief association, he was equally unpopular among other blues addicts. Like Perls, he had a reputation for being petulent and abrasive. Worst of all, he did not belong to the blues fraternity; therefore the fact that he was the only figure who brought any direct benefit to blues singers did not count with them.

Blues singers still belonged nowhere in the field of contemporary entertainment, which had no real niche for them. There were no bookers to handle blues talent. There were three or four American blues labels in existence, all of them one-man vanity operations. In the midst of what was supposed to be a blues revival, Skip James' first album had sold merely twice the number of copies his first reissue had sold twenty years earlier on the Steiner-Davis label. Only an amateur like Waterman would have attempted to make a go of a blues booking agency, or prove patient enough to put up with the idiosyncrasies of blues singers.

Waterman gave the impression of someone who wanted to have blues singers dependent upon him. He was most attached to Son House, a hapless derelict who could not be entrusted with a pawnable guitar, and had reached the stage of advanced alcoholism known as "wet brain," where a few gulps of wine were sufficient to make him drunk. Yet for three years, Waterman managed to make a concert performer out of the emotional cripple who was Son House, who could not travel alone, or perform without being given infusions of wine, the poison he referred to as "my medicine." Whether it was in House's best interests to pursue a career under such circumstances is another matter.

For the first time, a full year after his rediscovery, James had a legitimate record label. In keeping with its image as a company elevated above crass commerce, Vanguard formally took the name "Vanguard Recording Society Inc." Founded in 1950 for the sake of recording classical music, it had become the leading folk label of the period. Vanguard was decidedly classy by comparison with the scruffy Folkways label, thanks in part to the elegance of its co-founder Maynard Solomon, a classically trained pianist and cellist whose original interest in folk music had been stimulated in the 1940s, when he attended college with Woody Guthrie. A singularly scholarly figure within his profession (he eventually authored several biographies of composers), Solomon had great respect for authentic blues artists. "They all developed something special at a single moment of their lives," he would reflect, "and they didn't grow beyond that, because what they developed was *them*. That was very true of Skip James." Three decades after recording him, Solomon would summarize James thusly: "I think he was a supreme artist. A very great artist. That high keening mode he went into, it was extraordinarily affecting." James approached him with some trepidation. He suspected that Solomon was merely a front man for Arthur Laibly, the man who had recorded him for Paramount. Laibly, he believed, had absconded with Paramount's funds, and was working incognito for Vanguard.

James' Vanguard sessions took place in the company studio at 71 West 23rd Street in Manhattan on January 10 and 11, 1966, four days after he appeared in New York at a Village coffeehouse, the *Cafe Au Go Go*. "Mr. Salomon said it was the best [session] he ever had in the 15 years of Recording," James afterwards wrote the author. "He was very pleased with it." The release of Vanguard's *Skip James Today!* that August did not make him much more marketable than he had formerly been. The record sold poorly, as did a September release (on a Verve-Folkways anthology) of two songs he had recorded at the *Au Go Go*, *Devil Got My Woman* and *I'm So Glad*. However, its reception neither surprised nor dismayed Solomon, whose aim had been artistic rather than commercial. The album sold "about as well as we had expected," he later said, and he would recall being "quite satisfied" with James' small sales totals.

James' commercial stature loomed so small that his appearance that year on another label was not even noticed by Solomon. The unusual forum these records took was the archaic 78 record, resurrected by a prominent blues collector, Bernard Klatzko, who considered James among the five greatest recorded blues artists of all time. Klatzko issued two 78s as specialty items on the Herwin label, drawn from material James had recorded in 1964 in Boston: *How Long/Four O'Clock Blues* (both featuring piano), and *Illinois Blues/Drunken Spree*. He sold 290 of the 300 copies he pressed, and found that they sold more slowly than similar items offered by Son House and Booker White. "I don't think he was as popular as they were," Klatzko recalled.

Having been told to expect a royalty statement in six months, James expected Vanguard to reward him with a royalty check. He had no concept of a recording advance being deducted against a royalty, and was confounded when his statement duly arrived, informing him that he was as yet entitled to no royalty payments.

In an angry panic, he dashed off a letter to the author, whom he had begun to rely on as an emissary:

> Phila Pa
> 5274 Jefferson St
> 3-2-67
>
> Dear Stephen
> I got a Slip Statement from Vanguard This Morning But No Money I dont understand What This is All about. So I am Sending This to you To see What You Can Tell Me about it, and you Check it With Him and Let me Know what it Mean. I was expecting Money to Meet my obligation—With my Rent and Phone Bill and Dr. Bill are all Due He Told me I would be Hearing from Him on the 27 or 28 of Feb so I was expecting some Money as the Record Has already Been on the Market 6 Months and I am Suspose to get and acct. every 6 Months But so far I have got no Royalties as yet. You call Him and Call me Collect. Let me Hear From You at once . . .

Although James was by far the lesser light in Vanguard's roster, Solomon never gave him any sense that he was a secondary attraction to John Hurt. Waterman, however, lacked such discretion; as if he were afraid that James was going to bolt from his booking agency, he would frequently brag to James about the bookings he was securing for his two main blues attractions, Hurt and House. Instead of thereby seeing Waterman as a man of great connections, James felt slighted and envious.

He constantly complained that Waterman was not finding enough work for him. When James and other acts in Waterman's retinue found themselves on the same bill together, a good part of their time was spent comparing sour notes about their dealings with him. He was roundly accused of being a thief. One Chicago bluesman greatly gratified James by confiding that he was going to arrange for a local lowlife to "take care" of Waterman.

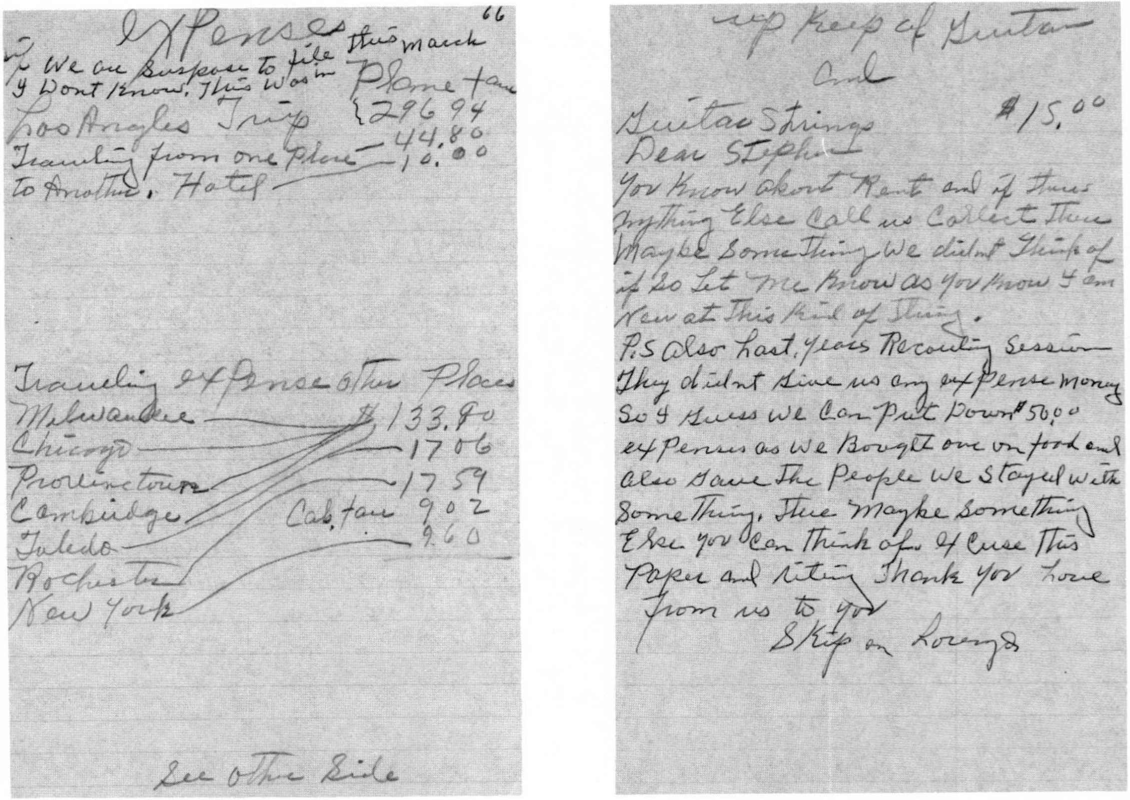

James' list of 1966 travel expenses

James' violent denunciations of Waterman were marked by
periodic pledges of confrontation, made more difficult by the
fact that the manager adroitly used the more conciliatory
Lorenzo as a buffer between himself and his artist. A pathetic
ritual would ensue. James would threaten to have it out with
Waterman; when the manager would eventually appear at his
apartment, James' nerve would falter, and the tough talker replaced by a stammering supplicant. James' anger was all too
clearly the result of his dependence; Waterman represented a
solitary lifeline, lowered at periodic intervals with only enough
frequency and cash in the bucket to keep him from starving.
A year after signing James, in July, 1966, he was to write to
the author: "I guess that Skip feels that I'm not getting him
jobs but he has a $300 concert at Lehigh in October and a
$325 one in Cincinnati in April, 1967."

Waterman would attempt to mollify his semi-starving artist
by paying effusive compliments to his art. In general, he tried
to give the impression of being on a mission of love for blues,
a posture that only instilled mistrust in James.

Waterman had as many complaints about Skip James as James
had about him, to the point of regarding himself as a virtual
martyr to the cause of Skip James. Pestering letters from the
author on behalf of James brought forth a self-pitying diatribe:

October 16, 1966

After getting your letter yesterday I didn't know
whether to answer it, laugh a lot or just shake my
head. I finally decided to do all three.

The complexities of managing (?) Skip James are
many. First of all, understand the family problem
brought about by Skip being with John Hurt's niece.
Everytime that I go down there for John, Skip makes
acid remarks about "Oh yeah, I sure don't need any
babysitter for me. You just give Skip the word and
Skip can get there by himself. I don't need anyone
to be fetching me and carrying on for me like I was
a baby!" He's right, of course, but the little item that
he is missing is that John is an artist in demand. I
don't argue merits of the different musics. I plainly

and simply don't manage anyone whose music I don't love myself. They are *all* equal to me, and I stand by that statement. I have refused Mance Lipscomb, wouldn't touch Lightnin' Hopkins or Brownie & Sonny simply because I don't like their music enough to listen to it myself and could not, in good faith, urge others to employ them. The facts are this [sic]: Skip James lost money for the Fret, John Hurt has always made money there. Skip James lost money at the Gaslite, John Hurt has always made money there. Skip James lost money for the Ash Grove, John Hurt made money there and on and on and on. The best that I can get owners to say is that, after his record is out, they will see if there are any mentions among the customers and maybe try to get him one more time. Also of importance is the fact that Skip's music, albeit brilliant technically, is depressing and melancholy, and club owners don't want to hire depressing musicians. The customers won't order food and drinks and there is little or no return business. I know this from running clubs myself.

Skip is not the easiest guy to get along with. I have never heard Skip say anything optimistic and he regards me as an instant miracle worker on short notice. He borrowed money from me last Fall ($100) on a personal loan and promised to pay me back from the Vanguard advance. . . .

Club owners are simply wary of him because he has never made money for them. The guy from the Main Point [a Philadelphia coffeehouse] calls all the time for John Hurt, John Hurt, John Hurt. I can't make a Hurt-James package for different weeks because he'd rather not take John than take Skip when he knows his customers won't come for Skip. Manny Rubin at the Fret is vague and says "Maybe I'll try him again sometime and Mr. Hood [John Hood] at the Gaslite says the same thing.

. . . This whole routine sounds like a big negative blob. But remember that I love his music, urge people

> to hire him and feel genuinely badly when they look
> away and try to change the subject.
>   . . . Money, hell, I just want to keep my sanity.

The tenor of James' basically bland performances actually had nothing to do with his dismal reception on the coffeehouse circuit. Above all else, folk audiences wanted familiarity and inclusivity in musical form; James had been rediscovered because his unfamiliar, exclusive style of music excited the most critical blues listening faction. The very notion of a "folk" song was a song that was familiar, through wide performance circulation. Originality, in the peculiar "folk" scheme of things, suggested artistry, which was exclusive to artists.

The real "folk" of the folk music scene of the 1960s was the audience that patronized the music: a small but homogenous mass seeking an identification with performers. This identification was most readily established by artless amateurism, or a lack of special aptitude that distinguished the performer from the audience. The more amateurish a musician sounded, the more readily the coffeehouse audience could project themselves as vicarious performers of whatever was served before them. The surest way to become unemployable on the folk circuit, in fact, was to display astounding ability along the lines of Jose Feliciano, the brilliant guitarist who appeared at the 1964 Newport Folk Festival and had even less success on the coffeehouse circuit than Skip James.

Because they were sung by black voices that were not easily approximated by folk aspirants, blues were inherently unpalatable to the coffeehouse crowd. Blues guitar, à la Skip James, did nothing to compensate for this handicap; James' guitar was incoherent when lifted from the context of the singing it was meant to adorn. It sounded thin and jagged by comparison to Mississippi John Hurt, who had developed a smooth, full-sounding, facile picking technique to make up for his puny voice, which had doomed him to amateurism in his original Mississippi environment. Because Hurt's wispy singing largely adorned his playing, and was racially nondescript, it posed no barrier to his "folk" popularity. His guitar playing, while novel in technique, had all the prerequisite familiarity necessary to engage coffeehouse patrons, thanks to its pattern picking and its almost incessant alternating bass. That Hurt was largely locked into a single rhythmic accompaniment meant nothing to the melodically-oriented folk fan; rhythm was a jarring attribute of the rejected rock and roll idiom.

Thanks to James' acute loss of rhythmic facility, Hurt was (in the 1960s) the better guitar player, not only smoother-sounding but able to play faster. To appreciate James one had to relish seemingly disconnected blues guitar sounds, fragments without a set pattern beyond the basic pattern that was blues. The only blues sounds that folk audiences appeared to have the slightest taste for were those produced by a bottleneck.

The coffeehouse for James was simply a cul-de-sac. His rediscoverers had openly lauded him for the very attributes that alienated the audience that was now necessary to his survival as a rediscovery. Had James been able to discern this discrepancy he would have recognized that the peripheral, almost forgotten aspects of his repertoire—a meager assortment of bottleneck songs and "rag" pieces acquired from Henry Stuckey—represented his only prospect of success. But James had no perspective on his coffeehouse audiences; he was simply dispatched to clubs, and not (as Waterman invariably discovered) asked back for encore engagements. His tunnel vision was further constricted by the aggressive acclaim he was sure to receive from the isolated handful of blues fans who patronized his performances, and were totally unrepresentive of his audience at large.

The idealized view of the "country blues" singer as a purist rather than a success-seeking performer prevented James' various managers from ever suggesting any alterations in his approach, which James had already taken upon himself to adulterate in the interests of attaining concert success. In reality, his managers functioned as mere bookers, and James' communication with them was largely perfunctory. They invariably patronized him in the awkward fashion of the ordinary blues fan of the period.

Waterman's realistic assessment of the artist's popularity was not one he espoused to Skip James, who appeared to be little more than window-dressing to legitimize what was in reality John Hurt Productions. Like virtually all of the white people who associated with blues singers (including the author), he acted as an inverse Uncle Tom. It never occurred to James that Waterman was simply afraid of hurting his feelings by even intimating his own insignificance. Hearing only the manager's overdrawn accolades of his music, James interpreted Waterman's failure to find him work as willful neglect on his part.

If it was possible to fault Waterman for his management substance rather than style, it lay in his effort to promote James on the coffeehouse circuit, a forum that was not unfriendly to James so much as to blues music. Despite their presentation as "folk musicians," blues singers held almost no appeal to the adherents of the illusory idiom. Waterman's myopic preoccupation with the penny-ante folk circuit prevented him from exploring the far more lucrative and hospitable forum of the college concerts that performers like Sleepy John Estes had begun playing a year before James' rediscovery.

Most colleges of that free-spending era had substantial entertainment budgets. The students who were placed on recreation committees often faced a problem of how to spend the allocation they had at the beginning of the semester. Typically, a student who headed an entertainment committee (and thus controlled the concerts at his particular school) did so in the interests of fostering the appearance of one or two favorite performers. Once he had managed to place his pet performer on campus, he would not much care who else his committee sponsored. If a featured musician was someone whom he would never think to champion, this fact would make his dominance of the recreation committee more palatable.

College students had no idea what the prevailing market was; if a blues singer could be had for $300 or $350 he was considered a bargain. This rate was well in excess of the $100-125 a singer like James stood to make for a stint at a club like the *Cafe Lena* in Saratoga Springs. To a manager, dealing with college students who were not looking to profit from the appearance of a performer was far easier than dealing with a crabby, house-counting coffee house owner. For a performer, playing a single set was preferable than working multiple sets at a coffeehouse.

James, the most articulate blues singer of the era, made for an ideal campus act. He could have obtained dozens of engagements at college campuses. Yet Waterman did virtually nothing to cultivate the only conceivably viable market for James. This inflexibility partly rose from the nature of the one-man operation that was Avalon Productions, which now ran to half a dozen featured artists. Merchandising James to a college recreation committee involved submitting a tape, a thumbnail biography, and, if possible, a photograph. Waterman had no such press kit; he was either unable to afford one, or unwilling to invest in one. His single-page brochure lumped all of his featured acts together.

Desperate for bookings and, by his own lights, "below the crackerbox" in May of 1966, James contacted the author with a plea to find him a musical engagement. He could not pay his rent for the coming month. I hastily arranged for Goddard College in Vermont to sponsor a concert for James.

In the midst of James' performance, I fled the entertainment center, mortified by his incoherent pell-mell keyboard attack during *22-20*. I envisioned angry students storming my dormitory like the movie peasants who charged Dr. Frankstein's castle, this time in response to the singer's Frankensteinian recreation of *22-20*. But afterwards, it appeared as if the student attendees had not noticed James' mistakes. Partly because they were not obliged to pay money to see performers like James, college audiences were unfailingly appreciative, even to the extent of fawning, in the fashion of a letter to a school paper after James performed at Wesleyan College in October of 1966:

> Dear Mr. Charley:
> Friday night a black angel sang to me. His name is Skip James.
> Now I'm sitting here, staring at my typewriter, hoping for an inspiration; none is forthcoming. When he sings a chasm is exposed—love-inspired hate, the drowned sorrow of bad whiskey, torn anguish of love lost—which lays waste to a whole year of freshman English and grammatical structure. What Skip James was Friday night is a personal thing and admits of no disclosure. However, because he is a little bit of each of us, he has something to say to all of us.

> ... He's humble, he tells us that it is a privilege
> for him to be here; other way around. Too much
> polite applause; the Wesleyan cool. Sometimes you
> can't understand what he says; doesn't matter; if you
> really hear him, you understand him. He plays en-
> cores because he loves his music. He gives me his
> address and invites me over any time I'm in Phil.
> That's the kind of guy he is.

Though outwardly gracious to his audiences, James derided such
accolades as "air puddings." "I can't live on air puddings," he
complained.

The money James received for the Goddard College concert
(some $350) enabled him to obtain a telephone. But it was only
a temporary respite from the ever-looming "crackerbox." In the
midst of the so-called "blues revival," James could not make a
living wage. He could only pay his rent intermittently. A few
weeks after the concert in Vermont, he put forth another desperate plea for assistance:

> ... I do not mean to be a pess or worry to you
> all, at all but you know how I stand here, and the
> condition things are with me as a new comer or
> neighbor in this city. Now I hope not to be evicted.
> Since I have move here and got eranged in trying
> to make an be comeforted - but I am really below
> the cracker box now ... now you know my condition
> as well as I do. There isn't anything else for me to
> do but depend on you, and my work to do for sup-
> port and with that. Life is a blank to start with ...
> so I would appreciate very much if you all would
> be that much in sympathy with me.

James was not the only scuffling blues artist; in a letter that
July, Waterman noted that "the craze (?) is past and everybody
is digging hard right now."

The coffee house circuit was, in fact, drying up. The promise
of the 1964 Newport Folk Festival was unfulfilled, as both blues
music and acoustic "folk" music were all but swept away by
the tidal wave of rock.

PART SIX

32. *The Age of Aquarius*

In the 1960s, the music labelled as rock became, for the first time, the mainstream sound of youth. Just as folk singers readily jumped on the rock bandwagon, so did various white blues guitarists who had begun as disciples of performers like Skip James. From Memphis, Bill Barth informed me in December of 1965: "I am starting to make some money at last. I am getting a beatle haircut, an doing the whole bit. it's absurd, but we might get a job in las vegas or something, an that will mean more money than i ever thought i'd see. a nice change from fucking around with ungrateful ol blues singers . . ."

Although success eluded Barth (who was to record a rock version of *Special Rider* for Capitol Records in the late 1960s), it did not elude Henry Vestine, who became the lead guitarist of Canned Heat. Thanks to the orientation of its rhythm guitarist, Al Wilson, the group made a specialty of re-recording old blues pieces in rock form. They also made a practice of attributing these songs to themselves, collecting thousands of dollars in the process.

The advent of The Beatles and, with it, media focus on "rock" had garnished old blues singers sudden prestige. The contemporary view of them as the predecessors of The Beatles was enshrined in a full-page cartoon appearing in a June, 1965 issue of *Life Magazine*, one of the most widely read publications in America. It purported to show the lineage of rock music. At the top of the cartoon sat the Beatles, their limousine spewing money. At the base of an arrow that pointed towards their car stood a shack labelled "Blues" and dated "1875." Seven names were inscribed on the side of the shack; the first was that of Skip James.

Since rock and roll was not a pronounced musical form or even a mandatory style of music but a retailing term affixed to music merchandised to teenagers, it was actually a rootless genre. It was not until the 1960s' conversion of "rock and roll" to "rock" that musicians drew on specific blues techniques, rather than simply sing blues songs. This indebtedness was a natural consequence of the rock emphasis on guitar: blues had been the only vocal medium that made much use of that instrument. In the exaggerated vibrato and single-note work of most 1960s rock artists one could easily see the lineage of Lonnie Johnson and B.B. King. The facial contortions that accompanied the typical rock vibrato had come courtesy of Muddy Waters.

Rock riffs of the period drew not only on blues technique but on its tonalities, to such an extent that the minor thirds and sevenths that were characteristic of blues soon became mainstream pop sounds. With this absorption, blues was no longer a culturally alien music. It had been the non-diatonic quality of blues, above all else, that had thwarted its utility in Tin Pan Alley four decades earlier, even after W.C. Handy's *St. Louis Blues* (1914) had belatedly become a pop standard, and inspired songwriters such as Irving Berlin to compose Tin Pan Alley blues. The notes of the blues scale sounded jarring to pop sensibilities. Significantly, in the 1950s, Chuck Berry had frequently used blues phrasing, but had altered its tonality and given his songs a sweet tinge by replacing minor thirds with major thirds and minor sevenths with major sixths.

Yet as blues sounds seeped into rock, the blues song as such had little appeal to mainstream audiences. The teenage hippies who constituted the market for 1960s rock had no aversion to blues as played by blacks, and none of the stiff-necked prejudices against blues that often existed in the folk circuit. For the most part, they simply never heard the music; rock dominated FM radio. Although they tended to react favorably to old blues, it simply wasn't loud or frantic enough to compete on any level with the reigning rock sounds. Moreover, blues were relatively rigid and repetitive, and translated poorly into long-play production. For that reason, there were actually more blues hits in 1950s rock and roll, a medium of three-minute 45s, than in the 1960s, when rock and blues were coupled by the media.

Most blues artists openly sniggered at rock, and at the long-haired youths who abounded in the era. Like the parents of hippies, they tended to dismiss rock as "noise" and view the hippy hair style as effeminate. It was probably because he heard such commonplaces from the mouths of common blues singers that James took a relatively indulgent view of these tempting targets. A disparaging remark about long-haired hippies would prompt him to comment that Jesus had long hair. As for rock and roll, he simply stated, with a casualness that was unusual for him, "I don't like rock and roll."

James' exposure to students convinced him that "only some few are interested in real music. They like just a touch of it, just enough to do these here late styles of dancin' stuff—jackin' and jumpin', frogs and fishes, and so forth." Hippies and their music were beneath his dignity, and he barely acknowledged their existence. Basically, he was dumbstruck by the mores and, most of all, the breezy affability of hippie types. Although he was the beneficiary of their libertine attitudes—anything he did was accepted in an age of indiscriminate affirmation, signified by the superlatives "groovy" and "out of sight"—he had the opposite outlook, making a virtue of wholesale rejection. Inevitably, he was to assess his student fans as "emotionally on the negative side about life." He added: "I don't confide much in these students now; quite naturally I don't have the time to be contaminated with 'em."

He had already experienced his fill of contagion in such places as Dallas: "You go to Dallas, Texas," he told the author, "there's a place where you can pay fifty cents and see anything you want. Some guys there would sell their brothers. Crimes against nature: make you sick to your stomach. Women eating women, men drinking men, men beating women, and so forth." The promiscuity and sexual forwardness of college-age females similarly affronted him. "You see women now with sometimes two pieces on, to hide their privacies and perhaps their bosoms and all. Some don't even do that. Well, some day they'll be walkin' the streets buck-naked. Now that's a temptation to a man's weak spot . . ."

The sexual revolution of the 1960s struck him as a triumph of weakness. "... The 'sports' part of the world has just about taken over," he reflected. "... the 'sport' part has the day, right now. Even students are just out for feelin' all kinda 'sports'...."

For the most part, James apprehended "hippies" as being "students," his invariable term for the white youths in his audience, whether or not they attended school. Although James accused "this modern age" of being "rigid" by comparison with its old-fashioned predecessors, it was he who saw morals in terms of unmitigated black and white, and saw degeneracy everywhere. "The devil has got a lot of power, an' it look like to me that all this young generation is just full of it," he was to say. "Criticism, infidelism, Phariseeism; science. All that 'ism'—just devilism." He dismantled "science" with a single rhetorical swipe: "Does science wake you up in the morning? Did science divide the light from the dark? Did science put every star and element in its place? Did it create the mountains, put them in their place? Scoop out the mountains, scoop out the dry land, and make seas?"

This view of science was ample testament to James' impoverished, rustic background. In Mississippi, the hand of science was less evident than the hand of God, in the form of natural wonders and plagues; James did not even know the meaning of indoor plumbing before he came North. At the same time, he took a dogmatic debator's view of science: "Science teaches man is no more than a dog; neither have a soul ... Science teaches a lot of stuff when it's not." (As to what a "soul" consisted of, James had dissected the matter in a Dallas seminary: it consisted of a man's mind and breath.) Like other Fundamentalists, he saw science as a sinister encroachment on God's world: "They keep a-messin' around with the sun and the moon—do you notice every year, the atmosphere and the season gets more hotter and hotter?"

The basic "ism" that affronted James was modernism. Unlike many elderly people, who railed against contemporary society as they relied on its gadgets and reposed on its creature comforts, James had no use for such things as television. A casual glimpse at the soap operas his wife watched on a daily basis was enough to convince him that television was part of a social conspiracy. "It gives people ideas about love," he said scornfully of television.

Love and marriage, James thought, were for the birds. On seeing a "Just married" sign on a passing car, he snorted: "I'll bet you won't hear nothin' like that when they get divorcted."

In James' view, disaster always lurked around the corner, and it was a disaster he heartily welcomed. In a period of economic boom, he was convinced that the stock market was about to crash. What James really wanted was a reprise of a Depression-style catastrophe that would punish the populace.

This humbling disaster would not only clear away human debris, but put an end to the undesirable social progress that vexed him, such as the lurking ascendency of women: "Eventually the women are going to preside over everything. They're getting to a place now where they're getting the best high position in offices. They're in the promotion business; drivin' taxis, in the police department, and then in the churches the women are going in for preachin'."

Possibly owing to a racial double-standard, James had little against the young white females who patronized his concerts, other than to invariably refer to them as "tackheads," meaning "idiots." Rather, they seemed boring to him. "Women don't have anything mysterious and strange for a man today," he once pontificated. "They make themselves too common: all they know how to do is get in the bed and have babies." He was against racial intermarriage.

Civil rights marches struck him as "a racket" and "a fuss" that were not worth troubling about. He was less concerned with improving the lot of blacks than with having black youths he saw on his corner walks to the local liquor store properly punished. He thought they would benefit by being forced to perform plantation field work, there learning "discipline," and sometimes imagined that such a fate—decreed by God—was imminent.

Most of all, he had no reverence for non-violence, or peace. On May 4, 1966, he had appeared at a Cambridge SDS "People For Peace" concert with Judy Collins, Tom Paxton, Phil Ochs, and Tom Lehrer. The audience James serenaded would have cheered the sentiments of T-Bone Walker, a postwar bluesman now relegated to obscurity:

> Write your letter pretty mama,
> Tell your friends to do the same
> Tell the politicians pretty mama
> To stop bein' so insane.

(Vietnam)

They would have recoiled at the reactionary attitudes of Skip James, who saw the Vietnam war as simply a welcome confirmation of the Bible: "Now the people are talkin' about these wars," he said. ". . . The Bible particularly says that they'll be wars and rumours of wars. So when these wars come and arouse, the people shouldn't be so excited, 'cause it's got to be." As protests over the war were at their height, he remarked: "I wouldn't mind playin' in Vietnam." In the spring of 1966, he was given to rant that young blacks in Philadelphia—whom he generally referred to as "reprobates" or "frenetics"—should be drafted, sent to Vietnam, and used as "cannon fodder."

In James' view, wars and catastrophes were a good way to cut back on the surplus of people: "Right here in New York you can't hardly walk the streets. Then the biggest of them is just ignorant and won't take advice: just born and turned loose. The police can't take care of 'em, the jailhouses are packed, and the insane places are packed. And people are runnin' loose like rabbits.

"Regardless of all the incidents, accidents, and whatever the 'dents' it is that happen to make away with people, it still seems like you don't miss 'em."

While wholesale disasters struck James as desirable occurrences, he could not abide crime. At a time when most of his youthful audience derided police as "pigs" and thought of police in terms of "police brutality," he was obsessively concerned with "crime in the streets," a phrase that had yet to enter the political vocabulary. He saw a conspiracy between the "men in power" and the criminal. "If these men that is in power would take an active part in this [fighting crime], and do as it seem like to me it ought to be done, these guys that is commitin' these unlawfully crimes, they'd back up: they'd stand in fear . . . But as long as they do these dirty crimes and they give 'em sentences for maybe one year, and they serve about maybe three months, and then they parole 'em out, they get out there and do five times as worse...

"When they parole 'em out, that little bit of time he served will stir up that other envy and anger and onery that is already within him. And he gonna double that stuff. . . .

"These men that is in power, they *should* electrocute a few of 'em, or either take some to the Nero's chopping block and get their heads off 'em, or chain 'em to some of these fast vehicles and drag 'em up and down the streets and through the countries and through the rurals everywhere, until they just drag 'em all to pieces. You just get 'em to doin' that just once, and the rest of these crooks see about it and hear about it, you'll see how much calm it will be, and how quiet things will get."

At the time James uttered these remarks, crime was not a political issue, or a popular preoccupation. There were no Dirty Harrys or avenging Charles Bronsons taking cinema revenge against murderers or muggers, and James sounded like a solitary crank. Two decades before the controversy over Bernard Goetz erupted, he griped: "The mens in power, they'se after the innocent man more so than they'se after these criminals: if you defend for yourself against this dirty stuff, the man that's in power will wanna penalize *you* for it . . . I think somebody that's in power should take some immediate steps to stop that, because it's gonna be some terrible stuff goin' on. There are some people ain't gonna stand for that."

James' criticisms of "men in power" did not extend to the occupant of the White House, who was universally detested by students. He expressed a wistful desire to play in the White House, which was then beseiged by angry anti-war pickets. To him, Lyndon Johnson was a fine person: "President Johnson, he wants every man to be on an equality to a certain extent," he said. "If you get ten dollars a day, ten dollars an hour, he wants me to have it. My family got to be supported just like yours. I got to pay what you pay. Now their bodies got to be sustained like yours and mine; I need good shoes like you do. I have to eat; I just can't stay on the crackerbox."

It was not the War on Poverty alone that commended Johnson to James. "You'll notice he quotes the Bible very frequently," James said. He had similar praise for Billy Graham: "I see he's been doing some very active recruiting of dissenters," he remarked approvingly, after reading about one of Graham's crusades in 1966.

For someone who was a virtual cauldron of hidden aggression, and whose ideas embodied nothing so much as a desire to strike out and smash people, James would acquire a surprisingly temperate manner when he drank. Drinking actually had a calming effect on him, and his rages of discontent were partly brought on by his inability to absorb his anger through alcohol, thanks to the presence of his wife, who rarely left his apartment.

Disclaiming the horrendous state of the world was also gratifying to James as a means of deflecting his own attention from himself. The worse the world seemed, the less shabby a figure he himself would cut within it. Though James claimed confidently to have been "one of the best men who ever walked," none of the things he actually took pride in involved his own conduct or character. He spent dozens of hours discussing his life with the author, who was attempting to document it: never did he mention doing anything remotely resembling a good deed, or an act of kindness on his part. How threadbare the bag of good deeds he expected to tote to his maker would be is indicated by his attempt to impress the author with an example of his generous nature. This deed consisted of feeding pigeons in a Washington, D.C. park.

He had more pity for pigeons than for people. Jack Owens was certain that James had borne a son; James never mentioned the existence of children, except to decry the refusal of parents to punish them physically. He stated that if he had a disobedient child, he would murder it, setting an Abraham-like example for others. The legal consequences of such an act did not concern him; he spoke grandiosely of being assassinated on stage as the result of singing a spiritual, shrugging: "Sometimes you have to die for truth."

In his hospital room, he had lain beside a patient suffering the agony of a terminal illness. "You shouldn't feel sorry for him," he told a visitor. "You don't know what kind of life he's led." Had James been more fond of himself, no doubt, he would not have had such reflexive severity with others. He was an egotist without an ego.

If James sought solace by bringing the world down to his own level, the afflicted conscience or self-contempt this action would imply appeared to have been aggravated by the inertia of old age. He had largely lost the capacity to perform his previous misdeeds, or to do much of anything. Now he was forced to live with himself. In response, he became a devout deviant, expressing his defiance of society with verbal condemnation, couching his bitter contempt for mankind in Christianity. He used his faith to flail the world; it was never a cause of celebration. Rather than induce content, it opened a bitter chasm of discontent. It was almost impossible to imagine James in his original musical environment, entertaining a "house frolic": he seemed to be the death of the party.

James was far more interested in discoursing on the state of society than in discussing music, or recalling any particulars from his own past. Although bereft of small talk and banter, he was a non-stop windbag when he was in the company of someone who was susceptible to his sweeping social generalities. He was all the more anxious to deliver grand pronouncements because he could not use the concert stage as a podium from which to make them.

In addition, he had the typical eagerness of the half-educated egotist to constantly assert his intellect, in the process illustrating his pet sayings of the period: "I ain't the *biggest* fool in the world," and "*every* black thing come out of the South ain't a fool." He was apt to complete an obtuse observation by saying: "I may be a little bit of a fool—but not too big a one, what you bet?"

James was not such a fool as to think he could air his acrimonious attitudes in public, or in the company of frenetic "students." And he was not such a fool as to think that the ingenuous friendliness of his fans was anything more than a slick facade.

In his own sordid culture, he had kept a baleful eye cocked for ulterior, underhanded motives at the onset of any effusive goodwill gestures: he had long since learned that disarming friendliness was sometimes accompanied with a poisonous drink. When youths who did not even know him took the typical hippy tack of affecting instant fellowship with him, James divined devious designs beneath their surface sociality. Once a group of fans invited him to go out in a boat after a Provincetown concert; he politely refused. Later, he confided that he had been too cagey to go along with such a scheme, which would (he thought) culminate in his being thrown overboard.

Instead of throwing him overboard, his new generation of admirers threw him a lifeline. This occurred in the form of Cream's rock version of *I'm So Glad*, released on the album *Fresh Cream* in December of 1966. Already its lead performer Eric Clapton, a 21-year-old prodigy with three years' professional experience, was hailed as a great guitar player. Although he had listened to James' original recording, which had been reissued the previous year by The Origin Jazz Library, Clapton based his adaptation on the simplified rendition that had recently appeared on Vanguard. He had no inkling of its pop predecessor, then unknown to record collectors.

Taken together, the two versions of *I'm So Glad* form a unique document, illustrating the striking difference in blues and rock musical languages. No other song was transfigured into such myriad forms, spanning two races and eras. Each unique expression of the same basic musical motif contained real musical value. Its elasticity was made possible by the basic simplicity of the original 1927 composition by Art Sizemore, *So Tired* (with lyrics supplied by George A. Little), the crux of which was a four-bar air blown up into a sixteen bar refrain set in an A-A-B-A pattern. It enjoyed a curious multi-faceted musical existence in the form of a hit 1928 rendition by Gene Austin, one of the day's most popular crooners, a jazz-styled dance rendition by the Jean Goldkette Orchestra, "race" renditions by Lonnie Johnson and the Dallas String Band, and finally, an ambitous rearrangement by Skip James in the form of *I'm So Glad*, which comes across as neither a pop nor blues song, but something completely unique.

Taking his cue from its simple melodic core, James converted *So Tired* into an astounding vocal and instrumental tour de force, in which his guitar playing existed to augment his voice. The anemic vocal ambience of the original was completely uprooted; James sang with a wild intensity that was rarely achieved in any vocal music of the era. His wailing voice and the surging guitar it suddenly triggered completely upended the mood of the original; it was like the difference between a 1930s Hollywood movie (perhaps with Fred Astaire) and a surrealistic horror movie. One could almost picture, in fact, a scene of musicians in tuxedos playing the Goldkette version at a posh country club, only to be disrupted by the howling voice of James, a musical werewolf lurking outside in the dark, out to avenge himself on high society, his keening falsetto shattering champagne glasses and creating pandomonium among the brilliantine-haired musicians. But the frenzy and fervor James exhibited was something other than undisciplined chaos; its effect was particularly striking because of the refined sense of musicianship that accompanied it.

To listen to the Cream version is to inhabit still another universe, that of the spacey 60s. Like many contemporary rock songs, it was a theatrical musical expression of the culture it adorned, to such an extent that it was almost necessary to decode the song through the peculiar argot of the era. For example, it dramatized the pervasive acid-induced catchphrase "I'm going through changes" in its sudden introduction of unexpected effects, such as a gratuitous interlude of silence (actually borrowed, it is likely, from Bobby Freeman's *Do You Wanna Dance?*), the deployment of two distinct vocal styles (a simpering monotone set against a chorus, and a shout), and an a cappella conclusion involving a vocal trio. Jack Bruce's chant-like incantation of a single phrase ("I'm so glad") that was set against a background chorus echoing the same words in an ascending melodic phrase was a seeming invocation of the nebulous, enigmatic mysticism promoted by The Beatles, and embraced by contemporary hippies: the song appeared to be about transcendence, but did not expressly articulate any theme.

As an ensemble piece, it reflected the "do your own thing" credo of the age, Ginger Baker's drumming and Clapton's lead guitar simply proceeding on their own. This lack of interplay and cohesiveness in a band of de facto soloists was completely

gauche by comparison with the Goldkette orchestration, and
would have resulted in a mediocre example of Sixties' helter
skelter were it not for the disciplined contribution of bass guitarist Jack Bruce, whose unusual drone-like melodic line formed
a responsive echo to his vocal.

The Cream version attempted to replicate the frantic fervor
of the James Paramount, which was the basic quality that gave
James' tune its potential rock currency. The rock version, however, was more controlled and inhibited. Rock of the period
was celebrated for its "energy," and this commodity was supplied
by Baker's drumming; Clapton's $31\frac{1}{2}$ bar single note guitar
break (cut almost to pop song dimensions) was basically me-
andering filler, lacking either a theme or a percussive punch.
It was completely insipid by comparison with James' original
breaks, but more spontaneous, in keeping with rock playing.
The performer was hamstrung by his rhythm-and-blues-based
flatpicking approach, which made James' fingerpicked runs inaccessible. The only outright suggestion of James' playing occurred in its fingerpicked introduction (a four-bar phrase descending three frets to the tonic, given a repeat), which conventionalized the most conventional and least ambitious figure
of James' tune. But this unprepossessing figure was skillfully
used to invert the absent crescendo effect of James' original
Paramount, creating a decrescendo. The imaginative nature of
the overall arrangement more than compensated for the lack
of instrumental technique, it being more difficult, ultimately,
to arrive at interesting music than to play impressive guitar licks.

Unlike such rock impurists as The Rolling Stones and Canned
Heat, who appropriated composer credits for copied blues
songs, Cream freely credited blues singers for the compositions
they recorded. The result was that James, who in reality had
made only an arranger's contribution to the song, and had dis-
honestly failed to acknowledge its derivation (perhaps from
Gene Austin's Victor recording), received the only monetary
windfall of his career. Eventually, he netted between $6,000 and
$10,000 as the album became a million-seller. He also drew roy-
alties from another version that was unfamiliar to him: Deep
Purple's outright copy of Clapton's rendition, which appeared
on their 1968 debut album. In both instances James was the

beneficiary of the piggyback effect of having a composition appear on a best-selling album which was not purchased on the basis of his own marginal contribution to it.

Without this windfall, he would have virtually starved on the decimated folk circuit of the period. When *I'm So Glad* appeared, James could not even afford the postage required to send a copy of his own Vanguard album to a female fan in France. The month before its release, on November 28th, he had written the author: ". . . if you all can get a concert at some place very soon maybe I can get by until January. That will be better than droping a pegion (smile) but any way I am down on the dam craacker box for real . . . and Christmas is near and I cant get any work."

The death of Mississippi John Hurt the previous month had deprived Avalon Productions of its only saleable commodity, and with it, the opportunity to bootstrap James to Hurt.[*]

In a sense, the position of blues to popular music had not changed since 1950, when Leadbelly's *Good Night Irene* had become a pop hit, its original performer remaining a nonentity. But James was not bitter that a rock group had garnished a mass audience for one of his pieces. In some respects, he was too much the plantation darkey to voice the commonly-heard complaint that white performers could enrich themselves by playing black music. If he had ever formed the opinion that he might have been passed over by audiences because of his complexion, this situation would have struck him as the inevitable state of affairs, and one he did not protest. He actually told the author: "I don't expect you to treat me like I'm white." A lifetime of Jim Crow had eroded his expectations.

It was owing to his racial timidity that James pretended to have no reaction to the Cream's rendition of his work. He was willing to talk up his superior talents when they exceeded (by

---

[*]James was playing in Milwaukee when Hurt died. "I was enjoying myself fine until we got the news about John" he wrote the author on November 10, 1966. "I was deeply shocked and felt hurt for a while but as you know the show must go on. I dedicated 2 nos. and make a short talk in his memory." This rhetoric was doubtless intended for the benefit of his wife; James had no regard for Hurt, whom he claimed to have first heard near Itta Bena as a twelve-year-old.

proclamation) those of another blues singer. To disparage a white rock group, however, was another matter.

But the Cream version rankled him to the extent of causing him to refer to it on his death bed, when his opinion could not effect his fortunes. "They got it ass backwards," he insisted. "They don't have the harmony, the rhythm; I doubled-up on it [the rhythm]. It's too good a song to mess up like that."

He consoled himself with the concluding comment: "No one will ever play it like me."

James' sour reception of *I'm So Glad* actually would have been gratifying to most blues enthusiasts, who almost universally believed that whites routinely prospered by "ripping off" black music, or performing pallid, inauthentic versions of "the real thing." But Cream's rendition was actually an exotic rearrangement of an exotic rearrangement, both completely unconventional within their genres. In truth most rock renditions of blues conformed to the law of the musical jungle, which was no different from the dynamic practiced by blues singers themselves. Just as animal predators gravitate towards the old, weak, or infirm victim, so did white musical opportunists (and the black blues-players before them) unfailingly single out the black artists who presented no real threat or competition. They were the first ones to extol the blues "greats" from whom they borrowed music or drew inspiration. The white musicians who copied the likes of Muddy Waters, B.B. King and Albert King had discreetly selected mentors and models who could never show them up. On the other hand, a true virtuoso like Snooks Eaglin would remain a virtual untouchable: had a highly acclaimed "rock virtuoso" ever attempted to perform his music, it would soon become obvious which guitarist was the real virtuoso.

That Skip James had tempted the rock imitator was actually a testament to his own ineffectuality as a musician. By the time Cream's *I'm So Glad* appeared, his own musicianship had degenerated to the point where he was getting even his most simple tunes "ass backwards." Increasingly, as he performed he would attempt to complicate his pieces with spontaneous single-string fills. He would begin an impromptu riff, and not know how to resolve it; the riff would simply sputter out. Even when he managed to play an extended riff that didn't contain faulty notes, his departures tended to make his rhythm disjointed.

James' tendency towards slapdash instrumental embroidery was basically an attempt to cater to the white blues fan of the period. No one in his new-found audience reacted openly to his singing; rather, it was his guitar-playing that elicited admiring comments. His discoverers had been typical white blues students, transforming the vocal medium that was blues into an instrumental medium, owing to their inability to sing. Largely because they (and others on the scene) aspired to play blues guitar, they would react immediately to any unexpected instrumental flourish James displayed.

James had already begun pandering to this sensibility with his first appearance at Newport, when he had lacked the ability to hazard anything more than rudimentary flourishes. As he regained his fluency, he indulged his rococco tendencies to the fullest. Every one of his performances was marked by as many improvised guitar licks as he could cram into a song.

But James' impromptu excursions were not cohesive. He had never been a riff-oriented guitarist, à la Blind Lemon Jefferson, and he was far from being a virtuoso guitarist. His embellishments had a hit-or-miss quality: he would characteristically embroider a guitar phrase to the point of being unable to resolve it, and return hastily to the tonic chord as the phrase dangled uncertainly, the tune threatening to degenerate into chaos. Basically, he was simply practicing on stage. The best that could be said of James in the 1960s was that he had the ability to bastardize his own tunes, which most blues players, being rote musicians, did not.

One of the reasons James' playing eroded was because the fawning attitudes of white blues fans made it unnecessary for him to put any real care or effort into his musicianship. He could readily count on receiving the same plaudits whether he played capably, or atrociously, performed in earnest, or merely went through the motions. Instead of inspiring him, white appreciation had a corrosive effect on his playing. In this respect, James was no different from virtually all of the blues players who were to become "legends" as they were placed on the white respirator.

James was well aware of the tendency of the white blues fan to thoughtlessly acclaim his work. Once after he played a series of guitar riffs, he asked me: "How do you like that?" When I responded with the rote compliments of the blues enthusiast, James shook his head and sneered slightly.

"That wasn't any good," he said, more disgusted with his undiscriminating fan than with his music.

When the author hazarded jejune guitar efforts before James, the latter rewarded him with effusive praise. "Oh, that's good," he would say. Once he began to acquire proficiency, James stopped commenting on his playing. To James, compliments were simply encouragements of the sort given to children as they attempted something for the first time.

What lay at the root of James' banality as a blues rediscovery was simply the fact that it had not been his own idea to launch a musical comeback. Although the blues fan of the period imagined that James had somehow been rescued from tragic oblivion, this was a fancy produced by white chauvinism. He had quit playing music of his own volition. Like all professional blues-players, he had been unable to separate his music from the lifestyle it fostered and had been designed to facilitate. His music had been a ticket to enable him to indulge his squalid youthful appetites, and escape the drudgery of manual labor. Once he rejected the blues lifestyle, he simply stopped playing blues music. Merely playing music for its own sake gave him no inner satisfaction. When his career was rekindled, his main concern was to invest as little time and effort in his musicianship as possible. His basic apathy was illustrated by his 1964 comment: "Myself, I try to satisfy the listeners. When I satisfy my manager and the rest of 'em, then I'm perfectly satisfied."

At home James almost never played blues, except to occasionally dust off a forgotten piece with a view to presenting it at his next concert. The songs he regularly played for recreation were spirituals.

James' indifference towards secular music had grown so acute that he did no practicing whatsoever before traveling to New York to record his second album for Vanguard in the summer of 1967. As he bungled song after song, his producer Maynard Solomon appeared delighted with every take. At the end of James' performance of *Lorenzo Blues*, he beamed: "Mrs. James, you've just been immortalized."

Lorenzo Blues, his most recent composition, was probably the poorest piece of doggeral James ever invented, and Lorenzo herself was far from flattered by her husband's mock descriptions of her: "She stumbles when she talks, she wobbles when she walks . . . She's shaped like a Coca Cola bottle . . ."

As Solomon agreeably passed on a succession of seemingly unredeemable takes, the author was aghast: he wondered how an album could possibly ensue from such erratic playing. Actually, the producer was already prepared to mend James' mistakes. The ensuing album, *Devil Got My Woman* (released in May, 1968), was a seamless product. It was typical of the company to present what Solomon describes as "something of an idealized performance" via splicing: "We applied classical editing to folk music." Afterwards, he did not recall James' session as having been exceptionally error-ridden.

Despite the rock success of *I'm So Glad*, the white audience for blues singers remained as marginal as it was sycophantic. On paper, James had a prestigious career, replete with effusive press clippings; *Cavalier Magazine*, in fact, had labelled him "the greatest blues singer of all time." In actual life, he did not even make a subsistence wage as a blues rediscovery. He would file no taxes, and receive no royalty statements from his records. His income was low enough to qualify him for welfare, an expedient Lorenzo flatly refused to consider.

The rhetorical acclamation he received was itself a symptom of his lack of popularity. It was as if writers and fans were attempting to assuage a bruised ego, or compensate for his lack of popularity with devout recognition. Outwardly self-effacing in 1964, he became spoiled by his fawning fans and grew to accept acclamation as the natural order of things; a typical Jamesian reference to his reception reached the author via a letter dated November 10, 1966, describing a recent Milwaukee concert:

> The Program was a Terrific Success and they want
> me back soon. They say they have never heard any-
> thing like it before. The place was full every night.

In the 1920s, the black record producer Mayo Williams had
brushed off the blues singers who looked for compliments by
telling them: "We only know how good you are by your sales
figures." Maynard Solomon feted James as an artist; when he
did not fete him with fifty dollars in expense money after his
second session, James became enraged. He announced his intention of writing a song denouncing the producer, who had
no idea that James was owed such a sum. On June 28, 1967,
six months after completing the session, James wrote: "now I
dont know just What Stepts to take to consult With Mr Solomon.
Because I feel just like bursting him in his Dam nose. Whenever
I do meet Him if I live and the Lord Bless me he is Going
to pay me off something or mighty Damn fast talk or something
Going to happen."

After "consulting" with Solomon over the phone, James
learned that his expense money had been doled out to Dick
Waterman. Now he was ready to go on another rampage. On
July 7 of that year, he wrote the author:

> . . . he and Solomon give me such a nasty deal
> about my $50 exspences when I come to N.Y. to re-
> cord for them so I call Mr Solomon and also wrote
> him abut the matter and he told me and my wife
> that he had made the check out in my name . . . he
> must have give that check to Dick Waterman. Now
> he tell me he sent the check to some Dr. William
> Keng . . . Now Dick just about borrowed some money
> from this man or some plum bank or owed Dr. King
> and forged this check on me. So now you can see
> what a hell of a manager I have.

If nothing else, this episode demonstrated the negligible communication that existed between James and his manager, who
was less concerned with the niceties of bookkeeping than a
Southern plantation owner. James had to accept all of Waterman's statements on faith, because he was never paid directly

by his employers, and (aside from Vanguard) never saw any contracts with them.

He was surrounded by people who seemed to recognize that their importance to him was inversely proportional to the state of his finances. For example, his financial plight could have been alleviated by the simple step of registering him with Social Security, but this was not done by his manager. Were it not for the timely arrival of a check for *I'm So Glad*, James would have had a final confrontation with Waterman. He never saw Solomon again, so was left to comment, bitterly, on his deathbed: "If I'da known he was a Jew I never woulda recorded for him."

33. The Imposter

As he toiled half-heartedly on the folk circuit, James was acutely aware that he was no longer the musician he had been in 1931. He remarked that he was unable to play *I'm So Glad* as he had originally done. When he listened to the single battered copy that then existed of *Hard-Luck Child*, a tune he no longer played, he shook his head and said simply: "I just can't play like that any more."

In this respect, James was no different from most of the blues has-beens of the period. What distinguished him from performers like Son House, however, was that he had the technical ability to execute most of his original pieces. He was simply unfocused and apathetic, even as he played at home, far removed from the concert setting that still made him uncomfortable.

Because blues music is not intricate enough to remain interesting without a performing aura of passion or energy, his detachment amounted to a more severe debilitation than the alcoholic tremor of Son House. The perceived greatness of Mississippi blues had rested solely on their palpable intensity and forcefulness. Though James at his peak (in *22-20* and *I'm So Glad*) had displayed genuine instrumental brilliance, it was his drive, speed, timing, and expressiveness that had borne this brilliance, qualities that had been fueled by emotion, not intellect. Now it was as if an inner light had been extinguished in him.

What had gone awry with James?

Before his death, James was to tell the author that he had considered blues sinful to perform. As a compromise, he had played with his "thinkin' faculties" but had deliberately refused to "put my heart in it." What James feared above all was becoming the kind of mesmeric blues performer he had been in 1931, and thus infecting others with the sin that blues represented. "Feelin' in music is electrifyin'," he said. "It'll infect people."

Evidently he had devised a courtroom defense to counter his coming celestial indictment as a blues singer: he hadn't really been a blues singer. Only in the technical sense had he been a blues singer. No one could have taken his efforts to heart, because his own heart had not been in them. The flesh had played sinful songs; the spirit had not.

What was striking about James' disclosure was not so much his calculated attempt to be cunning and thereby obtain the spoils of both worlds, but the failure of blues commentators to so much as sense that James had been striving to impersonate a blues singer, rather than become one. What was to James a swindle on his part had come across as an expression of heartfelt sincerity.

But religion was not the only barrier preventing James from achieving actual blues artistry. His emotional energy and powers of concentration were drained by his preoccupation with killing his ex-girlfriend in Tunica. He had already, in the mid-1960s, taken the first step towards her assassination by discovering her actual whereabouts, and lulling her (by what means, he did not say) into thinking that he was dead.

Even as James was consumed with thoughts of homicidal revenge, he raged against the criminal deeds that were the only items in newspapers to ever catch his attention. Reading about any homicide other than the one he hoped to commit would set him off into a tirade.

"I always believed in *right*," one of his typical tirades began, "and I always have been a law-abidin' citizen . . . But here's one thing about it: the law [police] don't seem to be doin' justice here [in Philadelphia] . . . You take a case I read about in the papers, and look at these cats doin' this dirty stuff. This one guy—kill his mother, kill his grandmother, kill his mother-in-law, kill his sister 'cause they didn't grant him the privilege to do what he wanted to do: to talk a lot of 'sociality' over the telephone. I don't believe in this sociality. If *I* got a phone, I got it for purposes of business. Now why did he take those innocent lives? It wasn't because he was an illiterate, or either because he was 'mentally ill'—that's just a 'git-by' [excuse] . . .

"And the people in power who got this influence, some of 'em knows it's not like that. But they take 'em to a doctor somewhere and they'll say: 'Oh well, we examined his head and his brains is bad.' Well now, if his brains are so bad, what's he doin' in school?

". . . Of course, you can meet some of the highest graduates just out of school . . . and they act the bigger fool than some country cat that ain't never been to primary or either kindergarten. . . ."

To complete his portfolio as a law-abiding citizen, James needed one thing: a gun. Periodically, he pestered the author to supply him with a weapon. Ever the rhetorician, he began his wheedling campaign with a propaganda speech on self-defense. "Can't nobody that means right hardly get a gun. . . . These 'jitterbugs' [criminals] get 'em and the innocent man can't get 'em what needs 'em in his home . . . I don't want no gun to tote in my pockets because I don't have no envy in myself whatever, enough to hurt the other man. But I don't want him to hurt me."

Although the crime rate in the mid-1960s was miniscule compared to present-day proportions, James represented himself as being in constant peril from hordes of local "jitterbugs." His ostensible interest in obtaining a gun was to mete out Mike Hammer-style justice to criminals, and thus right the social wrong of liberalism.

"If I got some 'protection' [i.e., a gun] I'm gonna protect myself," he declared. ". . . I catch one of 'em jitterbugs comin' into my house, or grabbin' my wife or somethin'—now it wouldn't be good for me to even *hear* of him, whichever way he went. The laws, all the polices in Philadelphia or anywhere else would have to cremate me, 'cause I'd go manhuntin'.

"And when I found him, it wouldn't be no use of sayin' anything. The law would do anything they wanted to me, but I would make away with *that* cat . . ."

In the conversation in which he had first revealed his determination to shoot his ex-girlfriend to me, James had concluded his remarks in similar terms, remarking that the law could kill him afterwards.

James' mind was in a constant ferment of violent fantasies, all involving lurid circumstances in which he would die in a blazing shoot-out. Sometimes he would actually mull over these scenarios with the author, who interpreted them as displacements of his basic desire to revenge himself against his Tunica tormenter.

In one of James' death scenarios, he imagined punishing a bratty child in his neighborhood for misbehavior, and being forced to "defend himself" by killing the child's angry, avenging parents. In another, he spoke of the consequences that would ensue should the police (for reasons he did not specify) visit his apartment in an effort to question me. The police would not have a warrant for this purpose, and James would refuse them entry because I was his personal guest. This refusal would lead to a confrontation between two implacable forces: soon he would be engaged in a shoot-out with his police adversaries, resulting in multiple deaths, the last his own. This chain of inexorable events was discussed quite dispassionately, as though James were merely a bystander at his own demise, and the targets of his wrath simply abstractions.

The homicides he envisioned were never singular. "If you kill somebody," he once said, "you know you got to keep on killin' till you get killed."

All the while, the imagined mass murderer continued to press me for a pistol with which to defend himself against "criminals."

In November of 1967, I received a letter from James. Attached to it was a postscript from his wife.

> P.S.
> Now this is from me and if you care anything for Skip you will not get him a gun because when he gets to drinking and get angry about anything he always saying if I had me a gun I would kill until I get killed. He will threaten me too. So you see its better for him to have temptation at his hand . . . Just make some excuse why you could not get it.
> Thank you. L.

Behind his back, Lorenzo James always spoke of her husband as though he were a great tribulation she had to bear. "He's not the hero you think he is," she scolded me. My visits would give her an occasion to unburden herself with whispered complaints about James: he was "thin-skinned," "hard-headed," and "mean and ugly." These remarks belied her claims that he was also a secret softie who would cry in her arms at night and beg her: "Don't leave me."

On the surface, theirs was a placid relationship, without friction. The single quarrel they had in the presence of the author was occasioned by one of James' oratorical blasts against "sancts." His sanctified wife finally burst in the living room and exclaimed: "A fine example you set! You smoke; you drink; you don't go to church." The pair had a raging argument as to which of them made a likelier candidate for the flames, ending only when James stalked out of his apartment for a drink.

For his part, James did not judge his common-law wife from a Biblical perspective. He simply saw her as another one of the barrelhouse women he might have met in Arkansas, or as one of the "damsels" he derided in his blues. Outwardly, he cultivated her, peppering her with periodic compliments ("the more she cooks, she better she looks") and never failing to address her as "baby," just as he had Mabel.

Privately, he evinced no feeling for her. Lorenzo, he confided, had simply taken up with him for money. As an example of this, he pointed to the small decorative knick-knacks she had purchased with the proceeds of his concerts. She was always buying such useless things, he said. She was simply a sponge who soaked up his money and was using it to support her sister "Tee." "I can't pull a train with too many cars," James said. "I already told her not to buy any more furniture."

Now she was quietly awaiting his death, at which point she would squander his royalty monies on another man. This was simply the inevitable consequence of their relationship: "A woman has a nature, you can't stop."

But James had a plan to circumvent nature. He wanted to make out a secret will, leaving his estate to me and my sister Maggie, whom he held in high regard.

Increduously, I listened to James' plot/counterplot, and the cold, matter-of-fact cynicism that lay coiled behind it. I had always considered James' windy speeches on women to be so much rhetoric, and had taken to tuning them out, though James was eager to enshrine them on tape: "Now regardless of what you got that she wants, and regardless to how pretty you think she is, you'll love her just to a certain extent and she'll love you just to a certain extent. But she'll lie and pretend that she loves you more than that . . . She'll find the course in life that you want to pursue, and she'll block it any way she can, because she wants to be in command herself. There's more and more of that type of woman . . ." James was actually discussing himself as he held forth on the deviousness of women. His wife had no idea that he held her in low regard. His distrust of women was no more than a projection of his own insincerity with them. Of his youthful sexual entanglements, he stated: "I wouldn't lay with a woman unless she had a gold-plated cock."

When he received a letter in 1967 from an English fan who remarked on his sorrowful face as he sang the blues, he sniggered: "How can you tell what's in a person's mind by what's on his face?"

His characteristic facial expression actually did provide a glimpse into his interior. When he listened to others his eyebrows were always arched skeptically, causing his brow to furrow. He conveyed that he was expecting to hear something dubious, or what he would term an "air pudding."

For the most part, James appeared impassively withdrawn from life, making no investment of himself in anything exterior. Whether this was because he was consumed by his core of inner violence or fragmented from a dualism involving warring lethal/litigurical impulses was impossible for any outsider to know. At any rate, his slippery strategy of putting on sham blues concerts only made him uneasy. "I do things that I know is contrary to God," he said, "but still there's a conjunction with Him I don't overlook. He doesn't accept those things. And I'm gonna get through with the blues part of my life very soon, I think. I like the spiritual part of the music I play better."

34. *The Barrel Of Crabs*

Outwardly, James appeared to have settled into a life of placid gentility. His apartment contained an upright piano, an admirer's gift he played only briefly every two weeks, and then at his wife's request. On top of the piano rested a framed color portrait of Martin Luther King, placed by Lorenzo. Another retouched photograph depicted his grandmother, a portrait James had obtained from relatives in Chicago while performing in that city. Next to it stood a photograph of his stern-faced father, glaring at the camera. It bore the words:

> The above is the likeness of
> Rev. E.D. James
> Pastor of The Macedonian Baptist Church
> Leeds, Alabama
> The Rising Star Baptist Church, Benham, Kentucky

On the wall above the piano stood an abstract painting, the gift of a blues fan, which both Jameses said they did not understand.

In his placid moments, he expressed mundane aspirations: he wanted to buy a Volkswagen, and looked forward to playing in Europe, a goal he would achieve the fall of 1967. Sometimes he spoke of going hunting, moving to Vermont, or of opening up a music school, an activity he claimed he could not undertake without obtaining a license from the police department. A local church had expressed an interest in using him as its pianist, but James had desisted. "You can't serve God and Mammon at the same time," he claimed. Yet this was precisely what James was attempting to do as a blues singer. No longer did he present himself with the introductory remark captured on a 1965 *Ontario Place* recording: "I'm just a blues man. An' of course I play some spirituals as a request but I'm just a blues fella all the way." Instead, he ceremoniously began each concert with a spiritual.

He rationalized his failure to take a more active interest in church by scoring professed Christians as deplorable hypocrites. "Nowadays the Christianity isn't pure," he claimed. "The people don't mean it . . . People get up now and preach some of the most powerful sermons from a scriptorial standpoint and then get right on the street and won't give you a dime to get a cracker. Step on your feet and won't speak to you to say 'Excuse me' even."

The energy he expended in traveling and appearing at a concert took the edge off his anger, and he enjoyed every passing diversion he was able to indulge in in his travels, such as a visit to Disneyland, or the San Diego zoo, or a ceremonial banquet the Mayor of Hamburg was to put on for touring American blues singers in October, 1967. But all too often he languished, left in the unrelenting grip of his own misanthropy. While he always appeared in complete control of himself, he said of his general mood: "I get so mad I wanna bust."

Almost anything was likely to touch off bilious thoughts. "Pennsylvania is the most reprobated state in the Union," he maintained, when he hardly traversed Philadelphia. He occasionally spoke of moving away from it, but mused: "It's bad everywhere."

Without his help, the world had gone to hell, and there was nothing he could or cared to do to improve it. There was no hope for the future; the women of the world were seeing to that. " . . . They don't even brood over their children like a hen; they're like cowbirds . . . the cowbird leaves their eggs for the sun to hatch. That's all lots of those women are—hatcheries."

He no longer struggled against his own darkness, seeking a rhetorical ray of light as he had in the anguished days after his rediscovery. Then his thoughts of suicide had been tempered by the recollection of an old poem, "concernin' a man and his wife, his dear companion. They had a dispute and they had a fallin' out. And they got divorceted. He decided he would

kill himself. . . . He went out in the woods; he had him a pistol.
. . . He went out in the ravine, woods, just to kill himself alone
where nobody be askin' where he was.

"... And when he entered the spot where he wanted to put
his gun and kill himself, it was a little bird. Sittin' on the branch
of a tree singin'. . . . Little bird was sittin' down on the branch,
his head up, singin' so lonesome, until he decided he'd consider
that little bird and pay a little attention . . . he wanted to draw
his gun to kill it.

"... And it attracted his 'tention so he stopped. . . . And that
little bird saved his life . . . From that on, then he take an interest
in singin' and 'came, I imagine, one of the most wonderfulest
songsters or Christians."

Now he had become smugly sour, consoled by the emptiness
he saw in everything outside him.

For an introverted character, he had surprisingly few inner
resources. His most characteristic pastime was "peeping out"
his window from his living room, or (if the weather was nice)
watching the street from the vantage point of his front porch.
He passed hours in this fashion, peering at passing cars on the
street. It was as if he were still on a plantation, where the sight
of a car was of major interest. "You'll see mostly any car that's
made come down this street," he said.

He had no patience or taste for other amusements. Once,
with great fanfare, he turned on his television set to watch a
Phillies baseball game. Instead of watching the game, he began
a soliloquy about his experience in Bentonia as an ambidex-
terous pitcher, detailing his assortment of pitches, a notable
shutout he once threw, and his early retirement, occasioned by
the fact that the gloves available to him were too thin to protect
the hands he applied to musical instruments. Having given this
account of his unrealized greatness, he abruptly turned off the
set.

This was James at his worst: an outright personification of
the solipsistic blues song, indifferent to anything that did not
directly concern himself. With childlike self-idolatry, he noted
a folk songbook that featured him: inside its front cover he
scrawled, "You will see me on page 56 and 64," and "read me
on 54 page." Underneath a drawing of himself on page 54 he

wrote: "Skip James in person." That there was such a thing as another voice worth hearing—in any musical genre—or an instrumentalist worth hearing—did not occur to him. Only once did he utter a favorable comment about any singer. "Ray Charles," he opined after hearing him on the radio, "he can really sing."

He rarely glanced at the two shelves of books he possessed, largely theological tracts obtained after his father died in Alabama. They included such titles as *Science, The Lore Of The New Testament, Modern Business English, Wisdom's Way, The Four Horseman of the Apocalypse, Beverly Gray's Return, God's Good Man, The New Applied Mathematic, The Preacher's Homiletic Commentary, Ancient History, The Science Of Life,* and *Conquering The Seven Deadly Sins.*

Except to make a daily trek to the corner grocery or liquor store, he never left his apartment unless it was for a concert engagement. Even his avid taste for beer was tempered by Lorenzo's disapproval, causing him to retort: "Sure I drink—moderately. Jesus turned water to wine, didn't he?"

Despite his standoffish character, he became increasingly clinging to the author. When the latter would visit him in Philadelphia, it would become awkward to leave, as James' disappointment became evident. "You ought to come and stay here for a month," James suggested. By then he had taken to calling me "son."

The only social life he had consisted of regular Sunday visits from Lorenzo's daughter, Rae Roots, her husband Sonny, and their six year-old daughter Volney. A truckdriver, Sonny had begun playing guitar after the discovery of John Hurt. He openly admired James and was always deferential to him, musically and socially, which ensured a smooth relationship between them. As he ventured such tunes as *See See Rider, Trouble In Mind,* and *Diddie Wa Diddie* on his electric guitar, James made no attempt to accompany him, or offer him anything other than rote compliments. The gathering would then turn into a spiritual songfest, with Lorenzo and Rae picking out their favorite hymns from songbooks. James would silently accompany Lorenzo as she sang songs like *I Want To Be More Like Jesus* in a soft, timorous voice; Sonny would accompany a duet between Lorenzo and her daughter, *Nearer My God To Thee.*

Sometimes Sonny would arrive with another neighbor named Ellis, who had learned guitar from Blind Boy Fuller in North Carolina. James would diplomatically flatter his efforts, while giving the impression that he was enduring his company. Hours later, after Ellis' departure, he would remark: "How you like that music? I didn't like that."

Periodically, James would encourage his wife's nervous son-in-law to share a stage with him at a future performance. Then he would disparage his protégé's lack of ambition. He also spoke of putting the author (an even rawer amateur) in concert. "I'll put you in a coffee house, let you make a start," he told me. By James' lights, I had all the requisite qualifications to succeed. "You know about these 'jitterbugs,' how to avoid them, and traps and pitfalls," he said. "You've seen some parts of the world."

I had seen enough of the blues world to know that it was exactly the barrel of crabs that Skip James depicted. The barrel included blues researchers.

As James performed at a Pennsylvania folk festival, I listened to a young folklorist fulminate against James. Skip was a liar, the man claimed: he claimed to have invented his own tunes, but they were really folk songs. He would soon prove it by going to Bentonia and finding other blues singers in the Skip James tradition.

I could not understand why the researcher was so irate. It was par for the course for blues singers to misrepresent themselves. The statements of blues singers were often laughed off by people who heard them, so ridiculous were they. No one got upset when Furry Lewis claimed to have invented bottleneck playing. James himself gave no credence to the palaver of blues singers; when told of a statement Son House had made about Charlie Patton, he replied: "If Charlie Patton were livin' today he'd say that same thing about Son House." He begged off interviews whenever possible. "Use your own ideas about that," he would sometimes say, deflecting my questions about his musical past.

I had pondered James' musical roots, without success. Referring to the attempts of various interviewers to penetrate his musical past, James said that it was "none of their business." He was right, of course; no one pestered prominent rhythm and blues, rock, or pop stars for personal information. They were entertainers, not historical exhibits.

In search of James' elusive "roots," I had sought out Henry Stuckey, and Stuckey had failed to claim credit for originating a single James piece.

I had been led to Stuckey by Gayle Wardlow, who had discovered James' mentor early in 1965 on Criswell's plantation between Bentonia and Satartia, where he lived in squalor with his wife, daughter, and grand-daughter. Still smarting from James' rediscovery by rival blues researchers, Wardlow was anxious to have Stuckey emerge as a better blues singer than James.

But the nonchalant, cigar-smoking cipher who was Henry Stuckey did not even display a competitive attitude towards James. He listened to my various comments about James with a sly smile, as though he knew better, but was not saying what he knew, or as though we were sharing some conspiratorial joke. He asked no questions about James, and answered questions perfunctorily.

His shack was foul-smelling, and full of flies. Finally, I could stand the stench no longer: I went outside and threw up.

35. *Scorpions*

When I recounted my meeting with Henry Stuckey, James said: "... he's too smart for these slicks who talk you into studying the music racket again."

Soon afterwards, in the summer of 1965, Stuckey was stricken with liver cancer. On March 9 of the following year, he died in Jackson at the age of sixty-eight. He left no musical legacy, and a claim that he had recorded near his home for a one-man outfit on the very day James had returned from Texas to Bentonia in 1935 was never substantiated.

Every three months or so, James dusted off another old blues tune to play in concert. His latest re-creation was a slow standard, *Sportin' Life*, which he mistakenly attributed to Bessie Smith and had previously played on piano, after learning it from a white folk singer.

This sportin' life is killin' me.

A *Blues Unlimited* item dated October 4, 1968 and attributed to a "Philadelphia reporter" (undoubtedly Dick Waterman) spoke of impending concerts: "Skip James is doing a small concert with Elizabeth Cotton in Philadelphia, and leaves after that for an extended tour including concert dates in Denver, Portland, Seattle and San Francisco and club work in L.A. and San Diego." But the previous month, after playing an engagement at a college in Bethel, Pennsylvania, he had taken ill, and began to drink heavily, in an attempt (his wife thought) to deaden pain. In this period, he slept most of the time. His wife appraised me of his condition in a letter dated October 20: " ... Skip has been in bed these last 2 weeks. He is better but will have to

go to the Dr tomorrow and then we will know whether he will
have to go to the hospital or not. We hope not so say a prayer
for him rite sometime." Soon afterwards, he checked into the
University of Pennsylvania hospital, where he was diagnosed as
having inoperable cancer.

He was sent home to die without taking radiation treatments.
In February of 1969 I found him confined to his bed, in continuous agony. He spoke deliriously of Johnnie Temple, who
had died the previous November. "Johnnie, your suffering is
over," he said. The two singers had not communicated after
James' rediscovery, but Temple had been kept abreast of James'
career by Gayle Wardlow. Jealous of James' greater recognition,
he had finally erupted at the mention of his mentor's name,
deriding him as an old "barrelhouse musician" who "didn't know
any real chords."

Soon, the former loner would be united in death with his
old competitors. "Most of the old heads are dying off," he said.
"All the old musicians and music philosophers are going: their
time has come ... I have another two-three weeks."

James looked as close to death as a living human could possibly look, and he was in such pain (unalleviated by morphine,
or any drugs) that death appeared to be an impending deliverance for him. "I'm skin and bones," he gasped. "I won't be
here when you get back." He passed his time in half-delirious
prayers. "Lord have mercy. Lord, please have mercy on me.
Take me to heaven or cure me." As pain attacked him he would
plead: "Take me to the graveyard."

His wife stood by and admonished him: "Don't feel sorry for
yourself ... Be thankful for life." She enlisted the services of
a faith healer, to no avail.

"Our faith is never strong enough," she sighed.

Out of his presence, she groused: "He's not the only one who's
sick. He feels sorry for himself."

As James slowly rotted, he had two explanations of his condition. Believing that he might be undergoing punishment for
blues-playing, he vowed to perform only spirituals: "If it please
the Lord to restore my health, I ain't studyin' no more blues
whatsoever."

At other times he was convinced that his final agony was the result of the hoodoo his girlfriend in Tunica had set upon him. In his last weeks of life he was perpetually picking at the stools in his bedpan and secretly scrutinizing them for reptiles. The bloody shreds he saw swirling in his water looked like living things to him. "Does that look like a scorpion to you?" he would ask me. The scorpions, he was convinced, were eating him alive.

36. *The Funeral*

The death of Skip James on October 3, 1969 did not occasion any mention in non-specialist publications, save for a thumbnail *New York Times* obituary. A Mississippi blues singer, in 1969, was a man of no consequence.

Although few people in James' neighborhood had known him, or even heard of him, the funeral chapel that prepared his remains was packed with local mourners. These were persons who regularly attended local funerals as a social event, and it was probably in anticipation of their attendance and its accompanying illusion of the illustriousness of the deceased that Lorenzo had engaged the J.V. Hawkins Funeral Home for the task of giving James his final send-off.

For this occasion, it was imperative that the corpse on exhibit make a good impression on the onlookers. Such was Lorenzo's foremost concern before the funeral.

Working from James' passport photo, the funeral director created a virtual wax dummy out of the hollowed, ravaged face of Skip James.

James' appearance in the sight of God was a matter for the cleric who was engaged to preach his funeral to burnish. In moments of anger Lorenzo had taunted him with his sinfulness, proclaiming her certainty that he was hell-bound. In response James would admit that the post-mortem path of his soul was uncertain, adding, as though it were a consolation: "If I'm going to hell I won't be the only one there."

By secular lights, he was a religious fanatic, or a self-deluded fake: a man of stern, unforgiving Christian words, but not Christian deeds. By the standards of the neighbors who had turned out for his funeral, James was simply another backslider, because he belonged to no church, but was not known as a non-denominational Christian. This made his funeral a political occasion, requiring a careful balancing act on the part of the pastor who presented him to his audience. As always in such situations, he was preaching to the living, while purporting to discuss the dead. He had to certify James' essential Christianity in such a way as to indicate that he belonged in a church casket, yet not cheapen the worth of staunch church membership by sending him off with the kind of salute the onlookers would receive when it was their time to occupy the casket. Otherwise, what would be the point of going to church?

Knowing how meager her husband's church credentials looked to the spectators disguised as mourners, Lorenzo had something special to show them. The opening remarks were to be delivered by Dick Waterman—a white man in a church full of poor black faces. Waterman would attest to the fact that it was not a nobody lying in a casket, but a real dignitary who was placed before them, perhaps too important to pass Sundays with them in a local church.

Waterman genuflected to the sensibilities of an alien audience as best he could. "He started every program with a spiritual," he stated, inaccurately. ". . . He always said that God had to get first place in his program or it would be a failure . . . He played in London, California, New York . . ." But James' career consumed only a momentary digression: "He said that education without salvation was damnation."

The well-meaning manager had inadvertently managed to draw attention to what the more constant Christian spectators knew to be James' coming fate, for the man who spouted these great truths had been working as a blues singer. He had not given God first place in his program; his attendance record at church had been zero. He had obviously made a certain amount of money, without giving any to the church.

Having thrown these ill-chosen Christian sops to the audience, Waterman concluded by telling the gathering what had personally impressed him most about Skip James: "He was his own man. He took pride in his work . . . He had dignity." As though this summary of James were insufficient eulogy, Waterman concluded by characterizing him, oddly, as a "marvelous person." He had no inkling that James had gloated over the idea that a Chicago thug might "take care" of him.

"He was a *horse*," sniggered James' second cousin George Roberts, who had driven from Baltimore to attend the service.

Now it was time for the preacher, Earl H. Jackson. A resident of nearby Osage Avenue, Jackson was a small, thin, light-skinned man with a mustache and a nervous smile. He disdained the title "Reverend" and did not have a formal church affiliation; rather, he was known as "Elder Jackson." Before joining the church he had been known as Young Sporting Blood, and had actually supported himself in some fashion by dancing to Cab Calloway records played on the jukebox. Easy-going localites considered him a good preacher, because he did not condemn people merely for smoking or drinking, and his tolerance made him the ideal mouthpiece for the moment. Just the same, Lorenzo was fearful lest Jackson mount the pulpit, become carried away by the size of the audience, and begin to showboat and filibuster.

But though the spirit was doubtless willing, the flesh needed something substantial to feed on, and Jackson had not known James, except as an ailing voice over the telephone, receiving a remote blessing. The particulars of his subject's life did not much matter to him, for, in his enlightened view, "everybody is good and bad." Jackson was too cynical to exalt any human being; he viewed Martin Luther King as a man "making money." Of the latter, Jackson had little, at least in his capacity as minister: he worked as a trucker, along with Sonny Roots.

At first it appeared as if Jackson were in over his head. He gesticulated nervously as he read a succession of Biblical passages prepared for the occasion—John 11:25-26, 1 Timothy 6:7, Job 1:21, 2 Corinthians 2:3-4, 2 Corinthians 1:37-8, and finally, Psalm 90. He stumbled during the reading of the Psalm: "For all our days are passed away in thy wrath: we spend our years as a tale that is told..."

Setting the Bible aside, he repeated, "Life is a tale told," waiting for the weight of these words to sink in. "This is the age of preparation," the off-the-cuff preacher continued, "and like Skip's manager said, he was always prepared." He allowed that he hadn't known James well, but had prayed for him over the telephone. "If Alexander Graham Bell could see the uses to which the phone was put, he woulda been amazed." Then he brought the telephone into a theological framework: "You have faith in the telephone, why not have faith in God?"

Sitting as the second white person present, the author suppressed a snicker as he recalled how Mary Baker Eddy had been buried with a telephone, in the belief that she would awaken underground and need to dial for deliverence. The preposterous words of a spiritual, *Telephone To Glory*, echoed in his mind.

He listened as Jackson tried to tie James, like the telephone, to God. It was not a good connection.

"And he had one spiritual, one record—that was called

Look at the people!
Yes, look at the people, they got to be tried.

"And he wanted to join the church . . ." Here the upbeat Elder left his thought dangling unfinished, possibly because he sensed that he was now treading on theologically dangerous ground. The true believer hadn't joined the church . . . Why? Because he was a truer believer in money, or in whiskey? Jackson could not claim that James had led a Christian life, so he ducked the subject. That he died a believer was enough: "He called me 'Preacher,' he said: 'I'm ready to go now.'"

In her pew, a neighbor who had never met James concurred, using the Adam Clayton Powell-style rhetoric of the times: "He hung tough and kept the faith."

In Fundamentalist circles, true believers were not supposed to have to "hang tough." The lingering, agonizing—"hard," in old-fashioned parlance—death James had endured was popularly taken as a measure of God's displeasure with the life of the supplicant, a preliminary ass-kicking before the sinner was sent down to Satan for the final fiery brutalization that would last foreover.

No one appeared to be meditating over the content of Jackson's rambling remarks, least of all Jackson himself. Whenever he sputtered out momentarily he would point to the wax dummy in the casket and say: "He's not dead; he's just asleep."

With considerably more enthusiasm, Elder Jackson announced: "I told Mrs. James she has a son, and her daughter she has a brother...."

At this, Sonny Roots turned to a companion and guffawed: "He better watch that stuff!"

All Lorenzo cared about was that Jackson keep his remarks brief. She was mollified when his sermon soon sputtered out, thanks not only to her sharp preliminary warnings but to Jackson's inability to weave a Christian context around James' little-known life. His game but feeble rhetoric would have left no doubt in the mind of any regular church-goer in attendance that James' unexamined life had taken a wrong turn somewhere, and that its wheels had not been turned in the proper direction in time to avert a post-mortem crash at St. Peter's gate, which would throw him in the opposite direction.

Afterwards, the Elder mingled with the family at the James apartment, vainly seeking the connections between James and Christianity that had eluded him on the pulpit. When James' cousin George commented, "You couldn't chastise him"—indicating that James was a godless man—Jackson quickly replied, as if to smother the insinuation: "He was his own man, that's right—he wasn't a hypocrite."*

The cousin agreed. "Like the fella said, he was his own man. If he liked you, he let you know, and if he didn't like you, he let you know that, too."

He turned to the Baltimore Orioles, a subject of greater interest to him than his departed cousin. After making lukewarm chitchat, Jackson turned to leave, telling George ironically: "We had a good discussion—of *baseball*."

The Elder knew how to get a point across.

No one at the funeral had said anything about James' experience as a minister, or made anything of his musical talent. Cousin George had mulled the matter over, and concluded: "He woulda been better, but see, what messed him up was—people tried to shame him outta singing blues. That's what kept him from getting to the top."

---

*James had formerly insisted: "... any person who won't stand chastisement is a bastard—now that's in the Bible."

37. *The Burying Ground*

It was time for the mourners to say good-bye to Skip James. Lorenzo was greatly miffed that George hadn't bothered to hang around for the finale, but had quickly excused himself during the reception. He had not been there to witness her belated collapse later that night, when she tearfully told her company that James was a truly good man, which was why she had loved him.

"He had a hard life," she said, as though her primary emotion for him had been pity.

The next morning, the mourners returned to the funeral home, heard a reading of the 90th Psalm, and watched Hawkins step up to the casket. He offered to open it to give the audience their final look at Skip James. Lorenzo ambled up to the opened casket and sobbed hysterically until she was led away by her daughter.

Abruptly, the director began gathering up the flowers that surrounded James' casket. As the pallbears bore the casket to a hearse outside, he poured the water from each flower vase on the highway.

A seven-car procession followed the hearse, each car with its headlights shining lusterlessly in the grey morning. In keeping with an unexplained custom, the caravan made a detour to pass James' apartment en route to Merion Cemetary, the privately owned 22-acre graveyard on the Main Line in which James was to be buried. When the procession passed the Merion High School that stood nearby, a group of football players waved.

Three wooden caskets had preceded the procession, still waiting to be installed in their respective plots. A James pallbearer noted that they were destined for Potter's Field and that Merion was the only local cemetary with a Potter's Field.

Two workmen in tattered clothes hoisted James' casket from the hearse and placed it on top of a metal frame lined with rickety boards. Flowers the mourners had plucked from the vases were thrown on a hill of freshly dug dirt piled next to the grave. When the guests assembled around the casket Elder Jackson read aloud from the book of Common Prayer, and then invited them to repeat the Lord's Prayer. At the conclusion of the Lord's Prayer, the funeral director pushed a button, causing the casket to lower on rollers. As it descended into the open pit, Hawkins ordered the onlookers to return to their cars.

Eight years later, Lorenzo would be lowered in the same plot, alongside the common-law husband who insisted she would run away with another man.

The young blues enthusiast, who had been one of the pall-bearers, sat beside two middle-aged men who had known Lorenzo James.

"You don't see many wooden caskets—they use mostly concrete now," one of them remarked.

"Well, I done somethin' I never done before," said the other. "That's be a pallbearer."

"It's twenty after eleven—it didn't take too long, did it?"

"No, it doesn't take long to plant you."

James' gravesite.
(Courtesy Skip Henderson, Mount Zion Memorial Fund)

38. The Man Nobody Knew

On his deathbed, James told me: "There's a lot of things I never told you. There's a lot you don't know about me."
A moment later, he added: "I fed you on babe's milk." His voice began to trail off. "You weren't ready for anything but babe's milk." He did not elaborate on these statements.

James' deathbed non-confession made no immediate impression on me, and it was not until long afterwards that I began wondering what he had concealed about his past. It had not seemed possible that he had euphemized his life story, considering some of the episodes he had already related. But primarily, his comment had not registered with me because I was vastly less concerned with the subject of James' personal history than with the musical history he only ladled out in scraps and at long intervals, between massive doses of religious rhetoric and social commentary. The real secrets I had been seeking to draw from him lay in his musicianship. This was because, being a blues fan, the music he spoke through said nothing to me. I had not learned that its messages and meanings lay plainly within it, as with all music; I was hoping that some magical words of his would give it a meaning it did not intrinsically possess, to a consumer who knew nothing about music. His actual life as a human being meant little to me, particularly as I had no sense of life as it lay beyond adolescence.

Such a lack of perspective was and is peculiar to blues addicts, who are blinkered by nature, and adolescent in outlook. In my case, it was exacerbated by my envy of James' guitar-playing, which blinded me to all else about him. He had a skill I despaired of possessing, and wanted to obtain on my own terms.

By learning about his attitudes I imagined that I would somehow learn what it meant to play authentic blues.

Above all else, there was a uncanny, perverse chemistry between the two of us that led me to accept him completely on his own terms, which was one of the reasons he extended the palm of patronage to me. It is almost as if we both saw each other as the persons we would have been, had our races and social positions been exchanged. Viewing me as someone to mold, James pitched his values with the objective of guiding my thoughts in life. He plainly felt that no one had ever understood him, and as he slowly grew more enamored of having a ready ear at his disposal, he began to reveal a past that had originally been papered over with the conventional rhetoric of blues singers. Sentiment had nothing to do with his career, or with his life, except apparently, insofar as it related to his father.

Shortly before he took ill, he hinted that great revelations were to come. "I've got a lot in store to tell you; I haven't even begun. I don't know if you're ready for it."

Once the subject of blues lost its juvenile mystique, and I was able to reflect upon James from a mature perspective, I found myself pondering the implications of his sphinx-like deathbed statement.

One of the secrets he had in store for me likely consisted of a confession that he had literally sold his soul to Satan. The outlines of such a story (had one been in the offing) would have been similar to the one that Tommy Johnson told his brother Ledell, who imparted it to Gayle Wardlow. As a young blues-player in the town of Drew, Johnson had carried his guitar to a crossroads at midnight, where he had met a large black man. The man asked Johnson for his guitar, played a song on it, and handed the instrument to him. This figure, Johnson said, had been Satan, and by accepting the guitar he had sealed a compact with him that enabled him to master any song he wanted to play.

Such a scenario was likely enacted by cynical conjurers for the benefit of credulous blues-players who visited them, for a requisite sum of money. A conjurer would need only examine the hand of a guitar player and note its calloused fingers to detect a prospective customer for such wares. James had played in Drew as a teenager; he mentioned that the town contained "wise people" (conjurers). If he had fallen for such a scheme, which would have done short-term wonders for his musical confidence, this circumstance would explain why he was always so evasive when discussing his musical background, and fended off what he called "crazy, complicated questions" about his musical development. In his own mind, learning a song from someone like Henry Stuckey may have been a technicality: his real mentor was unmentionable.

But such a story would be something only slightly stronger than babe's milk, considering the vast amount of Biblical acreage he had since tilled. What he had really excised from his life story, apparently, was something he was unwilling to risk acknowledging, lest it either put a strain on our relations or cause him to lose face. The omission would be something that would likely make him appear treacherous or untrustworthy.

This missing link in his life, I concluded, must have involved significant acts of criminality, ones that he recognized as crimes. The crimes would involve not the readily-rationalized homicide, but naked aggression or duplicity: armed robbery or theft.

His musical career afforded ongoing opportunities to further a surreptitious criminal profession. It would have been easy for James to make a practice of robbing Johns, prostitutes, gamblers, or even "house frolic" owners. If he had a taste for larceny, he could have stolen farm equipment or cattle on any number of plantations, although Jack Owens said that the James he knew did not steal. On occasion, he could have worked badger games like the "pigeon drop," a favorite reference of his, the knowledge of which he claimed to have acquired by having been one of its victims.

To my knowledge, James was the only blues singer who habitually carried a gun, and it is a reflection of my youthful naiveté that I never thought to consider the implications of this fact. Nor did I sense other incongruities in his story that could have suggested a hidden crime career. For example, James was the only Southern blues singer on the 1960s' circuit who appeared to have a real emnity towards the caste system. Yet, although many of his relatively apathetic peers had left Mississippi for northern climes, he had stayed put. Moreover, he had let a year pass between the time he had been urged to contact H.C. Speir for a recording session and the time he actually did so, while giving contradictory explanations of his failure to record in 1927, when he had been offered a session. He said offhandedly that he had been hospitalized with influenza; in the 1960s, he hated hospitals to the extent of seeking out a conjuring cure for cancer. If James were in fact engaged in high-risk crimes, he would not have been eager to gain publicity as a recording artist.

He could not possibly have attained his level of fluency as a pianist if he had only the restricted access to that instrument he spoke of having, in Bentonia or Jackson. From the evidence of his 1931 recordings he must have been playing continuously for several years. My guess is that he did not want me to know where he had been living when he acquired this proficiency.

Once I began considering James in a hypothetical criminal light, his puzzling personality readily became more explicable. James would casually mention the existence of unspecified "enemies," as though they were as plentiful as friends: ". . . I would like to know of some things that will befall me in the future, as a warning. You know if you be kinda precautious, you can avoid, sometimes, trouble. Let's say that I leave here and I'm goin' to Boston. Say: 'Well, Skip, I wouldn't to to Boston if I were you . . . If you've got to go *through* Boston, it's all right, but I wouldn't stop, because there is some trouble awaitin' you there.' It could be enemies is expectin' me." This was the sort of conversation that could only come naturally to someone who was either paranoid, or had ample reason to look over his shoulder. James was not paranoid in any recognizable sense; his enemies were always hypothetical ones, except for his girlfriend in Tunica, and in that instance his delusions had a cultural, as well as physical, basis to feed upon.

Moreover, James lacked the earnesty and impracticality of a delusionary individual. He had all the dishonesty of a classic psychopath, out to sow false impressions. Had I not gotten to know him better, I would have come away with a completely false portrait of him. The first time I taped him, he stated: ". . . My mother always told me not to practice totin' a gun ... I always has been a child that would obey very much; take heed to instructions. I never did practice totin' a gun; mighty few times ... just a few times." It turned out that he was rarely, if ever, without a gun.

Such gratuitous disclaimers (I had not asked him if he toted a gun or obeyed his mother) typically accompanied his references to disreputable activities. "I never tried to drop a pigeon but I always tried to protect myself," he volunteered. At the same time, whenever James referred to people who were involved in illicit activities, he made a ringing endorsement of them. Professional gamblers were among "the most progressive people of both sexes"; his pimp mentor Will Crabtree "very studious"; his bootlegging father, a "very skillful" man. He lavished no such laudatory language on any other occupational class, including musicians and ministers.

James used his superior verbal facility to create an impenetrable screen around himself. His verbosity on a vast assortment of subjects prevented me from recognizing that he rarely referred to his past activities in any concrete sense, even on the most mundane level of anecdote. In youth he was secretive to the extent of developing a peculiar script, which he called "overhand" writing, and used for the sake of concealing messages. "The police can't even read it," he said proudly.

Even James' high level of verbal skill is subject to a dark interpretation. Nothing he said about his past explained how he had acquired an immense vocabulary for a black Southerner of his period, and used non-idiomatic words with such precision. During the entire time I knew him he never so much as looked at a book. At some point in his life, however, James must have carefully studied a dictionary. Scouring through dictionaries happens to be a favorite pastime of convicts, both to alleviate boredom and to acquire a cultivated air that enables them to function more effectively as criminals by appearing innocuous.*

---

*When Truman Capote began corresponding with one of the protagonist-killers of *In Cold Blood*, the latter "... immediately requested Webster's *New World Dictionary*, which, along with the thesaurus that followed, became the source for the high-flown words he loved to use—and often misuse. To Perry a letter was an epistle, good weather was salubrious ..." Gerald Clark, *Capote: A Biography* (Simon and Schuster, New York, 1988), p. 344.

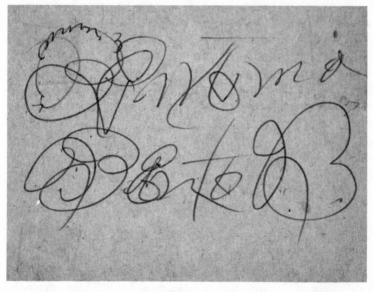

"Bentonia," written in James' secret "overhand" script

James had an air of calm self-possession; he appeared to be permanently detached from his surroundings. The only time I saw him completely lose his aplomb was on an occasion when he realized he had mentioned something to me in an unguarded moment. As he told me about a drunk and disorderly stint he had served in Tunica County, I interrupted him to say that he had already heard told me about the episode.

"I didn't tell you that," he insisted.

"Yes, you did," I replied. When I repeated the conclusion of the story his face took on a look of actual fright, and he fell silent for a few moments, as if wondering what other things he might have let slip.

The one time I saw James appear truly fascinated by a subject was when he began recounting the story of a botched Mississippi bank larceny. A black customer had hidden himself within the premises and looted the bank after closing time. The police suspected a white culprit, James said, because they didn't credit blacks with having the intelligence to commit that sort of crime. A few weeks after the robbery, they discovered an abandoned car, which led them to the criminal, who had panicked in his flight.

James recounted this story in great detail. Then he explained how he would have done it. He began with the strange statement that he would have stopped the vehicle and robbed the criminal of his proceeds. Then he would have buried the money quietly on the plantation he lived upon, making it a point over the next month to ask his bossman for periodic handouts. Finally he would tell the planter that he couldn't make a living on the premises, and would leave after retrieving the money. He would give the plantation owner a false forwarding address.

Most Southern blues singers lived in a single state. James, though never a nomad, had ranged over virtually the entire Deep South. He had lived in all of its states except, he said, Louisiana. He claimed to have shunned that state entirely, because of its racism. It was not until after his death that the author noticed that James had recalled seeing a storied blues singer named Blind Joe Reynolds in Sun, Louisiana in the late 1920s, and that he had mentioned paying visits to Algiers. But

Blind Joe Reynolds

for some reason he wanted others to think he had never been to Louisiana.

Such was not the impression he would have made in 1931 with the lyric:

> I'm goin' I'm goin'
> Comin' here no more
> If I go to Louisiana mama lord they'll
> They'll hang me sure.

James had explained this lyric as a lynching reference. But no one who heard the song in 1931 would have understood it as one. When I first heard the couplet, before succumbing to the myopia of the blues specialist, its meaning had been evident: the singer was wanted for a capital crime. The line had intrigued me, and I wondered who "Skip James" was.

I still wonder.

Afterword

As he lay dying, Skip James prophesied: "Music is gonna be at a low ebb. . . . The old original country blues are absolutely gonna stand forever." By this he meant that the brand of music he represented would never be improved upon.

Over the years, blues would gain increasing acceptance with white audiences, to the point where it now enjoys the middle-of-the-road status that Dixieland jazz earned back in the 1950s. In the 1960s, Skip James' notion of playing blues in the White House sounded grotesque; today such an appearance would have nothing extraordinary about it. A blues act like Cephas and Wiggins is able to garnish as much in a single night as James had managed to earn in a year of scuffling on the dreary coffeehouse circuit.

No longer is blues patronized as folk music, or seen through any particular ideological prism. It has become legitimate entertainment, enjoyed in its own right. To a large extent, its hard-won acceptance reflects the gradual respect extended to blacks that was largely withheld (or expressed insincerely) in the 1960s. But another reason that blues enjoys its current respectability is that its living ethnic representatives have little in common with the vintage blues singers of the Skip James era. Were the great Skip James of the 1920s to suddenly spring to life, along with fabled singers like Robert Johnson or Charlie Patton, the consequences would be devastating to the cause of blues, in its current civilized guise.

Devil Got My Woman

Appendix: Idioms

bad: Lawless; used in *The Pilgrim's Progress* (1678), where it was said of hanged criminals: ". . . had it not been well if their crimes had been engraven in some plate of iron or brass . . . for a caution to other bad men?"

barrelhouse: James provided a faulty definition and etymology of this word: "'Barrelhouse' simply means where they're barrelhousin' . . . In olden times it used to be that they'd call them 'barrelhouses' because the people was rough, and they'd dance and fight and cut up." The term actually arose from the archaic "barrel," meaning liquor, and appeared as an American colloquialism as early as 1883, when it signified a low-class tavern.

black: Exceedingly dark-complexioned, as distinct from "brown," "yellow," or "red" featured: ". . . He thought a heap o' his Black Woman. (Dats what he called her)" (80-year old Mississippian quoted in *Slave Narratives*; Federal Writers Project, 1936-1938). In James' era, this adjective was invariably used as a term of opprobrium:

> I'd rather be the devil
> To be that black woman's man
> (1964 version of *Devil* on the CD *She Lyin'*).

caps: A reference in Robert Johnson's *32-20*, apparently based on a misapprehension of James' reference to "Mister Cress":

> "I got a 32-20, got to make the caps all right."

Johnson misconstrued the pistol as a cap-and-ball revolver firing black powder and round bullets; these were typically .44 caliber guns manufactured by Colt between 1836 and 1872. The caps were fired prior to shooting as a means of cleaning residue from each cylinder.

cherry ball: This idiom for cherry wine or brandy (corrupted by James in *Cherry Ball Blues*) drew its original meaning from the obsolete slang use of "ball" to mean a drink of liquor, in which sense it occurs in Crane's *Bowery Tales* (1894): " '. . . th' on'y thing I really needs is a ball . . . But as I can't get a ball, why th' next bes' thing is breakfast . . .' "

child: A still-common idiom in black speech, where it can be equivalent to all three singular personal pronouns. It probably derived from the English dialect *chiel*, a "familiar term of address to adults as well as children" (*English Dialect Dictionary*).

clown: To show off, usually in an obnoxious manner. A once-conventional black idiom occurring in Lucille Bogan's *That's What My Baby Likes* (1935):

> I'm a long tall mama they call me chocolate brown
> Give me two drinks of whiskey and you can see me
> clown.

cock: A black colloquialism for female genitals.

Coonjine (*Coon Shine*; *Coon Giant*): An obsolete dance enshrined in the eight-bar ditty of the same name. The musical theme associated with it was excerpted in Gottschaulk's *La Bamboloula* (1847), and printed in *Slave Songs Of The United States* (1867) among four Louisiana plantation tunes "for a simple dance, a sort of minuet, called the *Coonjai'* . . ." When James learned the tune it was already associated with inept amateurs, as a reference by John Stark in his ragtime publication of the period (*Intermezzo Magazine*) indicates: "Keep it [improper fingering] up a while and your case is hopeless. You will have to line up with the coonjine artists."

coozie: A black colloquialism for sex organs; more familiar as "cooze" and ordinarily applied to females.

crow jane: The original sense of this idiom as slang for "black girl" emerges in Foster and Harris' 1928 record *Crow Jane Alley*, which unfavorably contrasts a "crow jane" with a "brownskin" woman. As a term for a young female, "jane" was conventional slang in the 1920s.

dozens: Stylized taunts invoking the mother of another person, particularly in a denigrating sexual context. The example given by James was dramatized in Zora Neale Hurston's *Their Eyes Were Watching God* (1937), rendered in song form:

> Yo' mama don't wear no Draws
> Ah seen her when she took 'em Off
> She soaked 'em in alcoHol . . .

drop a pigeon: To deploy the "pigeon drop," a confidence game involving the sham discovery of a bag of money that a swindler offers to share with the mark who has witnessed the find. After the mark is induced to put up a "good faith" investment so as to share in this bonanza, he is left "holding the bag," which has been rigged with a layer of bills atop worthless paper so as to give the appearance of being stuffed with money.

drop sand: To stir up trouble; a variant of "to raise sand," meaning to create a disturbance by arguing, which Sylvia Clapin noted as an American idiom in 1902. The expressions imply that the trouble in question is manufactured.

dry long so: An obsolete black colloquialism meaning "for no reason" invoked on *Hard Times*:

> Let me tell you people just before I go
> These hard times will kill you, just dry long so.

By implication, it meant wrongfully; Willie Moore reported: ". . . Just like I come up and do something to you, an' you hasn't done nothin' to me: now you done it 'dry long so.'" The term was probably a corruption of "dry so," a nineteenth century Southern idiom meaning unadulterated, or plainly.

Fall Off The Log: This barrelhouse dance was alluded to in Papa Charlie Jackson's *Mama Don't You Think I Know* (1925):

> Takes a long-tail monkey, short-tail dog
> To do that dance they call Fallin' Off A Log.

fanfoot: A dated black pejorative for an unkempt barrelhouse floozie, described by Gary Davis as a woman who "gets drunk, falls down in the street . . . don't care who get on her; don't even know lots of the time." The prefix of the term probably derives from *fen*, an archaic English slang word recorded by Grose (1796) for "a common prostitute". The suffix has a similarly archaic basis in either *foot*, a term for an act of copulation belonging to Shakespearian times, or *footy*, which Grose gives as meaning "despicable," and the *English Dialect Dictionary* (1898) records as obscene or base. A blues reference to it occurs in Blind Willie McTell's *Your Time To Worry* (1933):

> You drink your whiskey, run around
> Get out in the street now like a fanfoot clown.

flatfoot: An intensifier meaning "really."

Georgia Skin: A card game fashionable among black levee, lumber and turpentine camp workers. James described it thusly: "To play Georgia Skin you have all the cards in the deck but what you call the joker; the 'bad man.' If I'm the 'president man' — the dealer—then I have the last cards. All the cards that come off before mine are called 'fall' cards. I can charge the drawers [other players] whatever I want: five or ten dollars apiece, to draw out of my deck. Then it's my turn; after I get my bets laid, I turn the first card. If my card is the lowest, then I beat those other cards." Jelly Roll Morton said of it: "Of all the games I've ever seen, no game has so many cheats right in front of your eyes . . ."

hair like drops of rain: Kinky hair, an idiom used in James' *I Looked Down The Road*:

> I don't want no woman, got hair like drops of rain

In Jim Thompkins' *Bedside Blues* (1930) the line is completed as:

> Oh the girl I like got hair like a horse's mane.

hard times: A conventional colloquialism for the Great Depression, found in Caldwell's *God's Little Acre* (1933): "There wouldn't be so many candidates for the few offices open, if it wasn't for the hard times."

house frolic: A commercially organized dance held in a private residence, usually by a bootlegger. As a colloquialism for party, the term "frolic" dates to at least 1645: "I intend to wait on you and give you a frolic." (James Howell, *Letters*). Franklin's 1755 *Autobiography* reported: "I spent no time in taverns, games, or frolics of any kind."

hustlin' women: As a term for prostitute, this expression derives from the nineteenth-century slang usage of "hustle" (copulate). The association of the verb with prostitution occurs in Faulkner's *Sanctuary* ("'I'll take you back to Memphis Sunday. You can go to hustling again.'") and in Edmund Wilson's diaristic description of a New Orleans prostitute "–Worked in a store in Atlanta, then was in Macon hustlin' " (*The Twenties*.) Blind Willie Reynolds' *Third Street Woman Blues* (1930) also uses the term:

... Where my Third Street woman gone?
Believe to my soul she will hustle everywhere but home.

jukehouse: A synonym of "barrelhouse" drawn from the black idiom "juke," meaning to dance or fight, which itself was derived from a Scottish dialect verb (variously spelled "juke," "jook," and "jouk") dating to the 15th century and expressing various types of motion. (Cf. Jamieson's *Scottish Dictionary* (1825), Wright's *English Dialect Dictionary* (1898), and even Samuel Johnson's 1775 dictionary, which treats it as standard English.)

law: A policeman. The term occurs in Hambone Willie Newbern's *Shelby County Workhouse Blues* (1929):

Lord the police 'rest me, carried me 'fore the jury
Well the laws talked so fast didn't have the time to
say not nary a word.

misery: Bodily pain, a meaning occuring in 19th century English dialect and perpetuated in Little Richard's *Long Tall Sally* (1956):

Gonna tell Aunt Mary about Uncle John
He says he has the misery but he has a lotta fun ...

monkey man: A favorite blues singer's pejorative for a male who "lets a woman make a monkey out of him" (Son House). The term was undoubtedly drawn from the pre-1890 American phrase "to monkey," meaning to behave effusively towards a pretty

girl, construed as obsolete in Partridge's *Slang To-day And Yesterday.*
One of the blues references to it conveys the meaning of the term:

> I'm goin' now, find my monkey man
> I'll get all he's got now, then find my regular man.
>
> (Lottie Beamon: *Regular Man Blues*, 1924)

musicianer: One who plays music for a livelihood; standard English till at least the turn of the century.

notoriety: An obsolete black colloquialism for a person with a reputation for being dangerous. Gary Davis explained "notoriety" as "a person that has a outstandin' record or a bad reputation, a great long court record."

on the crackerbox; on the hog: Broke. The derivation of these phrases is obscure. The latter appears in *Black Gal.*

on the killing floor: In dire straits. This idiom first appeared in Arthur Petties' *Two Timing Blues* (1928):

> A two-timin' woman, keep you on that killin' floor
> How can you love when she's always in the wrong.

protection: Weaponry, with the implication that it is borne for self-defense. The expression occurs in Pink Anderson and Simmie Dooley's *Papa's 'Bout To Get Mad* (1928):

> You better go find yourself some good protection
> 'Cause sweet mama, papa 'bout to get mad.

put that baby to bed: This catchphrase was probably derived from an obsolete music hall expression, "put to bed" (to defeat).

rest: An archaic synonym of sleep occuring in *Devil Got My Woman.* William Byrd's *History Of The Dividing Line* (1728) notes: "... being shut up so close quite spoiled our rest..."

rider: A plantation overseer. James said that this figure was commonly called "'Mister Right Off'—right off the horse and on the nigger's ass."

Roll the Belly: A reference to this barrelhouse dance occurs in Lucille Bogan's *Crawlin' Lizard Blues* (1930):

> Crawlin' lizard's got a crawl they call the "Belly Roll"
> He can crawl, all in my door.

spiritual: The original term applied to black sacred songs, derived from Ephesians 5: "be filled with the Spirit; Speaking to yourself in psalms and hymns and spiritual songs . . ." It is likely that this term was bestowed by whites in an effort to semantically segregate the songs from "hymns," many of which formed the basis of black "spirituals." Although white hymns were largely composed and transmitted through hymnbooks, spirituals often originated as performance pieces, belatedly (if at all) collected in book form.

sport: A sexual libertine; a gambler who pimped for a living. The sexual connotation of the term was once standard English, appearing in Shakespeare's *Othello* (1602): " . . . the blood is made dull with the act of sport." The association between "sporting" and pimping probably arose from the predominance of gamblers in the latter profession, "sport" having been conventional nineteenth century slang for a gambler.

studious: Thoughtful. From the archaic English "study" (to ponder), found in Shakespeare: "You make me study of that: She was of Carthage, not of Tunis."

style: To call or regard as; obsolete standard English, found in *The Journal of George Fox* (1649): " . . . they styled me an honest, virtuous man."

tackhead: The likely idiomatic basis of this pejorative is indicated by an Alex Hill piano instrumental, *Tackhead Blues* (1928).

teaser brown: James' variant of the conventional blues phrase "teasin' brown," defined by Gary Davis: "That's just a woman don't mean nothin' she says and nothin' she do . . . You mess around with a woman like that, you understand, she cause you to be throwin' rocks, shootin' pistols, usin' pocketknifes . . ."

wild geese: Canada geese. William Byrd's *History of the Dividing Line* (1728) reported: "Now the weather grew cool, the wild geese began to direct their flight this way from Hudson's Bay . . ."

wise: Skilled in soothsaying or conjuring and thus possessing surpassing wisdom; obsolete standard English occuring in *The Merry Wives of Windsor* ("the Wise woman of Brainford").

Subject Index

Nixon, Hammie, 268
Norwood, "One-Legged Sam," 134

Ochs, Phil, 317
Old Liberty Church, 209
Oliver, Paul, 220
O'Neal, Hank, 290, 295
The Ontario Place, 274, 277, 281, 339
On With The Show, 97
On The Road, 257
Origin Jazz Library, 217, 220, 249, 261, 322
Owens, Bessie, 128
Owens, Jack, 112, 175, 209, 210, 212, 232, 236, 320, 356
Owens, Nettie ("Net"), 99

Paramount Records, 4, 133, 136, 158, 160, 162, 163, 199, 250, 301
Patton, Charlie, 41, 92, 133,140, 158, 170, 217, 243, 258, 260, 262, 342, 365
Paxton, Tom, 317
Perkins, Carl, 261
Perls, Nick, 241, 299
Peter Paul and Mary, 256
Phillips, Washington, 178, 187
pigeon drop, 357, 371
Polk, Buddy, 212, 213, 225
Polk, Lincoln, 13
Polk, Martha, 31, 166, 245
Polk, Willie Mae, 162
Powell, Irving, 53
Presley, Elvis, 215, 261
Primitive Baptists, 178
Prohibition, 80-81
Pullum, Joe, 192

Rainey, Ma, 136, 199, 219
Rabbit Foots Minstrels, 99
Rachel, Yank, 268
"rag" songs, 42, 95
Ramsey, Frederick, Jr., 219
The Record Hunter, 261
Red, Tampa, 218
Reynolds, Blind Joe, 134, 361
Roberts, George, 349, 351

Robinson, Oscella, 107-112, 118, 125, 151, 176
rock and roll, 258, 261, 307, 313-315

Roll The Belly, 71
Rolling Stones, 324
Rollingberg, Mack, 181-82
Roots, Rae, 294, 341
Roots, Sonny, 341
Roots, Volney, 341
Rose, Biff, 234
Rosenthal, Gene, 273
Rust, John, 208

Sam Goody's, 261
sanctified church ("sancts"), 189, 192, 297-98
Seeger, Pete, 280
Serge, Marshall, 132
Shackleford Good Roads Bill, 56
Shimmy-She-Wobble, 71, 101
Shooters, S.T., 66
Sigles, D.C., 163
Sims, Charlie and Jesse, 30
Simmons, Benny, 246
Sizemore, Art, 322
Slader, Adam, 209
Slader, Burd, 209, 212
Slow Drag, 31
Smith, Bessie, 7, 138, 158, 199, 219, 296
Smith, Charles Edward, 218-19
Smith, Clara, 138
Smith, Mamie, 39, 138
Solomon, Maynard, 300, 302, 329, 330, 331
Soul Stirrers, 192

Spann, Otis, 228
Spaulding, Henry, 43, 140
Speir, H.C., 133-4, 136-7, 138, 158, 159, 162, 163, 168, 200, 208, 358
Spires, Arthur, 95
Spottswood, Louisa, 287, 293
Spottswood Music Company, 290
Spottswood, Richard, 242, 287

Song Index

Other titles of interest

THE ARRIVAL OF B. B. KING
Charles Sawyer
274 pp., 99 photos
80169-8 $12.95

BIG BILL BLUES
William Broonzy's Story
as told to Yannick Bruynoghe
176 pp., 4 drawings, 15 photos
80490-5 $10.95

BIG ROAD BLUES
Tradition and Creativity
in the Folk Blues
David Evans
396 pp., many illus.
80300-3 $15.95

THE COUNTRY BLUES
Samuel B. Charters
288 pp., 45 illus.
80014-4 $12.95

BLUES FROM THE DELTA
William Ferris
New introd. by Billy Taylor
226 pp., 30 photos
80327-5 $11.95

THE BLUES MAKERS
Samuel Charters
New preface and new
chapter on Robert Johnson
416 pp., 40 illus.
80438-7 $16.95

BLUES WHO'S WHO
Sheldon Harris
775 pp., 450 photos
80155-8 $35.00

BOSSMEN
Bill Monroe & Muddy Waters
James Rooney
163 pp., 42 photos
80427-1 $11.95

BROTHER RAY
Ray Charles' Own Story
Updated Edition
Ray Charles and David Ritz
370 pp., 30 photos
80482-4 $13.95

LOVE IN VAIN
A Vision of Robert Johnson
Alan Greenberg
New foreword by Martin Scorsese
272 pp., 9 photos
80557-X $13.95

SCREENING THE BLUES
Paul Oliver
302 pp., 8 photos
80344-5 $13.95

WOMAN WITH GUITAR
Memphis Minnie's Blues
Paul and Beth Garon
368 pp., 50 photos
80460-3 $14.95

I SAY ME FOR A PARABLE
The Oral Autobiography of Mance
Lipscomb, Texas Bluesman
as told to and compiled by
Glen Alyn
Foreword by Taj Mahal
508 pp., 45 illus.
80610-X $16.95

Available at your bookstore

OR ORDER DIRECTLY FROM

DA CAPO PRESS, INC.

1-800-321-0050